The Political Economy of
America's Environmental
Dilemma

The Political Economy of America's Environmental Dilemma

Michael J. Brenner
Harvard University

Lexington Books
D.C. Heath and Company
Lexington, Massachusetts
Toronto   London

Library of Congress Cataloging in Publication Data

Brenner, Michael J
  The political economy of America's environmental dilemma.

  Includes bibliographical references.
    1. Environmental policy–United States. 2. Environmental protection–
United States. 3. Pollution–Economic aspects–United States.
I. Title.
HC110.E5B7   301.31'0973   73-11685
ISBN 0-669-90910-6

Published simultaneously in Canada.

Printed in the United States of America.

International Standard Book Number: 0-669-90910-6

Library of Congress Catalog Card Number: 73-11685

To L. S.

List of Tables

Preface

This book expresses both strong personal feelings and scholarly interest Provoked by an individual response to the threat environmental degradation poses to communal amenity and health, it assumed the shape of a scholarly exercise to explain how our public institutions could be so negligent as to permit this drastic dereliction of our habitat.

The environment is a special sort of issue. As one begins to pull on the thread of analysis it presents, one is soon obliged to unravel much of the institutional and cultural fabric of our industrial society. There is good reason for the reiterated and now perhaps clichéd claim that the environment is a distinctly cross-cutting, if not transcendent, social problem. This work is an attempt at separating some of these threads and at determining their nature, while examining the pattern they compose. There are three facets to the study: an assessment of programs and policies to manage the environment, both those in force and proposed; a critical analysis of characteristic features of American public institutions as they bear on the environmental issue; and an examination of dominant political and economic theories that emphasizes their inadequacies for conceptualizing this new problem. Often using characteristic and influencial works of political and economic analysis as points of critical reference, the book enunciates and develops a number of themes about the challenge environmental needs pose for American public values and institutions.

It is basically a work of policy analysis, with the visible emphases and theoretical preoccupations of a political scientist. Given the author's pronounced feelings about the subject, there are also elements of exhortation and even an occasional touch of polemic. Inevitably the analysis contains assessments about the practicality of policies, the efficacy of institutional arrangements, and the relative virtues of academic theories. A conscientious effort has been made throughout, however, to distinguish personal preference from the neutral evaluation of policy consistency, effectiveness, and purpose.

The introduction lays out the dimensions of the subject, briefly sketching the four facets of the environmental problem: pollution as health hazard, as disamenity, resource depletion, and, collateral to these physical conditions, disaffection from the organizational environment. Part 1 seeks to establish and to elaborate on the connection between institutional characteristics of the industrial system that explain its neglectful attitude toward environmental conditions and our dominant social beliefs as expressed in formal theory and doctrine. Chapter 1 stresses that adverse conditions are necessary, if inadvertent, outcomes of the way in which we conduct our public business and define social objectives. Chapters 2 to 4 explore the reinforcing bias of dominant political and economic concepts, while suggesting the influence they exert on governmental approaches to environmental problems once acknowledged.

Part 2 moves to a detailed assessment of the public initiatives that have been taken in recent years. Its main point of critical evaluation is the postulated need to integrate those intersecting elements of public policy that impinge on environmental management. Chapter 5 examines the structure and powers of the Environmental Protection Agency from this perspective, judging its capacity to achieve the paramount authority that we see as a requirement for successful environmental action on a systemic scale. The case study of transportation policy in chapter 6 is a look at a policy area central to environmental reform that both highlights the issue of institutional bias and provides a basis for judging the likely impact of present programs. Chapter 7 considers PPBS (Planning and Program Budgeting Systems) and related budgetary approaches as an alternative to incremental policy-making, and suggests how political assumptions and social preferences must be made explicit for its scope to be extended and for it to become a technique that offers the basis for the congruent planning indicated by environmental need.

Part 3 extends the empirical portion of the study. Chapter 8 on ways and means is concerned with two questions: What is the most feasible way to proceed with remedial pollution control measures? and, Who should pay the bill? It assesses the diverse approaches that have been offered to defray the costs of pollution control and the expense of providing amenities given political requirements, established corporate structures, and likely social effects. Chapter 9 introduces discussion of the relationship between science and technology and their influence on the direction of the industrial system. In reviewing recent proposals associated with technology assessment, we are obliged to consider both the recurrent problem of how to create mechanisms for concerting diverse areas of policy, and the special problem relating to the social impacts of specialized research and education.

Our theme that one cannot talk meaningfully about environmental policy without raising fundamental questions as to the allocation of resources, the criteria for establishing social objectives, and our capacity for directing society's long-term future leads to a consideration of the practicalities of environmental politics in Part 4. It stresses that the environment cuts across conventional categories of interest and party loyalty and thereby creates both new antagonisms and possibilities for major innovation. Chapter 10 analyses the strain between environmental objectives (and supporters) and more conventional types of social reform. With the juxtaposition of environmentalists and welfarists as its point of departure, the analysis considers conflict over images of democratic politics as well as economic interest. Chapter 11 has a dual purpose: to look critically at efforts to fit the environment into a broader mold of radical thinking on contemporary society, and to establish the association between the alienated state of mind and environmental concern.

Part 5 moves from analysis to advocacy with a menu of proposed reforms. Chapter 12 concentrates on recommendations for institutional change and suggests specific programmatic and structural initiatives. Chapter 13 is concerned with the sphere of values and education. It specifies the kind of education and training that would modify the present logic of the industrial system, proposes curricula likely to endow society with appropriate skills, and takes up an earlier theme as to the place of organized knowledge in modern society. Chapter 14 poses the classic question of individual value and social responsibility as it is raised by the present circumstances of degradation of our surroundings. What are the strains between the quest for individual meaning and an agreeable private way of life and the communal obligation to pursue some proximate objective of social reform? How might they be reconciled and what are the costs of doing so?

Finally, let me thank some friends and colleagues: Sam Devons, Alan Sindler, Paul Hohenberg.

Fleury-Le-fôret
29 July, 1973

Introduction

There are intriguing elements of paradox in our current environmental dilemma. A culture that prizes rationality and logical control permits enormous systemic irrationalities. It is applied reason that has fashioned the forms and tools of our society, yet we base public policy to an inordinate degree on myth, convention, and habit. Our institutional techniques for performing the myriad tasks of industrialism are artfully conceived and carefully constructed, yet the physical condition of our collective life seemingly defies management. Everywhere there is organization but we live in disorder. These cryptic aphorisms state the paradox of our times and suggest the full dimensions of the environmental issue.[1]

The environment as a public issue is that rarest of phenomena, something new in the arena of political debate and academic analysis; so much so that we still labor with only partial success to formulate what we have in mind and to delineate with some degree of rigor its several dimensions. There is no more striking evidence of our neglect of the environment than the inadequacy of our social theories for making comprehensible as formidable a condition as this drastic dereliction of our urban and natural habitat.

We can most easily say what sort of problem the environmental crisis is not. It is *not* a question of our capacity to manage the economy in order to routinize prosperity. Neither is it basically an issue of how to distribute the bounty. Political and economic analysis today is so preoccupied with matters of efficiency and reward that we are disposed by an almost Marxist reductionism to define all social problems in terms of production and consumption. The environmental issue is not that tractable. It is rather concerned with the unintended by-products of a society where industrial expansion and economic well-being are the overriding objectives. The inattentiveness of men and institutions to their surroundings—as they relentlessly perform the self-defining tasks of the industrial system and indulge a seemingly insatiable appetite for disposable private wealth—gives rise to those environmental ills that orthodox social belief has such difficulty in explaining.

The problem exists at three levels and has to be conceptualized accordingly. In order of concreteness, they are: (a) the physical conditions themselves; (b) the system of beliefs and institutions that created them and has shown itself largely unadapted to the requirements for remedial action; and (c) those dominant doctrines and theories with which we explain social reality and direct our collective behavior. The first, most tangible aspect of the issue is the unhealthy and aesthetically displeasing degradation of both natural surroundings and our communities. Here, in turn, we should distinguish between pollution as *health hazard* and as *disamenity* (hereafter we shall refer to the former as Environment I, and to the latter as Environment II). By pollution as health hazard we mean the introduction into the air, the water, and the soil of potentially injurious by-products (chemical and biological) that are created by industry and population concentration. The discharge of noxious wastes from a paper mill into a stream; the auto emission of sulfur oxides or nitrogen dioxide into the atmosphere; ash particles created by a power plant; the use of lakes and harbors as receptacles for poorly treated sewage; or the dumping of imperfectly sealed radioactive residue onto the ocean floor—all are examples of environmental pollution.

The social amenity dimension refers to the enormous discomfort resulting from congestion, noise, and unsightliness on the grand scale that we find today, especially in our cities but by no means limited to them. The reprehensible condition of mass transportation; the destruction of the urban center by the automobile; the despoliation of the landscape—whether by billboards, arbitrary road construction, or overconcentration—are examples of disamenities grown to such proportions that the terms of daily existence become unpleasant, disorienting, and often painful. Of the two types of environmental conditions, pollution is easier to recognize and to evaluate. We can measure the amount of waste material generated annually, or the level of air pollutant emissions. We can estimate, albeit with an appreciable margin for error, their consequences for the life cycle of a lake, the residue of toxic metals in fish, or the accentuation of respiratory diseases.[2] Although our technical instruments in many of these areas are surprisingly unrefined (itself a reflection of the limited interest manifest in environmental problems), we nevertheless are in a position to lay out the causal sequences that lead to hazardous conditions and increasingly are able to establish standards of risks and tolerances.

Conditions of disamenity are less liable to measurement, and their effects on human behavior more difficult to assess. Judgments about individual and social psychology are normally more tentative than evaluations of physical conditions. Inevitably there is a high element of subjectivity in determining what constitutes an intolerable level of congestion or noise, and it entails aesthetic preferences that cannot readily be given numerical values. Uncertain and divergent standards of worth complicate the problem of calculating tradeoffs between the desire for greater amenity and the disinclination to restrict economic development, e.g., construction of (presumably) commercially lucrative skyscrapers in already overcrowded areas or the building of convenient highway connections through parkland. Questions of lifestyle and cultural value do enter into Environment I problems as well, particularly those which involve both pollution and disamenity, as is the case with discharge into waterways. Environment I and Environment II concerns intersect in a number of other, less obvious ways, as we observe throughout this essay. To mention one pertinent example, the reduction of auto-caused air pollution might well require a greater reliance on mass transit. The development of public transportation facilities is itself a major facet of any serious effort to create a more appealing urban setting.

Notions of what constitutes the good life are always in the near background of discussions on environmental conditions. To suggest an aesthetic component to environmental criticism is not to detract from the problem's cogency. Cavalier dismissal of aesthetic criticism as frivolous, unworthy of consideration on the same plane as "serious" matters of technological innovation and economic reward, misperceives the circumstances in which the citizenry of the affluent West live. We are not equating a salubrious skyline with the essentials of food and shelter. We are, though, several degrees of collective wealth removed from scrounging the survival requisites. The poor among us are victims of gross misallocation, not insufficient means. The practical tradeoff is between amentiy, convenience, and attractiveness on the one hand; and a second color TV, 2 1/2-hour supersonic flights to Europe, and 'first-day covers' from the moon (besides redundant weapons systems) on the other.

Moreover, aesthetics mean more than a jaded patrician's contemplation of a textured garden *or* the tourist's unobstructed scenic view of the Grand Canyon and his marvelling at the pristine waters of Lake Tahoe. The condition of the physical surroundings we inhabit is at once an expression of our communal personality, and itself a determinant of how we address our environment. As psychological studies inform us, the temperament and disposition of workers is perceptibly influenced by the setting in which they are employed. It is by no means an unwarranted extrapolation to suggest that the present condition of our communities aggravates the alienation and isolation, two of whose manifestations are compulsive consumption and an arrogant disregard for collective amenity.

Both the amenity and pollution facets of the environmental problem are intimately linked to *pollution increase.*[3] The growth of the United States from 150 million in 1950 to 207 million in 1970 represents a 38 percent expansion of the society's requirements for power (and the air pollution it engenders); transportation (most of it in the form of smog-creating automobiles); housing construction (characterized by the serried rows of ticky-tacky development that transforms greenswath into slurbs); and all of those consumer items whose manufacture's by-products—and whose disposal—befoul the air and water. Even had the standard of living, consumption levels, and technology remained constant throughout this period, the demographic arithmetic would have dictated a sharp rise in industrial activity, and an expansion of the gross national product. The compounding of population increase with the strong societal commitment to a philosophy of unhampered economic growth assures that the sources of environmental damage will intensify and become more profuse. Zero population growth will not in itself solve environmental problems. It would permit more reasonable discussion of means to curtail industrial expansion. Without controls on population, modulated economic development can only be introduced at what is now the unacceptable expense of reducing or at least stabilizing standards of living. With it, proper attention to environmental conditions, and the absorption of costs to remedy present damage, becomes economically that much more feasible.

It is worth noting that the relationship between population growth and pollution is not linear. As Barry Commoner has demonstrated, the drastic postwar increase in environmental damage is out of proportion to the rise in population.[4] Not only has industrial expansion grown at a faster rate, but the new technologies associated with it (e.g., plastics, complex pesticides) are far more pernicious in their ecological effects than earlier technologies.

Commoner draws the qualified conclusion that population control is not central to a program of intelligent environmental management. When restricted to Environment I effects, the argument is pertinent if not conclusive. However, disamenities do stand in direct relationship to the concentration of people. The burden placed on our already inadequate means for planning the urban environment by ever concentrating population in metropolitan areas is undeniable. The unmanaged, if not unmanageable conglomerations that ensue are a clear source of congestion, unsightliness and discomfort. Furthermore, whatever the degree to which population levels are correlated with both forms of environmental damage, it is an economic fact that the costs of simply maintaining increased population in basic needs and facilities detracts from the resources available for pollution control and the creation of amenable facilities. One aspect of our growing reliance on refined technologies is that an increase in the available working force does not add proportionally to productivity, while it does generate proportional demand, and, in many cases where the "critical mass" effect occurs, causes disproportionate environmental damage.

Commoner's evaluation has touched off an acrid exchange between himself and Paul Ehrlich as to the relative importance of three factors in the equation of environmental deterioration: population, affluence, and technology. Their wide-ranging and pointed debate is unusually informative for an academic joust. Commoner holds to the position that the three are separable, in theory and practical effect, and that population increase is the least consequential among them. Ehrlich argues, with what appears to be greater persuasiveness, better logic and more substantiation, that our accelerating impact on the environment is comprehensible only by reference to a complex pattern of development entailing each of these components in elaborate, reciprocal interrelations. He notes, for example, that increasing pressure on a traditional resource (tin) or technology dictated by increasing affluence and population, can force substitutions and innovations that are disproportionately harmful to the environment (plastics). Furthermore, even the more intensive employment of old technologies can produce drastic alterations in environmental conditions. (This is surely the correct interpretation of the severe ecological damage caused by the automobile).

Another facet of the environmental dilemma is the threat of *resource depletion.* Periodically for the past quarter of a century our attention has been called to the finitude of the earth's natural resources. The Club of Rome study conducted at MIT is to date the most extensive, if still preliminary, attempt to demonstrate the dangers inherent in unchecked population increase and industrial development.[5] It differs from earlier, similar appeals in its elaborate use of refined analytical techniques. The more profound impact of this venture, though, owes more to the study's coincidence with a heightened concern over environmental affairs generally, and resource need in particular (the energy crisis). The impassioned debate evoked by the study has underscored how formidable is the task of assessing systematically ecological futures, and how controversial is any suggestion of pessimistic outcomes. (The ensuing confrontation also has pinpointed the methodogical and conceptual difficulties of such an undertaking.) The details of that debate need not detain us long, though. Pollution and disamenity are today undeniable problems whether in fact a life of high consumption will become unsustainable in the distant (2100) or the near (2010) future, and the requirement for resource planning of a character not now in force is overwhelming.

The dire predictions of food shortages and mineral depletion, in combination with population rise, do lend an ominous tone to our otherwise more prosaic consideration of the intellectual and institutional preconditions for the intelligent management of our collective existence. For whatever the disagreement on particulars of magnitude and timing, there is nothing but faith to place against the incontrovertible principle that the earth's carrying capacity is limited and not infinitely elastic. The real possibility of depletion strengthens the case in favor of a broadly conceived, and integrated planning for human use, and the unreasoning opposition to any pessimistic analysis of our condition is further evidence of the imperative need to attenuate the Faustian impulses that move modern civilization.

Ancillary to these aspects of the environmental issue is the widespread and deepening estrangement from the formal organizations which make up our institutional environment. This estrangement is most easily recognized in the form of alienation from the efficiency minded bureaucracies whose emphasis on standardization and specialization reflects the industrial order's requirement for routine, efficient performance. Organizational alienation can be interpreted, from the behavioral perspective, as the most vivid evidence of a more pervasive disaffection from the dominant values and forms of our society. Although the phenomenon of organizational alienation and cultural disaffection is associated with the other elements of the environmental problem, and will recur in various portions of the essay, the individual psychology of alienation is not a major theme of literature on the environment. The institutional environment is, though, germane to our subject in several respects.

First, personal alienation detracts from social engagement. Without an active concern for the broader conditions from which personal stress derives, we are handicapped in trying to move collectively to fashion an environment that is an object of affection and the recipient of attentive care. The rejection of existing political forms as being unresponsive to the concerns of its citizens produces a strain between the organizational requirements for effective public action and the quest for personal meaning, usually through private withdrawal. That same quest can be seen manifest in the call for direct democracy and participation, a yearning for personal engagement, per se, that can be largely satisfied without appreciable changes in public policy and societal conditions. At the same time, it gives evidence of acute interest in changing the process' outcomes—the state of the environment prominent among them. The reconciliation of the two ingeredients of alienated social attitudes is a condition for ultimate success in meeting the environmental challenge.

Second, the bureaucratic organization of government is an impediment to imagination and innovation—both of which are essential if we are to fashion the public means to deal effectively with dereliction of our habitat. The fragmentation of public authority into organizational fiefs diminishes the system's capacity to view social needs comprehensively and to act concertedly. Rigid bureaucratic structures reinforce conventional wisdom and assure a narrowness of vision. The same specialization of function, and routinization of behavior, that render the modern organization so efficient an instrument for performing specific tasks implicitly defined for it by the industrial system, make it unsuited to view critically premises and purposes. Whether one speaks of the corporate technostructure or the government bureaucracy, they are largely mechanical bodies exhibiting all the failings of institutions weak in conscious will and direction.

Third, organizations rigid in their conception of mission are poor instruments for implementing new policies, especially when those policies diverge in objective and programmatic format from what had been the accustomed mode. One of the gravest impediments to acting with concert for the alleviation of adverse environmental conditions is the inherent resistance of administrative structures to a shift in the direction of their organizational missions, and to a new obligation to divorce themselves from old constituencies. Life within the organizational universe can be as frustrating of superior political will as it is alienating of individual sensibilities.

Part 1
Institutions and Ideas

1

The Problem As System

By the environment issue we normally mean the physical degradation of our surroundings as expressed in pollution and acute disamenity. At another level of explanation, however, the problem can be conceived as our prevailing system of public institutions that are peculiarly unsuited to monitor collective needs or to formulate government policy with a comprehensiveness that matches the scope of the problem. Environmental concerns are so intricately woven into the fabric of the industrial system that new programs and proposals for change touch nearly every aspect of public policy and national politics. As recognition of the problem's severity and multiple facets increases, and practical initiatives acquire specificity, the wider implications of remedial action are becoming manifest.

It is increasingly clear that we cannot talk meaningfully about pollution abatement or providing for the amenities of urban life without also considering: levels of tolerance for unbridled economic growth; the ratio of public expenditure to private consumption in the allocation of national product; and the criteria for establishing the priority areas for public expenditure;[1] as well as our institutional and intellectual capacity for planning our long-term future.

It is one of our main contentions that a major impediment to coming to grips with this medley of interlocking issues is our inordinate reliance on mechanical procedures and incremental judgment for setting social objectives. We have been moving toward an industrially determined future with a piecemeal planning that generates change without assessing comprehensively its consequences. The refining of our practical knowledge, techniques, and organizational tools to domesticate nature and exploit its riches has the quality of a self-renewing process that reflects the premiums that have been placed on growth, rational procedure, and economic efficiency.[2]

Nearly all of our institutions—corporations, universities, and especially government agencies—meet the requirements for sustained activity through marginal adjustment of their organizational structures and programmatic purpose, routinizing change in such a way as seemingly to render superfluous any contemplation of ultimate objective. Galbraith powerfully demonstrated in his study of the corporate technostructure how little comprehension of the whole of its operation there need to be for it to achieve narrowly defined ends.[3] The same principle can be applied to government where the dissociation of powers and a highly pragmatic approach to policy manages to meet immediate obligations without reference to longer term goals or critical scrutiny of premises and implicit priorities. As a result, relatively little attention has been paid to the

3

cumulative side-effects of industrial production and mass consumption on the environment. A political system responsive to the slightest marginal changes in agricultural prices, or the level of investment in industrial plant, has had no mechanisms by which to register and to measure the fundamental alterations in the quality of air, of water, i.e., of the very things on which human life depends. Only within the past few years, with the nation vividly poised on the brink of major ecological disaster, has the public eye been fixed on the state of the physical environment we inhabit. And only within these past years have the public institutions of our society, our governmental agencies, noted these same realities and begun to respond in however desultory a fashion.

That these profoundly damaging conditions could go largely unnoticed is a misfeasance suggesting how remarkably insensitive our communal institutions are to even the most palpable developments so long as they are not defined by the standard economic indicators of value or endowed with political worth by our interest-based system of group representation.

The present structure of our public institutions is not a coincidence; it is nicely fitted to our social objectives. Our pluralist, democratic system of Keynesian capitalism is geared to perform certain kinds of tasks and does them very well: e.g., implementation of new techniques, productive expansion, maintaining political access for a multiplicity of groups and interests, and distributing wealth so that grievances over material reward are kept at a tolerably low level. Its broader cultural ends are also met for the most part: to fulfil the faith in progress defined as growth, to allow practical talents to develop, and to gratify the status inspired yearning after consumable goods. It is no secret that the routinization of affluence—and perfection of the economic management upon which it depends—are the paramount concerns of a democratic government in an industrial setting. Its institutions, its characteristic modes of acting, the behavior of the officials who work the system, are keyed to accomplishing these ends.

Were the achievement of communal harmony as highly prized as group and personal enrichment, were maintenance of a congenial natural environment placed above technical innovation, and the cultivation of life's aesthetic dimension given precedence over (or even equal weight with) regular increases in the GNP, the procedures of our political institutions, their manner of addressing public issues, the way of defining consequences would be different, as would their substantive policy outputs. The forms and processes of our public institutions serve to limit what becomes identified as an issue, as much as do the dominant beliefs and values of the culture. In the same way that prevailing attitudes trim and skew our perceptions of reality, so is an incremental process of policy-making in a system of factionalized authority disposed to pose certain kinds of issues in certain ways while excluding or downplaying the significance of others.

Democratic politics in our liberal pluralist system has three characteristics: (1) representation based largely on a plethora of organized interests defined by economic function; (2) a dissociation of powers intragovernmentally between branches and among executive agencies; and (3) a disjointed, incremental approach to policy that is skeptical of broad designs and plans. In combination, these features help to explain (1) the difficulty we have in recognizing communal problems that are not a reflection of our capacity to routinize prosperity or our criteria for distributing wealth among groups and classes; and (2) our reluctance explicitly to set priorities and to undertake the correction of public policy necessary to achieve them.

Legislation expresses in its nuances and stresses the outcomes of muted contests for preferential advantage among plural constituencies. Executive authority is in consonant fashion dispersed among administrative agencies which have acquired their clientele of associated groups and interests. The result is policy by bargaining and adjustment. Everybody gets a piece of the action, but there is relatively little sense of the whole. Interests are neatly balanced, but the balance between government's proper role in satisfying particular interests and its responsibility for the collective welfare of the society as a corporate entity is weighted toward the former. It is assumed that the government's little pieces of policy taken together somehow meet public needs. Disdaining comprehensive planning, the mode of action is reactive. Congressmen, bureaucrats and presidential assistants normally formulate programs and draft legislation in response to expressions of need or grievance by those interests, factions, or groups who are the active elements in the process (normally entailing an increase in some government benefit: farm subsidies, rise in the minimum wage, aid to defense contractors). Occasionally, an official will take the initiative to refine or to adjust a program already in force (the scheduling of tax credits on capital investment). It is less common for him to offer an original proposal to meet recognized needs in an innovative way (federalization of welfare). And only in exceptional circumstances, does he address a problem unperceived by the system's particularistic actors. The consequence is (a) neglect of problems that take the shape of general conditions beyond the ken of one or a coalition of interests, and (b) marginal adjustment on an expedient basis as the normal way of proceeding. Cross-cutting and conflicting interests, positions taken in reference to organizational ends, always militate against comprehensive policy-making. The plural structure of power does not necessarily mean that all coordinate effort is resisted. It does imply the prevalence of partial perspectives and narrow outlooks.[4] So conceived, public policy takes on the quality of a turgid, meandering stream that moves slowly along its circuitous course without giving much evidence of knowing its ultimate destination or caring how long it takes to get there. Each loop and turn is expedient adjustment to slightly altered circumstance of political topography. While carving out its course, it shifts time after time, leaving behind evidence of its previous efforts in the form of sloughs and crossbows that remain part of the (administrative and programmatic) landscape long after they have ceased contributing to the stream's progress. Only on those innovative occasions when the sluices are opened, are new channels cut, and speed and direction imparted to the flow.

The element of corporate conservatism in pluralist politics is discernible in the routine, semistructured coordinate relationships among the organized economic association, its legislative supporters, and its protective executive department. Consultative ties between government and interests stand as the institutional symbols of the public obligation to protect, and to engage in a dialogue with the significant component groups of the industrial system. The farm federations, trade unions, professional associations such as the AMA, and, of course, a legion of business interests (defense contractors, the highway lobby), have their blocs of supporters in the House of Representatives and the Senate. Their administrative counterparts are, in turn, the Departments of Agriculture, Labor, Defense, the Treasury, and Commerce. (Doctors, as a professional group, get by quite well with the acquiescense of such agencies as the Surgeon General's Office.) The practical requirements for economic management in the interests of efficiency dictate these clientele relationships.[5] A modern industrial society depends on the interdependent efforts of its productive and organizational parts for its successful working, and for the provision of individual and group benefits. The assumption by government of primary responsibility for economic management and welfare maintenance that has occurred since the Great Depression in all Western societies requires that links of cooperation and communication be forged between public authority and organized sectors of the economy. For economic management to be effective in a democratic society, organized representatives of the various producer forces are necessarily in regular consultation with those government authorities responsible for economic policy. Thus a rudimentary form of industrial corporatism has appeared, unplanned, but powerful in its situational logic.

The danger is that state responsibility tends to become defined *exclusively* in terms of synchronizing those organizational parts and of meeting the formal requirements for lubricating this highly mechanical system. The shortcomings of the present political arrangements are that narrow economic criteria of social need overwhelmingly dominate political life, and that there is little perspective on the environmental consequences of the industrial system's routine operation so structured. It is clear that there has been a *systemic* oversight of the pollution and amenity problems (systemic–not systematic; rather than a conscious, concerted effort to suppress information, there has been an unconscious failure to perceive the issue). Thus, while we know of public officials sensitive to the value of keeping employment in Detroit high, of others responsive to the market price of wheat, and still others attentive to the profit margins of aerospace contractors, no public official, especially within administrative departments, has served as watchdog for the value of reducing automobile congestion in the heart of American cities, nor was there one who had developed, as part of his departmental responsibilities, sensitivity for the discomfort of New York City subway riders. There is no avoiding the overwhelming conclusion that there are whole areas of social life that have lain outside of any official domain. Yet they are ones of acute, if not fatal, concern to millions of people.[6] They take the form not of natural disasters but of man-made conditions arising from the self-same workings of a society successful in other respects. Certainly, until the Environmental Protection Agency was created, there was no "Department of the Environment," expressing the government's overall responsibility for the condition of our natural endowment, and for the creation of amenable physical surroundings, with its well-established constituency in Congress and clientele interest groups. Environmental concerns do not meet a productive standard of consequence. They do not represent the pecuniary interests of one particular sector of society. They point to a collective condition. Moreover, to establish an executive agency like the Environmental Protection Agency as one bureaucratic agency among others, representing one set of special interests among others, misinterprets the problem. It overlooks the essential qualitative distinction between a particular interest that is part of the productive dimension of society, and a problem-area of a communal nature that concerns the relationship between the industrial system itself and the overall environment of life.[a] (See chapter 5)

The Problem As Theory

The institutional and cultural biases of society are reflected in its theoretical knowledge; and conversely, dominant social theories tend to reinforce and to

---

[a]Until recently, the environment was equated with "conservation" and treated as a special interest. Since early in the century, there have been agencies within the Department of the Interior concerned with conservation, and there have been conservation-minded organizations (e.g., the Sierra Club and the Audubon Society). Even on their own terms, they have operated on the fringes of government, organizationally weak and of limited influence. Indeed, agencies like the Forest Service seem more inclined to serve the demands of the lumber industry for access to national forests than to preserving wilderness areas, if not, as Representative Dingell caustically remarked, "a wholly-owned subsidiary of the timber industry."[7] Conservation was an idle indulgence of a society with other, more important things to do. Conservationists were viewed as curators who sought to preserve our remote, economically unproductive areas as a remembrance of an environment past.[8] Intelligent management of the urban environment, planning for careful resource use, and prevention of pollution were in no sense a major governmental activity or an object of public attention. Represented by weak executive agencies, supported by a constituency composed only of those few individuals for whom the condition of the environment was a salient problem, conservation could not compete in a political arena where maximizing production and arranging distribution were taken to be self-evidently what society and its public institutions were all about.

sustain the system's modal features. Our intellectual apparatus is part of the problem.

The conceptual bias exists at two levels. First, in the prevailing popular beliefs about the unqualified virtues of growth, progress, and technology; about the central place of material goods in the good life and the status generating effects of consumption; about the inappropriateness of increasing expenditure on public amenities at the expense of private income. Second, in the more formal, analytical knowledge of political and economic theorists who, in their writings, help to fashion over time the frame of reference in which we develop our collective understanding of reality.

The emergence of the environmental issue has been profoundly disturbing, not just of conventional belief, but of the intellectual systems on which economists and political scientists depend to explain the workings of a modern society. Often they are so stilted in their attachment to the existing organization of things and state of affairs that they appear to be more impediments to intelligent understanding of the issues at hand and to the elaboration of strategies of reform than sources of enlightenment and guides to purposeful action.

Change in our approach to the environment will depend on a revision of both popular belief and formal knowledge. Shifts in popular attitudes can be expected to occur gradually as part of a pragmatic response to new, observable circumstances. One major factor determining the scope and depth of the reappraisal will be the leadership exercised by public authorities in defining environmental issues, developing themes, formulating programs of action, and taking initiatives that entail a redrawing of priorities and budgets. A requirement for imaginative leadership, in turn, is a new vision of the industrial system such as only more structured theory can provide. Unfortunately, the most influential and widely held political and economic theory is built on principles that confirm the naturalness and desirability of our present institutional pattern. For political scientists, they are: pluralist versions of representative democracy; incremental approaches to public policy-making; and an aversion to broad philosophical views of public purpose. For economists, they are: the growth imperative, the marginality of environmental effects to cost calculation, and deep preference for the market mechanism, as opposed to state authorities, as the best allocater of national resources. Incorporating and purifying the conventional wisdom about social ends and means, they lend an aura of inevitability and logical correctness to the basic structures and processes of our industrial system.

2 Pluralism and American Politics

As a theory of democratic society and as a political doctrine, pluralism has enjoyed wide currency and favor.[1] However varied their formulation, the major strands of pluralist writings hold together surprisingly well. The ingredients of the pluralist vision are well known and can be expressed in these postulates: the primary public concern of the great mass of citizenry is the advancement of pecuniary interests and claims to status; groups rooted in the various sectors of the economy strive to influence government so as to secure preferential benefits; a constitutional system provides ready channels for the legitimate expression of their demands; these groups compete for tangible gain within a framework of consensus on democratic procedure and tacitly recognize the common interest to be practical cooperation within the prevailing system; national leaders are obliged to devote the greater portion of their time to questions of "welfare," and they are most highly sensitized to claims of economic interest. A concommitant to the preoccupation with welfare issues is a decline in old-style political combat between implacably hostile forces and the passionate ideologies that sustained them. The nature of individual and group desires is such that unrelenting class or party warfare becomes superfluous and, indeed, is distained as an obstacle to the steady expansion of industrial production which makes possible their satisfaction.[2]

Conflict is confined to the field of combat provided by the legislative and bureaucratic politics of industrial coordination and interest aggregation, a hauling and pulling among interest groups that seek to gain narrow advantage within the consensual framework. Liberal constitutionalism in the pluralist mold, therefore, is viewed and largely functions as a series of interlocking institutions that operate with a high degree of routine to perform satisfactorily the public functions of society with a minimum of self-consciousness and with a minimum of directive leadership. To a large extent, government organs are registrants of the outcome in group conflicts, and their officials are umpires who—although often showing preference and bias—enforce, and themselves act in accordance with the rules of the democratic game.

Leaders are not *entirely* slaves to circumstances, immobilized except to pivot from one special pleader to another. The executive, and in some respects, the legislator, is charged with defining the relationship to government of a plethora of groups in such a way as to reconcile comprehensive economic direction with a plurality of partial interests and quasi-autonomous institutions. He experiments with procedures to achieve these ends and uses the multiple forms of persuasion

9

available to him to secure the necessary commitments. For him, politics increasingly centers around alternative means for reconciling and coordinating diverse interests while maintaining equilibrium and an essential unity by compromise and consultation within a broad consensual framework. He is, though, not the man to anticipate crisis, to ponder long-term problems, to launch into a public debate over broad national goals, and rarely does he create a personal authority that transcends the immediate support of his party's coalition of backers. He does not address himself to the citizenry at large, but rather, characteristically, to clusters of interest groups. In a sense, he does not govern persons, but acts through a number of organizational intermediaries; he does not espouse an all-embracing political *Weltanschauung* but reflects in his thinking the preexistent and inherent harmony of cooperative industrial society. In most instances he does not deal with the passions of intensely committed individuals but coordinates particular interests and mediates the mild conflict of group and administrative feuding. His world is one of bargaining, negotiating, coalitions, and organizational encroachments and retreats.

The distinctive feature of a political system so constituted is that it depends on: (a) everyone doing what he is institutionally conditioned to do; and (b) a uniformity of goals and values. As long as the prime dispositions are to produce efficiently and to advance tangible interests, a political system geared for managing the infrastructure of an industrial economy, for implementating the complex network of regulations and rules that sustain it, and for responding to the claims for preferential reward made upon it by organizational interests is successful. Which is to say, it is successful in its own terms. Political rights are secured, access to government endows status and inspires a sense of political competence, progress in the growth of GNP continues, and its product is widely, if inequitably, distributed.

The exclusiveness of its preoccupation with gratifying private wants and its rote manner of operation carries with it equally severe liabilities. Outstanding is its neglect of communal needs and public goods defined by other than the conventional economic indicators; second is the structural deficiency in its lack of instrumentalities for recognizing unintended consequences; third is the failure to create a sense of the political whole or to provide a place for leadership with perspective on the role of institutions. Each of these traits is exemplified in the system's handling, or mishandling, of environmental problems.

Pluralism as both description and advocacy has not gone entirely unchallenged.[3] Most of the attack, though, has come from radical critics mainly interested in questions of equity and maldistribution. They have been keen to point out that: (a) not all groups in society have access to the decision-making centers; (b) those with limited education are disadvantaged through lack of organizational skills; (c) governmental procedures are not in fact always neutral but rather are used prejudicially for or against certain interests; and (d) the individual is denied a sense of political efficacy by being forced to act through organizational intermediaries. Much of this analysis was valid and remains so. Our criticism, though, is of a different order. We are primarily interested in the want of any affirmative conception of public or collective interest and the system's failure to provide proper place for instrumentalities to deal with problems unmonitored by interest-based, plural associations. The system is failing in areas where class or racial bias bear on the issue only tangentially, if at all.

Criticisms of pluralism that stressed its narrow focus and overly mechanistic character were made, usually in rather abstract terms, before the environmental crisis broke into public view.[a] Without reference to specific failures of the magnitude now observable (race relations aside), it was difficult to drive home the attack. In response to claims of systemic liability, the pluralist countered with the pugnacious challenge, "Prove it!" Pointing with satisfaction to the stability and accomplishments of the American system, he awaited a retort with smug assurance. Today there is overwhelming and mounting evidence of major failure. By any objective standard, our public institutions and leadership have been grossly unaware of, and unresponsive to, conditions of pollution and disamenity. Its obvious virtues notwithstanding, pluralism has failed in an important respect.

The disagreement between the plural-incrementalists and their environmental critics is simultaneously one of social value and political philosophy. There are genuine differences in the importance they attribute to pollution, disamenity and/or resource depletion. Orthodox pluralists tend to judge these problems to be less than urgent and so conceived they are relegated to a place relatively low on the scale of public need.[5] In other words, they both dispute the claim of dire crisis and ascribe less weight to acknowledged problems than the environmentalist does. The conditions themselves do permit, of course, for varying assessments and interpretations. We should, though, recognize a strain to consistency between the logical requirements of an intellectual system and the evaluations made on a particular issue that affects the viability of the broader doctrine. This caution hold for those on both sides of the argument.

---

[a]In the early and mid-1960s, there was a dimension to the academic critique of pluralism of an essentially philosophical character which differed from the radical criticism that focused on the inequities sustained by pluralist politics. Identified with political philosophers like Sheldon Wolin, it argued the virtues of a classic democracy where active citizens, participants in communal affairs, satisfied the individual's inherent need for civic engagement, while endowing the polity with both organic strength and greater sensitivity to the requirements for its collective well-being.[4] Wolin saw mass participation as a precondition to social health and later would point to the pervasive youth alienation and general estrangement from the political process, and the system's convulsive struggling with racism and militarism as evidence of its structural weakness. Defenders of pluralism, in practice and in theory, interpreted these problems as due to faulty individual judgment and mistaken policy, rather than reflecting systemic shortcomings. And often they have pointed to the critics, both radical and philosophical advocates of participatory democracy, as exacerbating the problem of managing a democratic society in times of social crisis.

In particular, many doctrinally committed plural-incrementalists still reject the idea that the environmental problem is severe and that any major failure in the system has been uncovered. Quite apart from the inclination of any theorist to resist evidence challenging his intellectual offspring, these theorists are like the actors they described, so much a part of the institutional mechanism (and its sustaining belief system) which conditions attitudes and behavior that they change no faster in their thinking than society or government does in its actions.

At the philosophical level, environmentalists and pluralists dispute where the outstanding danger to society lies. In his general outlook, the pluralist views protection of democratic institutions in the face of the recurrent threats of uncompromising, doctrinaire attitudes as the overriding concern at all times. For him the system is inherently fragile and liable to disequilibrium. It can only survive and flourish where very special conditions obtain. These include the aforementioned attributes: a pragmatic political culture that places premiums on compromise; a deep, largely unspoken agreement on political forms *and* social purposes; the plural organization of power intragovernmentally and among those groups that act on it; and an incremental approach to problem-solving. When these conditions are weakened, the democratic system becomes vulnerable. The environmental movement is seen, among other things, as a possible threat to the stable system built on these principles. It introduces passion into politics; it generates inflexible commitments; it implies planning and design; and not least important, it could ignite a bitter political struggle between steady-state ideas and supporters of dynamic industrial growth. The pluralist's conviction that democratic man's sense of status and attachment to rules of the game depend on regular increases in his material well-being leads the theorist to look askance at any suggestion of restricting the social lubricant of ever bigger paychecks (see chapter 8).

From the environmentalist vantage point, this school of analysis is so keen on asking "who gets what, when and how?" it has overlooked the fact that everyone is "getting it" collectively from a system preoccupied with preferrential payoffs. Plural-incrementalists have an essential fear of politics, except of the muted sort they find so appealing and which characterized the United States until very recently. The "bugbear" is uncompromising ideological politics, the intolerant passions it can engender, and ultimately the threat of totalitarianism it carries. Conditioned by the experience of the 1930s to suspect mass engagement in political action, they see a challenge to ordered government in an issue-oriented, energized politics directed at implementing a program that drastically challenges the procedural conservatism now in force. Were political commitment and involvement not controlled by that plethora of interest associations and party groupings that normally monitor popular action aimed at government, that whole governmental mechanism that cuts and trims, adjusts, mediates, aggregates, and moderates would be undermined. For the pluralist, those institutional arrangements are necessary checks on the abuse of power by willful majorities or overweening executives. Without them the concentration of power in irresponsible hands become a real possibility, and the prospect a temptation for power-seekers. Moreover, political action inspired by a clear ideal is seen as exacerbating the threat by introducing an element of doctrinal rigidity into the political arena.

What the environmental movement entails is more than just the introduction of another interest into the policy process. It implies at least a partial transcendence of the game of interest politics itself. For there cannot be effective action without a clear sense of priority, a concerting of governmental effort and the reinforcement of the public interest (and political authority) at the expense of private wealth and plural interests. The issue as the environmentalist sees it is the substantive product of the democratic system and its failure to address itself to certain matters of acute communal need. The attack on pluralist faith and incrementalist advocacy does not necessarily presume failure in other policy areas (although mounting political alienation and the movement for participatory democracy raise some doubts on that score). The thrust of the critical analysis is that the processes of policy-making that now prevail need amendment if progress is to be made toward improving environmental conditions. The process *qua* process, as mechanism and method, is not taken to be an indisputably central element of stability, the keystone of the system, that must be left untampered if representative government and political liberties are to be guaranteed. On this score it is the plural-incrementalist who is exhibiting rigidity and evincing a doctrinaire commitment to a set of political beliefs. In asserting that only an ultrapragmatic instrumentalist can produce intelligent, effective policy-making; in labelling rational planning as, at best, an unproductive exercise in intellectual wool-gathering, and at worst as a latent authoritarianism; and in associating the common good and public well-being with the routinization of private affluence; the theorist presents us with a self-contained intellectual system of his own. While stressing the flexibility of the political order so constructed, the analysis is strikingly insular in its imperviousness to contradictory evidence, in its arguing from first principles, and in its tendency to see any change in its particular features as a threat to the whole edifice of a democratic polity.

Incremental pluralists are in one sense like the French generals who have been accused of always planning for the last war while overlooking threats of the moment. Their deep, and abiding commitment to a conception of democratic politics that stresses the muting of political passion, the partial nature of all political loyalties, reflects a distrust of doctrine, policy design, and participation inspired by political philosophy. For them, the "last war" is the totalitarian politics of recent historical memory. It, along with the Great Depression, seems the decisive intellectual experience in their lives, and their abiding point of reference. The danger is that mass man, unrestrained by traditional loyalties and conventional belief, will abuse the liberties of a democratic system. The conditions they have largely been unable to perceive are those that grow out of the very system whose mechanical stability they so highly prize; organizational alienation, estrangement from a politics of compromise, disaffection from the acquisitiveness that seems to be the industrial system's motivating force and revulsion at the destruction of physical beauty and social amenity permitted by the blindness of the machine. The very strength of a pluralist democracy is its self-sustaining equilibrium which seemingly requires no conscious guidance for it to maintain harmony and order. It is just this implicitness, its reliance on unspoken purpose that is also the source of many contemporary ills.

The indictment of "pluralism" as a political theory is that it has demonstrated the same uncritical assumptions characteristic of the system it describes. Explanation and advocacy have been one. So completely is that so, that the adherents to pluralist doctrine have an almost perfect record of failure to anticipate the political problems that are trying us. Leaving aside the disruptive effects of the war in Indochina, which is tangential to the issue of theoretical weakness and bias, let us think for a moment of those political discontents that have been the focus of our attention and concern: the demand for participation—in organization and in politics; the environment; racial conflict and the compulsive status competition it has unleashed. None of these elements played any major part in the pluralist theory-building of the 1950s and early 1960s. Now that they have thrust themselves upon us, pluralism demonstrates a sad inability to conceptualize them and to reconcile them with the dominant features of the system whose details they have so finely analyzed and whose virtues they have espoused. Pluralism has taught us much about modern democracy; the accomplishments of the system to which it belongs are considerable and on the whole admirable. Its shortcomings are equally real.

Whatever the success of pluralist democracy in the American pattern in achieving continuity and stability for its liberal institutions, and in creating unprecedented affluence, it today must face a further test. Can a pluralist system so constituted effectively act to manage its collective environment? Where public policy is largely determined by the interplay of diverse economic associations and partisan groupings, the opportunities for consciously relating a particular program to a broader design are less than abundant. Can leadership accustomed to mediating muted conflict of interest politics think and act comprehensively? Prone to assume that well-being and stability require only gentle governmental steering and minor structural adjustment, can it begin to question purposes as a prelude to creatively controlling its industrial future? Can a citizenry whose involvement in public affairs normally is filtered by the economic or professional association that advances vocational interests collectively define public goals and act communally? How the system meets the threat of environmental crisis and the challenge of fashioning a more edifying social environment is being strongly influenced by conditions wherein our problems are comprehensively communal and our political identifications narrow and particularistic.

3

Incrementalism and the Distrust of Reasoned Policy-Making

Incrementalism is undeniably the characteristic *modus operandi* of democratic government and of our institutions in general. It is also the favored doctrine of social scientists interested in the processes of public policy formation and decision-making. The most prominent and influential writing on the subject takes this approach. Charles Lindblom is the name most commonly associated with *disjointed incrementalism*, as theory *and* prescription. Indeed, the term "disjointed incrementalism" is his invention. In a number of cogent works he has elaborated his ideas with verve and force.[1] They might properly be taken as the definitive statement of academic thinking on the subject, as well as being an articulation of attitudes that pervade our entire political structure.[a]

---

[a]The designation of Lindblom and Braybrooke as the point of analytical departure is dictated both by the clarity of their statement on incrementalism and its exposition as a principle of political as well as organizational decision-making. In contrast to the rich literature in the field of organizational theory and the highly nuanced (if not scholastic) elaboration of administrative decision-making models, surprisingly little critical attention has been paid either the boundary relationship (and mutual influences) of administrative and political authority or the characteristic processes of issue formation and policy choice at the highest levels of government.[2]

The overwhelming portion of the copious organization literature considers questions of internal structure and administrative management in a context that takes systemic objectives and policy goals for granted. More recently, the mounting concern and intellectual interest in the multiple forms of organizational alienation and widespread rejection of formal bureaucratic institutions has aroused a serious review of the requirements for effective performance and the tradeoffs between efficiency in achieving narrow goals of output maximization with the desirable and increasingly necessary cultivation of organizational identification, cooperative community, and personal meaning in the work place. As we suggest in chapter 8, there are connections to be made between institutional reform and modification of the industrial system's dominant purposes and uncritical belief in the virtues of growth and productivity. However, the types of issues about organizational structure and processes addressed by the bulk of the reformist literature fails to consider not only this aspect of the problem, but also the broader public policy role of procedurally conservative organizations adhering to, and supportive of, conventional wisdom about budgetary priorities, definitions of public interest, and other fundamental precepts of political economy.

Decision-making theory as an extension and companion subject to organizational theory has been only somewhat more illuminating of governmental procedure and its implications for public policy. Strikingly, it is in the context of foreign policy analysis that the most incisive and imaginative effort has been made to assess the policy implications of our bureaucratically structured public institutions. The work of Graham Allison on 'bureaucratic politics" has been particularly noteworthy in delineating the patterns of organizational interest and bureaucratically defined public purposes that skew the formulation of issues for political decision, impinge on the decision-making process, and influence their implementation.[3]

The incrementalist mode, and state of mind, introduced as a theoretical problem in this

For Lindlom, and those who support his position, incrementalism is a term of both analytical description and exhortation. Those writers do not use it merely to describe how governments function, but staunchly advance the belief that it is the most effective, and democratic, manner for conducting the public's business. There is no denying the correctness of the analysis or the acuity of the insights it provides. There are abundant reasons for critically questioning its advocacy.

The point of departure for their theory is an attack on what they call "ideal" or rational policy-making. As a theory (it is rarely observable in practice in the American system), it is described as an approach that sees government as a machine programmed to make rational choices on the basis of systematic analysis, choosing among clearly defined alternatives. As they understand rational policy-making, one treats policy questions as intellectual problems. For the incrementalist this is a wholly distorted view of the policy process that unrealistically attributes a purposefulness and logical rigor to public officials that, in fact, is absent. Moreover, it is argued, rational policy-making entails a formalistic rigidity that would make the policy process unresponsive to information conveyed upward in the political system and would be unaccommodating to shifting circumstances. The assumption is that the rationalist model depends on a fixed, doctrinaire view of the public good that is undemocratic and inflexible.

In sketching the very great discrepancies that exist between the rationalist ideal-type and the reality of policy-making, Lindblom et al, properly draw one's attention to the pragmatic instrumentalism by which government normally functions. But the problem they perceive is not the inadequacy of the system as presently constituted. Rather it is the dangerous and disruptive effects of trying to impose a rational method where it is inappropriate and undesirable. Disjointed incrementalism is for them not just an expedient alternative. It is the *preferred method* for making policy that both matches our pluralist democracy *and* will provide for a more perfect systemic rationality in the long run. In other words, we are not only disjointed and incremental by cultural habit and out of desire to avoid the abuses of centralized authority (and accordingly might accept a price in inefficiency and narrowness for it). Policy analysis à la Braybrooke and Lindblom claims that in fact we now enjoy pluralist flexibility *and* the added dividend of handling our problems and meeting governmental responsibilities

chapter (and which reappears in several empirical contexts subsequently as an impediment to concerted environmental policy-making), is at once a function of pervasive bureaucratic institutions and a more generalized intellectual and cultural disposition in our society. It afflicts both administrators who have undergone powerful organizational conditioning and elected officials who have experienced a more subtle socialization in a political system that enshrines pragmatism and the piecemeal approach of pluralism. The consequences, as we observe throughout this work, are to reinforce orthodox thinking about public ends and means, and to leave government temperamentally and intellectually ill-prepared for the task of strategic planning that seems critical to serious environmental programming.

more efficiently than we would if our institutions were self-conscious in stipulating objectives and systematic in relating ends to means.

What does disjointed incrementalism mean in practice?

It is decision-making through small or incremental moves on particular problems rather than through a comprehensive . . . program. The strategy thus sharply reduces the analyst's need for either a wide-ranging body of empirical generalizations or the propositions of a large formal theoretical system.

Lindblom and Braybrooke provide us with an artful description of the public officials' mental processes:

When a man sets out to solve a problem, he embarks on a course of mental activity more circuitous, more complex, more subtle, and perhaps more idiosyncratic than he perceives. If he is aware of some of the grosser [sic] aspects of his own problem-solving, as when he consciously focuses his attention on what he has understood as a critical unknown, he will often have only the feeblest insight into how his mind finds, creates, dredges up—which of these he does not know—a new idea. Dodging in and out of the unconscious, moving back and forth from the concrete to abstract, trying chance here and system there, soaring, jumping, back-tracking, crawling, sometimes freezing on point like a bird dog, he exploits mental processes that are only slowly yielding to observation and systematic description.[4]

He thinks and acts within a universe of organizational and programmatic givens. The consequences for the overall process of government policy-making are to emphasize its institutional conservatism and its *ad hoc* pragmatic response to new circumstances. The individual participant in the process operates on the basis of margin-dependent choice. What *is* serves as the point of departure for what *might be.* Attention focuses on "the increments by which the social states that might result from alternative policies differ from the *status quo.*"[5] Options are not developed on the basis of social principles or some stated conception of what government should do or what a situation dictates. Alternatives represent variations in the adjustment of ideas incorporated in programs now in place. The policymaker considers only a restricted variety of policy alternatives.[6] Whereas the possible courses of action objectively are numerous, recognition is accorded only to those that represent extrapolations from the *status quo.* No alternative that is independent of present policy therefore can enter into the policymakers field of vision; neither for that matter can a new problem area, e.g., environmental amenities (and, as a corollary, there are also a restricted number of consequences considered for a particular policy).

There is a strong tendency to neglect indirect effects, long-term cumulative effects, and any consequences whose monitoring is not provided for by the narrow definition of the established policy itself. Policy is formulated to meet a clear need with the least possible disturbance of established ideas, organizations, or ways of doing things. The system's ability to operate in this manner of fact may becomes one criterion of an issue's suitability for public action. So embedded are objectives in the incremental process of policy adjustment that they often become subordinate to existing programs rather than the other way around. Thus, in a classic sense, means come to determine ends.

As a political method, disjointed incrementalism only becomes intelligible, and its viability comprehensible, when placed in the context of the pluralist, interest-based policies of our industrial system. It is the assumption of an unspoken consensus on social purposes and political values that permits a procedural mode of functioning to act without reference to the principles on which it is grounded or the goals that move it. The presupposition that the stability of the system is assured permits a mechanical ordering of relationships. And it is the belief that incremental adjustment accommodates all interests and concerns that allows it to function free from disruptive conflict or challenges to its basic format.

Our criticism of the incrementalist analysis *cum* prescription is threefold:

1. It lacks any conception of the common good or "public interest" and thus neglects collective problems and systemic effects.
2. It offers no mechanism for effectively anticipating problems.
3. It biases the study of public policy in favor of the *status quo* and offers no substantive basis for critical assessment of alternatives.[b]

Let us look first at the proposition that the system they outline is one without substantive bias, and one which can accommodate itself to any range of circumstance and conception of social need. Because policy usually changes marginally, and only in reference to what is preestablished, the theorist assumes that the public good is being advanced by programs already in force. The public good becomes a *relational concept* that has no intrinsic meaning in itself. The incrementalist views it as associated with the maintenance of present procedures for their own sake, and as an indicator of well-being. No policy is *on its merits* preferable to any other since no social theory, design, or plan is self-evidentally the most desirable, whatever it might be. Established policies imply "correctness"—because they are an output of the procedurally defined system. Disjointed incrementalism rejects the notion that there is any acceptable standard for judging "ideals"; they can only serve as a source of disruption and

---

[b]We should make it clear that disjointed incrementalism is a succinct description of the way public policy normally is made. Those practices are also one of the reasons for our environmental difficulties. Incrementalists, though, too casually disregard the system's defects and do not recognize how it fails drastically to meet certain kinds of public problems. As with pluralists, their shortsightedness seems very much an aspect of the system they study and represents an extension of the same attitudes and ways of looking at the world that prevail among public officials.

19

dissension. Approvingly, they note that "if the analyst limits his attention to increments, it follows that he will also foreswear the extraordinary difficulties of finding a utopia of the maximum of a function and will ask himself only for evidence of a step forward."[7] But how is "forward" defined, and by what criteria?; only by reference to the direction implicit in ongoing policy. Since the bases and objectives of that policy never undergo systematic consideration, we might surmise that progress is defined situationally; that is, defined with regard to the properties of the political system and the unspoken belief in the desirability of their preservation. Looked at from this procedural vantage point, America's common good in 1953 included legal sanction of social segregation and the federal government's acceptance of local oppression of black citizens. By 1966 that same situationally defined good meant an end to legalized segregation, a concerted effort to oppose local discrimination, and massive programs to remove the social and economic differences between the races.

The system which serves as the point of reference for theorists of incrementalism is, of course, the American system understood as one character-ized by the muted politics of interest competition. Reading the discussion of disjointed-incrementalism from the environmentalist perspective, one can only be distressed by the self-confident manner in which the authors optimistically review its workings. Looked at from the conventional vantage point of those preoccupied with the traditional issues of industrial life, though, the system seems more efficient (if not entirely unbiased) and its products admitting of praise. The public interest in this context then becomes the satisfaction of as many group claims on government as is reasonably possible. Policy-making is largely the function of managing the interplay among economic associations and social strata while overseeing the performance of the industrial infrastructure upon which all depend for receipt of benefits. Government's responsibility is very much one of accommodation and adjustment under those conditions. The public policy-maker in effect assumes the limited function of economic gratification. As Braybrooke and Lindblom admit, he is engaged in satisfying rather than maximizing behavior. In this way, any common objective of a group of individuals can be thought of as a public good.[8] In a curious distortion of Mill's classic precept that an objectifiable common good will result from the individual rational behavior of citizens, the incrementalists reject the idea of common interest itself and substitute the sum of satisfied groups whose contentment is the only valid goal of public policy.

Keeping the distributive issue in mind, we can more readily make sense out of an incrementalist proposition such as:

In its preoccupation with increments, the strategy often makes it logically possible for analysts to agree on evaluation of alternative policies, regardless of their disagreements on ultimate values.[9]

Certainly, if the issue is one of expenditure on the poverty program or increases in social security payments, it is relatively easy for analysts to reach agreement by splitting the difference *or* casting aside one proposed program as being organizationally unworkable. In so doing, they hold in abeyance a possibly more fundamental disagreement over community control or guaranteed annual incomes. But the basic conflict is not resolved, and postponing its resolution can heighten antagonisms that eventually lead to violent confrontation.

An even more critical failure is disjointed incrementalism's inability to *identify* issues and to define them properly. It responds poorly, if at all, to problems not previously handled by the system and without an obvious, organized constitutency, e.g., environmental pollution, and more strikingly, environmental disamenities.

The incremental theorist claims that:

Where analysis and policy-making are serial, remedial, and fragmented, political processes can achieve consideration of a wider variety of values than can possibly be grasped and attended to by any one analyst or policy-maker.[10]

If one is speaking of the number of relevant elements that might be picked up in reference to a particular issue of detail, the statement is undoubtedly correct. With all the organizational interests affected demanding a piece of the action, a great deal is going to be said and heard. However, it is not self-evident that this swarm of incremental policymakers is a substitute for leadership with a wide scope of responsibility whose task is to recognize problems, anticipate consequences of present programs, and guide governmental action toward the achievement of some generalized social goals. *Marginal incrementalists,* by definition, are unable to discern values or problems except as they grow out of established policy.

The weakness of the incrementalist's intellectual position, lacking as it does any concrete conception of achievement other than a procedural one, is starkly seen in its futile wrestling with the problem of pernicious and/or unintended consequences. Some problems are just overlooked; others are created by a disjointed approach to public policy itself and equally neglected. Unable to perceive social reality except as it is filtered through the sieves of agency bureaucracy and ancillary interest organizations, the policymaker must hope that *somewhere* in the abstruse apparatus of government, *sometime,* it will show up. Having established no way of anticipating problems, the incrementalist attempts to turn a liability into a theoretical asset. Thus, he argues, "unanticipated adverse consequences can often be better guarded against by waiting for their emergence than by futile attempts to anticipate every contingency as required in synoptic problem-solving";[11] and he claims that the fiction that *it is better to answer as many questions as possible in advance*—is not an acceptable axiom for decision-making.[12] Presumably, the effort to do so would stultify the policy process by sucking policymakers into the frustrating quicksand of doctrine, planning designs, or just ideas.

The presumption is that unanticipated effects will be remedially dealt with. Such might be the case, in most instances in any event, if we are referring to interests that have been slighted. There the feedback mechanism of constituency-oriented agencies or congressional faction (or street riot) comes into play. But it is inaccurate to state with serene confidence that: "groups and government decision-makers become watchdogs for values they fear will be neglected by others, and each decision-maker develops great sensitivity to certain lines of consequences."[13] The present condition of the American environment belies that confidence. As we have noted previously, the keen attentiveness to certain kinds of developments is matched by a remarkable insensitivity to others. There is no basis for claiming that officials or groups took it upon themselves to serve as watchdogs for commuter needs or clean-air requirements. It is hard to see how they could have, given that these officials and groups define their responsibility by reference to the narrow interests they are organized to promote or that line of policy they are expected to implement. They are not privateers roaming the political system looking for targets of opportunity "neglected by others." Rather, they are an integral part of a process that delimits what enters the range of vision and is accorded status as a pertinent concern of public authority. It might well be true, to use Charles L. Schultze's accurate paraphrase of the incrementalist position, that "since our values and the weights attached to them are extremely subtle and complex, no attempt to articulate them in advance will encompass *all* their shadings and intensities." (Italics mine.)[14] But there is good reason to expect that some form of planning, as opposed to the "muddling through" of disjointed incrementalism, will point up *more* of the shading and intensity, and will identify a range of values overlooked by an overly pragmatic policy process.

We should be reminded that incrementalists have a deeply ingrained dislike for any discussion of priority or social purpose. Aaron Wildavsky has put it more bluntly than most:

It is impermissible to treat goals as if they are known in advance. If an order of priority is determined, it should be *ad hoc*. Hopefully, the question of priority can be entirely evaded by redesigning.[15]

Presumably, purpose and preference can and should grow organically out of the interaction of plural forces acting upon and within government. This view is inaccurate as description of present realities, in addition to being dangerous as advocacy. Schultze correctly asserts that it is "naive to think that in areas of tremendous complexity, the pure bargaining process can translate a loosely developed set of general values into meaningful operational objectives. While it is often strategically and tactically important for participants in the bargaining process to conceal their objectives from their adversaries, it hardly behooves them to conceal them from themselves."[16]

In fact, the process of policy-making as we know it is not valuatively neutral;

it is riven with bias and preference. Present policies favor some interests over others (e.g., trucking companies over commuters), they give considerate attention to some issues (e.g., the financing of highway construction), and barely recognize others (deteriorating mass transit facilities). To argue in support of a "priority-free" politics is to assert the naturalness of prevailing priorities. The conservative effect is pronounced. Significant change in the direction of greater public expenditure and accentuated effort in addressing conditions of environmental pollution, or disamenity cannot be accomplished through a process of marginal adjustment. Such an approach dooms us to years of their continued neglect. It is only by making explicit the values implicit in the present pattern of public expenditure that we can fully appreciate the present disporportions as to areas of government activity and the imbalance between heavy private consumption and negligible spending on community needs.

Awareness of the magnitude of the environmental problems and conscious attention to the programmatic requirements for resolving them are the precondition for their resolution. Disjointed incrementalism by contrast means pragmatic disregard for structural defects and systemic disequilibria. The more routine the policy process, and the deeper its commitment to procedural norm, the greater the strength of intellectual inertia. Conservatism of thought is a hallmark of bureaucratic structures and a managerial style of leadership. The pervasive incrementalism of our political system stands as a major impediment to those pressures that otherwise could evoke an imaginative response commensurate with the character of the problem. For it distains free play of the mind and rumination of alternative futures—preliminaries to actual innovation when adversity is met.[17]

Incrementalism and Social Science

Principled, or doctrinaire attachment to disjointed incrementalism, as *prescription,* deserves further attention. This attitude is so much a part of the intellectual scene (as well as an accurate expression of the thinking of practitioners), and exercises such a powerful influence on social analysis, that examination of its peculiar qualities is important for any study of public policy in our industrial system.

The most curious feature of our addiction to so odd a concept as disjointed incrementalism is that it runs counter to the dominant rationalism of the culture. Modern society is distinguished by its intellectual positivism. Whether we refer to our scientific knowledge of nature, our productive techniques, our economic organization, or our forms of constitutional authority, we properly term them rationalized. Seemingly, in all these domains there has been a conscious and desired increase in the element of calculation and logical control, with a consonant reduction in the ability of contingent factors to interfere with the ordered workings of things. For it is a feature of our times that premiums are placed on efficiency, practicability, and regularity. Predictive power in industry depends on a formal abstraction of the factors of production and establishing an unchanging standard of value and medium of exchange. Predictive power in the exercise of bureaucratic authority depends on the formulation of codified laws and rules that are applied abstractly without reference to individual circumstance. The desired capacity to act with formalistic assurance is at once a reflection of modern society's dominant values, and a factor itself militating toward the creation of a highly structured social order.

Predictive power is also highly valued by social scientists. In their emulation of the natural sciences, the disciplines of economics, political science, and sociology have striven to refine the methods by which they could acquire a similar capacity to predict on the basis of recognizable patterns and regularities. The emphasis on quantifiable data, the development of techniques to provide such data, and the elaboration of theories based on it, are reflections of the positivist thrust that has fashioned the mind of the social scientist for at least a generation.

Theorists of disjointed incrementalism, of course, are not quantifiers; they offer little in the way of method and recondite technique. What we do find is an inordinate stress on *process*. It is the manner of doing things that counts even more than what is done. Their theory is also a political method designed both to detect regularities and to create them. As theory, its capacity to explain and, within certain circumstantially determined limits, to predict, depends on a view of policy-making that emphasizes practices with an implicit order and regularity about them. By focusing on the continuity of an "ongoing" set of activities, by stressing the marginality of change and the narrow band of reasonable choice, and by thus affirming the logical correctness of customary procedures, incrementalists create a theoretical world amenable to intellectual management and to some degree of predictability. If follows that the role of ideas (ideology, doctrine, systematic planning) should be downplayed and often denigrated. Any broad conception of the whole, any purposeful behavior aimed at shifting the boundaries of public action, threatens that routine working of institutions that permits confident analysis based on the assumption of recurrent behavior. Thus, ironically, the theorist's disposition to achieve a rational mastery of his subject skews the analysis in such a way as to neglect the element of rational, conscious, goal-oriented behavior among the political objects of its study.

Advocacy then serves to confirm the theoretical bias by opposing the accentuation of policy based on reasoned design. What is initially noted as a characteristic of the political system becomes a convenient subject for social science method and finally a personal belief as to the desired state of affairs. The social scientist as advocate has an intellectual stake in rejecting those reforms in the political system that will increase that element which is least liable to a predictive method dependent on observation of an undirected systemic pattern. Prescription is thereby an adjunct to theory.

The incrementalist's dislike for policy planned with reference to a systematic set of ideas is matched by his aversion to leadership. The political manager is a mediator of muted interest contests and records their outcome in legislation. The administrator makes marginal adjustments to gradual shifts in bureaucratic circumstance and fluctuations in the configuration of interest politics as expressed in legislation. Nowhere is there place for a public official with a vision of the preferred state and the will to accomplish his purposes. Admittedly, relatively few individuals of that type are visible on the political horizon. But here again, description overlaps with prescription to disparage any appreciable change in the accent of public policy-making. And once again, method has a strong affinity for theoretical orientation. Leadership implies individual decision. To focus on the individual act, though, threatens to contradict the purpose of a generalized methodology which is to avoid explaining political events in terms of the particularities of each situation. Theory strives to extend the area of prediction by abstracting concepts from the welter of concrete facts and to make them applicable to a number of related phenomena. The element of individual decision is reduced to a minimum in an effort to avoid the slippery questions of personal motivation that arise in discussing innovative, planned policy as opposed to the established practices of existing organizations managing conventional programs. Where factors of personal value and conscious individual calculation are paramount, the incrementalist feels acute intellectual discomfort.[c]

---

[c]Pluralists and incrementalists are attached to the mechanical images of interest-based politics for analogous reasons. They share a very definite conception of the democratic policy. For them, democracy is a political method, a *modus precendente.* It is a method for choosing officials officials to exercise the authority of the state, while giving the citizenry a "say" in the selection process. It is a method for satisfying the demands on government of as many economic groups as possible. It is a method for organizing government and for making policy. Its success is measured by the stability of the system. Whatever seems to meet that objective is in the public interest. Everything else is of secondary importance, if not inconsequential.

4

Economics and the Externality Problem

The bias of economic theory is as basic as that of political theory. The "science" of economics is at once more pretentious than political science and simpler. As Kindleberger has recently explained:

This is partly because it uses a powerful hypothesis about economic activity— that human beings economize or, more precisely, seek to minimize costs for a given output, or to maximize output for a given cost or input. It is also because inputs and outputs can be measured in a single *numeraire* or scale: money.[1]

Kindleberger could have gone one step further to state: (a) the presumed goal of economizing activity—increases in material gain; and (b) how output is defined— tangible product. Modern economics has perfected its models and increased its predictive power by defining human personality as characterized by a uniform predilection for pursuing pecuniary self-interest. Economic theory applies best to those domains where we can correctly presume that the behavior in question is aimed at increase in tangible benefit. It is under those circumstances that money serves as the appropriate measure of costs and benefits, and where models of individual or group conduct can elaborate the rules of interest— maximizing behavior.

We seem to be saying simply that economic theory applies to economics. Indeed, we are; but most professional economists do not agree. They see their discipline as engaged in the study of choice and decision in nearly all social contexts. For them, all behavior is cost minimizing and output maximizing. If there is an appropriate monetary measure of the goods involved, economics can do its analytical job.[2] Unfortunately, economists tend to take an overly generous view of where an appropriate monetary measure can be found. They are also disposed to accentuate *that* aspect of a relationship that does permit economic calculus while, at the same time, conveniently overlooking the nontangibles. It is a form of economic reductionism whereby the world, by intellectual degrees, becomes one unbounded arena for exchanging utilities. This reductionist propensity is understandable given the discipline's history, as well as the normal inclination toward academic aggrandizement.

Economics, as we now understand it, neatly embodies the valuative biases of a modern democratic culture. Economists are among the truest believers in the ethic of progress and have committed their work to the goal of economic growth and industrial expansion. If for generations they were known as members of "the most pessimistic of sciences," that reputation owed more to their failings in fashioning theories adequate to the task of assuring prosperity than to any widespread questioning of purpose. Today, certainly, the profession as a whole (and with rare exceptions economists in their individual capacities) view their responsibility as the explication of the intricacies of their subject in the interest of furthering our capacity to advance economic growth. (Ancillary to this overriding objective, are the analyses of attendant meliorative problems on matters of distribution and equity.) It would not be an exaggereation to say that the social role of economists is generally perceived as that of advising the collectivity how it might most swiftly and efficiently enrich itself. Indeed, that is the function they normally perform.

As luminous a personality in the field as a former chairman of the Council of Economic Advisors, recently was reported to remark that he could not "conceive of an economics without growth."[3][a] Understandably so. Its assumptions about individual acquisitiveness, corporate growth strategies, and government commitments to guaranteeing routine increments of gross national product do not permit of steady-state theories. As Nathaniel Wollman points out, conventional economics almost never asks itself the question of what "the 'proper' supply of non-marketed goods and services" is.[4] It is concerned only that the aggregate quantity increase. Growth economics' near total dominance of the field is understandable given the cultural predelictions and objectives of the society at large. But its shortcoming are no less real for that identification; and its drawbacks for analysis of environmental problems are accentuated by the profession's uncritical acceptance of its underlying *raison d'être*.

The dominant formulations of economic science provide little place for environmental factors. First, there is the bias in its assignment of values. The pricing system measures accurately certain things, mainly tangible goods and services (and even the latter clumsily), and very inadequately others, e.g., physical discomfort, polluted air, or water. In his brilliant attack on "index economics," Ezra Mishan (one of a handful of economists who are not "growth-maniacs") develops a critical analysis of the ways in which economic theory does, or does not, take into account environmental costs in its calculus of comparative advantage.[5] These indirect costs, e.g., those external to the transaction, are normally relegated to the theoretical limbo of a catchall category labelled variously "externalities" or "spillover" effects. Unintended consequences such as pesticide contamination, scarred landscapes, and cacophonous noise, are not directly considered in the cost-benefit estimate. Under present theoretical conditions it would be very difficult to include them even where there were disposition to do so. Until recently, clean air, clean water, quiet, and natural beauty, have been designated "free goods." By *free goods* is meant those which are not scarce and which therefore are seen as possessing no

---

[a]This statement is the scholarly counterpart to the advertising of a West Coast power company that proclaimed, "Stagnation is the Worst Form of Pollution."

economic value except the cost of utilization. They are taken to be of "unlimited supply," for all economic intents and purposes. They are costless.[b] Whatever their potential misuse, the costs are borne by others than the actual user. The failure to attribute value to these goods is not just in the manner of an oversight. Rather it accurately reflects both the society's definition of worth and the awkwardness, if not impossibility of fitting them into the normal calculus of costs and benefits. Partly as a consequence, industrial growth and increases in individual consumption have been generally regarded as more worthy of attention than the physical condition of our surroundings. Actually, this understates it. As expressed in most economic theories and models, environmental amenities until very recently have had no priority *whatsoever,* since the free goods they depend on are not accorded any value. It is not surprising, therefore, that the only economic values we have are those that treat man as either a producer or a consumer.

Economists under attack are keen to point to their concept of externalities as evidence that they are, in fact, concerned about the "intangibles." But the very term *externality* states the problem; those factors are not integrated into the calculus of cost-benefit. As Mishan observes: "Economists tend to look upon them more as an obstacle to facile theorizing than as an existing social menace. They are: . . . side effects of uncertain magnitude rather than . . . central points of interest."[6] Recently, some economists have attempted to regain lost ground by contending that "externalities" as a category implies no theoretical bias or negligent disregard for environmental effects. In an interesting example of this counterargumentation, Richard Coffmann has claimed that "externalities" is not a slighting concern, but is a "neutral analytical term which refers to things economists *predict will be ignored by decision-makers . . .* It merely gives a name to something which may occur in the course of human affairs without implying desirability or undesirability." (Italics added.)[7] Economists, themselves, of course, have an influence on what decisionmakers, public and private, will or will not ignore. Moreover, the issue is not the economists' notation of desirable objects; it is a question of what economists consider consequential or inconsequential and, therefore, a factor to be weighed in analysis. Casual mentions in passing are not statements of significance.

---

[b]In the United States, this sense of limitless supply was heightened by our pioneer past, with its open vistas and perception of natural abundance. "Free goods" were also public goods in the sense that everyone was allowed to partake of them without reference to ownership. Conservationist attitudes retain the idea of "public goods" but use it as the basis for governmental regulation that attaches a cost for, or prohibits outright, their use. Pollution has been a cost we have escaped paying, relegating them to the economic nether-world of externalities. Automobile manufacturers and owners as an example are not forced to bear the full costs of its construction and use since they are allowed freely to pollute the atmosphere without being charged for the clean air they destroy, if in fact there was a recognizable way of ascribing its value. (The imagery here is an appropriate one in communicating·the idea of blind progress–exhaust is never considered by the driver since it is something that occurs behind him as he moves ahead).

The burgeoning subfield of "welfare-economics" is one area of theoretical modelling in which externalities figure more prominently. It has developed in recent years in response to a practical need for means to caluculate classic welfare costs and services like health insurance that do not readily fit into conventional calculations of financial benefit, if not cost. More recently, efforts have been made to adapt it to environmental issues, with very limited success. For, as Peter Self has succintly noted, "welfare economics is a purely notational set of concepts which provides a platform for criticising the 'narrowness' of the market or of financial accounting, but can offer no positive basis for the arbitration of conflicting economic claims."[8] It is social policy that established value in welfare or other externality-heavy areas, not a market; which is simply another way of making the necessary and basic distinction between public goals and private interests. Theoretical attempts at mathematical modelling of externalities that serve as amusing puzzles for econometricians should not be confused with theory proximate to the problem of ascribing worth and deciding the allocation of resources between producer sectors of the economy and environmental needs.

Welfare economics can be seen as a tacit recognition of the inadequacies of conventional economic theory to the externalities problem is to ascribe worth to environmental goods—health, comfort, and beauty—by calculating negative inability to take account of the externalities. Economics might pretend to be a "total system's approach to public decision-making," but it is one with very special built-in limitations and a narrow range of applicability. It is not acceptable to say that economics is "the study of all factors affecting choices" when there is overwhelming evidence that it has been systematically remiss in overlooking a whole category of factors.[9]

A related, and perhaps, more realistic, if selective, effort to adjust conventional economic theory to the externalities problem is to ascribe worth to environmental goods—health, comfort, and beauty—by calculating negative economic value. In the case of planned utilization of land now in its natural state, the basis for calculation is the potential value of development as determined by the market. As an example, there were plans to fill shallow portions of San Fransisco Bay as a prelude to commercial development. It was estimated that the reclaimed land would bring a price of $1000 an acre.[10] The potential economic value of the bay's surface could be estimated accordingly as a capital resource. The ultimate decision of state authorities to prohibit land fills and to leave the flats untampered is thereby interpreted as an economic decision to "pay" the costs of nondevelopment.

The difficulty with this kind of approach is threefold. One, it ascribes only negative worth to natural conditions, based on the costs of nonutilization, without reference to intrinsic positive worth. Two, so designated, environmental goods are viewed as appendixes to conventional economic calculations. The implication is that marginal changes in the commercial desirability of the property could, and should, in themselves dictate the status of that land. Third, by forcing environmental goods into the mold of conventional economic theory, undue emphasis is placed on the market system, with its utilitarian standard of value, for determining environmental policy, whereas it is more appropriately a matter of broader social and cultural value only one element of which is economic profitability.

In considering the attempts of economic traditionalists to master the externality problem, we again face the problem of differentiating academic theory as description from academic theory as purposeful guide to action. It is probably correct to say that the conventional economic analysis of the behavior of a corporation manager, bank representative, or Treasury official shows little evidence of attention to externalities in the choices he makes. However, a good deal of economic writing defines a situation or proposes courses of action and does not merely describe and relate. Moreover, economists are the most active and listened to of academic advisors. In neither capacity have they distinguished themselves by calling our individual or collective attention to "all factors" that might enter into the economic choices under consideration.[c]

The second major bias of economic theory concerns the *market mechanism.* A concept dear to amateur as well as professional economists, it in truth is a very imperfect instrument for allowing individuals and groups to exercise their discretionary rights. It does not offer unrestricted choice; rather it structures choice so as to exclude a certain range of objective possibilities (as we examine later in reference to mass transit).[12] Wollman has remarked that, "to the extent that people act on the basis of restricted information and inadequate understanding of the consequence of their acts, market transactions fail to achieve maximum human welfare."[13] The market system is not intended or organized to provide information on the quantity of sulfuric oxide that will be billowed into the atmosphere by a steel mill whose construction is under consideration. The executives and financial agents who make that decision are conditioned by present definitions of worth and ascriptions of value, and by their own sense of vocational obligation, to take into account only costs bearing directly on industrial performance and profitability. For potential workers in the plant, the choice posed is between keeping a well-paying job in an unhealthy atmosphere or living in a less polluted locale where work in uncertain (assuming

---

[c]There have been a few notable exceptions to "growth economics" preoccupation with resource exploitation to the neglect of resource management. The excellent work of the economists at Resources for the Future has been outstanding for its rejection of the casual theoretical assumptions about the practical infinitude and substitutability of basic commodities.[11] In recent years, they have broadened their analytical horizons to consider questions of environmental pollution. Although in the former area, RFF has pioneered in the effort to devise more realistic forms of resource costing, they tend to accept the conventional theoretical apparatus that devalues externalities, assumes the validity of orthodox economic accounting as represented in GNP figures, and join in the strong belief that the market is the most efficient mechanism for realizing environmental goals.

that knowledge about pollution levels and its effects is sufficiently widespread that he recognizes it as a problem). The market does not offer him the option of working in a plant whose pollution is controlled. Only political action aimed at putting pollution laws in the statute books and getting them enforced will create that choice. But public initiative of that kind lies outside the market's domain. It pertains to what are called public goods, in this case the health of the community's citizens. From this perspective, the neglect of externalities might be redefined as the failure of government authorities to assume responsibility for public goods. And, indeed, they have been derelict in meeting their responsibilities. Economic theory does share some of the responsibility, though.

First, economic theory has been very leery of permitting government too broad discretionary powers in determining what is a public good. We are routinely treated to warnings, mild or dire, that collective action to correct externalities should be avoided unless there is an overwhelming case that anticipated benefits will outvalue costs.[14] There is the fear that the convenient cost-benefit calculus of the normal economic transaction will be adversely affected if factors other than those associated with tangible elements of production and consumption are allowed to impinge. It is by no means coincidental that economists in the environment movement are most distinguished by their absence.

Concerted action to control pollution implies a major expansion of governmental powers to force economic actors to take account of externalities. Potentially, it could curtail industrial growth itself (and in so doing, if we accept the former CEA chairman's judgment, bring about the demise of the economic profession as we now understand it). Moreover, it would oblige economists to recast their theories so as to give significant place to environmental consequences. Given the inapplicability of their standard measures to these new factors, the task would not be an attractive one for many and an unrewarding one for most. If we consider as well that aspect of the environment we termed amenity rights, the theoretical problem is further complicated. The market-based monetary measure has trouble enough with estimating the costs of air pollution quite apart from the physical discomfort resulting from congestion or despoilation. What price beauty?[d]

The market concept is economic's counterpart to the political scientist's pluralism, sharing its inheritance of nineteenth-century liberal thought. They both express faith in a myriad of individual, rational choices to achieve systematic rationality. These decisions, based on the calculation of gain, are

---

[d]Mishan carries the skepticism about the market a step further in arguing that the commitment to growth destroys the possibility of creating a more engaging environment:

As the carpet of "increased choice" is being unrolled before us by the foot, it is simultaneously being rolled up behind us by the yard.[15]

Economic expansion and environmental well-being can be looked at as elements of a zero-sum game.

presumed adequate, and even necessary, to realize the broader objective of determining and meeting collective need. The recurrent failure of the market to routinize prosperity ultimately required the intervention of public authority to direct the movement of industrial economy in democratic countries. Liberal political theory has salvaged many of its postulates by substituting the group for the individual. As an academic concept, the market is apparently more impervious to changing realities. It lives on despite the oligopolistic organization of industry, monopoly unions, and of the manifest government role, now not only in infrastructure planning and administrative oversight but also in dictating areas of development (e.g., aerospace) and gross distribution of resources (as between private consumption and public expenditure).

(A recent article by economist Henry C. Wallich demonstrates the extraordinary lengths to which the market addiction is carried. Addressing himself to warnings of resource depletion, he seeks to establish that is is not "top priority today" by noting that "the economy will simply substitute things that are plentiful for things that become scarce. . . . In the course of centuries, more basic adjustments will probably be needed," but there is nothing we could or should do about it now.[16] Two aspects of this response are striking. First, it expresses a casual confidence that there are items to be substituted for those exhausted as if we lived in a world on unlimited means, for all economic intents and purposes. Second, it assumes a remarkable adaptability of the market that overlooks the prominent activity of government in encouraging and subsidizing exploitation of resources; and thus ignores the possibility of it encouraging changes in use patterns as well).

The second respect in which economic theory must share responsibility for our derelict attitude toward the environment is in the formal role of economists as government advisors. Sharing popular preferences, they largely have interpreted their charge to be the formulation of means by which to further economic growth. Employing conceptual knowledge and academic analysis that incorporates the intellectual bias of disregarding externalities, they have lent the aura of scientific truth to a manner of formulating economic issues that, in fact, distorts reality.

The predominant economic goal recognized by government, and to which economists have applied their expertise, is the promotion of conditions favorable to expansion, and to ameliorate the external welfare effects of exploitation, deprivation, and inequality. Other social objectives (balanced environmental management, steady-state production), entailing a different use of economics, have been downplayed by government and economists. Whereas public officials merely express the popular mood and translate it into policy, the economic theorist seemingly has the intellectual responsibility of acknowledging alternatives, outlining their dimensions, and assuming that the principles and precepts on which they are grounded do not reflect the bias of one or the other.

We have argued that economic theory as we now observe it is distorted in its conceptual constraints. Analysis and advocacy are even more egregiously bound to the conventional wisdom of established policy. Thus, in the discussion of budgetary means to meet the costs of pollution abatement, or provision of amenities, practical economics is prone to take for granted the present distribution of wealth: both as among social groups and between the public and private sectors (see chapter 8). The parameters of economic policy that have been implanted in a context that presupposed growth and individual enrichment to be paramount are thereby endowed with a naturalness that is entirely specious. To consider environmental policy with all the givens of orthodox analysis and practice still in place is prejudicial to environmental needs. It is also evidence of a theoretical failure to recognize the qualitative distinctiveness of the public issues this new problem raises, the challenge it poses to conventional economic doctrine, and the inherent weaknesses of that doctrine.[e]

Unconforming economists like Mishan, Wollman, and Galbraith constitute a fraternity adhering to what has become known as "the new economics" (or, more precisely in the profession, as the "new economics of resources"). Unlike the old-style conservationist, their major concern is not the husbanding of resources; it is environmental quality. They are interested in just those intangibles that their colleagues too readily have relegated to the tenebrous realm of externalities. The new economists are not wedded to the imperatives of growth, nor preoccupied with the mechanisms and meaning of attaining it. They are equally sensitive to the problem of deciding "when things should not be done."[17] Questions pertaining to the improved allocation of our national resources bulk as large as those connected with the issues of growth and equitable distribution of product. The new economics tries to put economics in the service of publicly defined social objectives in general, and the environment in particular. To employ the simple terminology we use in reference to planning: economics for human use is given a place commensurate with that reserved for economics as a technique for development and coordination of production.

Were the new economics to become the dominant motif, and were its apostles to enter the corridor of power, we would expect to find a new standard of social well-being come into common usage. Today we tend to equate progress with increases in the gross national product. This disposition to define the collective good in reference to the sum total of goods and services produced in society is an ingrained cultural trait. It is, though, by no means the natural or universal indicator of success and accomplishment. As the new economics argues, without reference to the sort of goods produced, the uses to which they are put, and the

---

[e]Modification of the economist's present advisory activities would place a new burden of intellectual responsibility on him. His worth and effectiveness would have to be reestablished in the face of new theoretical and practical problems. Although he begins with relatively high official confidence and with the asset of government's apparent dependence on his advice to achieve its residual, if then redefined growth objectives, he nevertheless carries the heavy freight of theories and models with built-in biases.

type of society they create, GNP (leaving aside its increasingly obvious redundancies and questionable notion of "product") is merely a gross measure of volume. Only our profound confusion of size with quality permits the casual assumption of so unsatisfactory a qualitative indicator of the common good (see Appendix A).

As presently designed, GNP is so imperfect a measure of overall social benefit that it includes as increments to wealth both activity causing pollution (resources and labor services) and that engaged in cleaning it up.[18] Thus the cost of alleviating pollution, e.g., the manufacture and installation of control devices, is added to the sum rather than subtracted from GNP. There is a real ambiguity here that poses serious theoretical problems, since from one vantage point both activities are indicators of economic potential. In the event of war, for example, the manufacturing plant of the "control-device" company as well as that of the polluter would be adapted to war production. As an indicator of productive capacity (and support services), therefore, GNP is reasonably accurate. It remains, though, to devise a different sort of index that can estimate, if not measure with precision, adverse environmental effects of that capacity's use and to balance those estimates with conventional output. As we have noted, welfare economics is inadequate to this task. For want of a definitive model at this stage, we might note a few benchmarks to guide the undertaking. One, it is necessary to distinguish among, and delineate the multiple facets of environmental effect: pollution as health hazard, disamenity, resource depletion. Two, general estimates that tentatively have been made of the costs of pollution cleanup should be refined in relation to source. These more specific sums might then be placed against the utility of that source. Third, a similar, if necessarily more arduous effort should be made with regard to restoration of amenities, and the price of preventing disamenity. Fourth, assessment of resource depletion might use as its point of analytical departure the original contribution of Kenneth Boulding in his essay, "Economics as an Ecological Science," where he outlines the elements of a "closed-system" economics model.[19] In the model, GNP is viewed as constituting the cost to a system (particularly with regard to nonrenewable resources) of economic activity.[f] With these ingredients in hand, we could proceed with the effort to develop a reasonable index of environmental well-being to place alongside GNP. Such an index would be one step toward

---

[f] As explained by the British ecologist, Dr. Robert Overbury, "In current 'open system' economics, consumption and production are generally regarded as 'goods in themselves' and 'gnp' measuring total throughput from 'infinite' sources of exploitable materials to the infinite sinks (both outside the system) is viewed as a kind of index of prosperity. In a closed system, throughput is required to be a minimum, and effectiveness is measured not by production and consumption per se, but by the 'stock' of welfare including capital assets and overall quality of life support systems, including human capital, attainable with the least possible turnover. Any technology able to achieve its objective of improving life quality with minimal human effort and use of materials, that is at minimum 'gnp' would clearly be a good technology."[20]

freeing social analysis from dependence on the inadequate conceptual apparatus of conventional economic theory.

Affinities of Plural Incrementalism and Market Theories

The birth of an assertive, new economics critical of environmental doctrine quite naturally has raised the theoretical hackles on the backs of the orthodox. Nothing is more resistant to change and sensitive to criticism than an intellectual position well staked-out with the powerful force of tradition behind it. In this case, the dominant theorists have the logic of a whole culture sustaining them. Indeed, the supreme air of confidence exuded by defenders of conventional wisdom suggests just how deeply entrenched the established forces are. It is only the more lively, and intellectually attentive, who even bother to sally into combat. Oddly enough, it is a political scientist, Aaron Wildavsky, the articulate mainstay of incremental pluralism, who has offered the strongest defense of economic orthodoxy. The argument he presents is all the more fascinating for neatly fitting together the propensities of established economic and political belief, and it therefore deserves attention.

With his characteristic force and pugnaciousness, he assails the new economics in a revealingly titled piece, "Aesthetic Power or the Triumph of the Sensitive Minority over the Vulgar Mass: A Political Analysis of the New Economics."[21] Wildavsky throws down the gauntlet in the first paragraph, where he makes his two main points crystal clear:

How does the "old economics" of natural resources differ from the new economics? The old economics was mostly economics. The new economics is mostly politics. The agonizing question confronting the new economics has troubled political theorists from the time of the Hebrew prophets to this very day: How shall society be organized so that the preferences of the morally or aesthetically sensitive minority will triumph.[22]

Those few sentences encapsule a good portion of those distorted perceptions by which the traditionalist disparages environmental criticism and confirms his own virtue. It is worth detailed consideration.

Wildavsky's first point is that the issues raised by the new economics are not comprehensible in terms of economic theory. In one sense this is true. Economics, as we have pointed out, is biased in its standards of valuation and its assumptions about human behavior. Furthermore, despite its protestations, it does not constitute a universally applicable theory of choice. Its utility is restricted to certain kinds of choices, those involving the calculus of material gain. The new economics represents an attempt to correct the fallacious reasoning built into the old economics. As such it does not presume the established tenets and categories of analysis to be inviolate. Second, is the new economics mostly politics? Wildavsky apparently means by this statement that its supporters have a preferred state of society in mind. That is true, too. But the substance of their concern is no way validates or invalidates their criticism of inherent bias in the economic theories they attack. Their motivation is not a proper basis for judging their logic.

There is, of course, a connection between theory and subjective value. It is thanks in good part to their environmentalist concern—as well as to the quality of their intellect—that they have discerned the distortions of established theory. For it is the environment that suffers from the way choices are now structured and consequential factors determined. It remains, though, logically consistent to accept the critical analysis of the new economics, even while opposing some if its proposals for affixing pollution charges or for prohibiting certain kinds of economic exploitation.

Adherents to the old economics are equally committed to a certain organization of society. They are free to use *neutral* terms of analysis in presenting *that* position. The terms of the old economics, though, are not neutral. It is certainly convenient to chastise one's opponents for not knowing economics because they reveal the inadequacies of the old economics—but it is not intellectually tenable. In effect it represents the appropriation of a scholarly discipline to defend one's preferences—which is exactly what Wildavsky accuses the new economists of doing.

Wildavsky's explicit commitment to an economics of enrichment leads him to another familiar position—that of rejecting as unfeasible and pointless proposals for reallocation of financial resources. The allocation issue presents itself in reference to: (a) the contemplated expenditures of considerable sums to rid society of pollution that otherwise would be invested in industrial expansion; and (b) the channeling of resources to amenity needs, e.g., mass transit, and away from private consumption of public prestige projects, e.g., the space program as now established. For Wildavsky, this is the "marginalist fallacy" whereby a select minority seeks to "accomplish highly cherished ends that could be justified if only people would wait a little longer to become richer.[23] It is a matter of introducing political factors to skew the market mechanism and thereby to deny the "people" fulfillment of their normal desires.

Elsewhere in this essay we discuss how the market serves to deny people the full range of potential choice. There is no reason to repeat that argument here. What is worth noting is the assumption that somehow the present pattern of allocation is immutable and God-given. To question it, and to suggest other standards for the utilization of national product, is to be accused of reaching for the heavens—or worse, of challenging the heavenly order itself. Gross comparisons of expenditure and consumption are not a species of idle gamesmanship. They get at the heart of the issue. The fact that we spend more on cosmetics than the federal government spends on mass transit or that the Pentagon's publicity budget is greater than the combined deficits of 25 leading private universities in their moment of direst need, says something essential about our social values, about the purposes to which we apply our wealth, and about the practical tradeoffs that could, and should, be made to alleviate some of our environmental problems. (These comparisons also reemphasize how ridiculous are protestations of insolvency when the costs of alleviation are discussed).

This distorting vision also manifests itself in a readiness to use a double-standard when considering *public action* in the environmental field. Thus Wildavsky inveighs against the undemocratic disposition of the environmentalists to use government as the instrument for making choices that significantly alter the allocation of resources. Reading Wildavsky, one would think that at present the only public expenditure that occurs is limited to: (a) the meeting of critical survival needs, e.g., defense, or (b) distribution of wealth among economic groups who use their political power to improve their condition. In fact, of course, the government funds programs to achieve all sorts of public ends. The expenditure of $40 billion on the space program is the most obvious example. In that instance, $40 billion of the national wealth is being allocated to meet an objective that is not essential to the collective welfare; neither is it dictated by a desire to redistribute wealth in the interest of social justice and welfare (although a certain redistribution does take place, inadvertently, with regard to regions and communities—South and West; to professions—aerospace engineers; and stockholders in aerospace industries). These programs also entail interference with the market, insofar as the free play of that market would not generate the economic motivation to invest in the project. Applying the standard of profitability that Wildavsky is keen to preserve as an essential element in the old economics, space ventures are not tenable. Government expenditure on mass transit, therefore, on pollution control and protection of wildlands, is of the same order of public activity as those other programs we accept as natural and uncontroversial.[g]

---

[g]It is interesting to note that there has been no overwhelming expression of popular support for space exploration, contrary to myth. The Apollo program was not the choice of the decisive majority (as contrasted with the preference of a "minority of aesthetes" pushing environmental programs). In a survey of attitudes toward government expenditures conducted through the Michigan Survey Research Center in 1961, i.e., at the height of the public "enthusiasm" for space probes, only 26 of those polled favored more expenditure, while 32 preferred less. As a preference it was twelfth on the list—just below "parks and recreation." (The table accompanies Wildavsky's "aesthetic minority" thesis, buttressed by the contention that: "There is no evidence to suggest widespread and intense support for drastically improving the environment.")[24]

Part 2
Programs and Proposals

5 The Environmental Protection Agency: An Attempt at Environmental Management

Our criticism of prevailing political and economic ideas carries with it the implied argument that effective environmental management depends on a systematic coordination of that medley of governmental policies through which our society largely determines its industrial future. The two essential ingredients of such an approach are: (a) clear commitment to the primacy of the coordinating agency (or agencies) and programs; and (b) redressing the present imbalance between the public expenditure on collective needs and private consumption. It seems appropriate to look critically at the recently created Environmental Protection Agency with these considerations in mind in order to judge its potential for serving as an instrument for accomplishing the task of concerted policy-making.

The Environmental Protection Agency is a functional agency with administrative responsibilities. Proposed by President Nixon on the advice of his Advisory Council on Executive Organization, it consolidated half a dozen executive agencies scattered through the executive branch that previously had exercised various powers of pollution control and environmental management. Enjoying a legal status similar to NASA or the AEC, the EPA, according to its enabling legislation, has as its "main role [to] establish and enforce standards, monitor and analyze the environment, conduct research and demonstrations, and assist State and local government pollution control programs."[1] In conception, therefore, the agency is the watchdog of the environment.

Its most significant role is as assessor and enforcer of pollution standards. In some areas, it is empowered to administer the legal codes contained in specific pieces of environmental legislation, e.g., the Clean Air Act, and the various regulations pertaining to water pollution. In other domains, it is invested with discretionary powers to set emission or effluent standards and to determine violations, as mandated by the National Environmental Policy Act.[a] The agency has the further responsibility for monitoring the actions of federal agencies for environmental effects. Section 102 directs all agencies whose activities raise a potential threat of environmental damage to submit a memorandum, e.g., the now

---

[a] Under the 1970 amendments to the Clean Air Act, the EPA is *required* to publish within 90 days a list of dangerous air pollutants, and soon after to set stringent national emission standards. Accordingly, air standards for municipalities were set in the spring of 1971, and performance standards for industrial plants in December. These procedures are outlined in *Environmental Quality*, the Second Annual Report of the Council on Environmental Quality, released in August 1971.[2] The problems of measurement and enforcement are considerably more difficult.

39

famous "impact statement,"—reviewing conditions, and outlining prophylactic and remedial measures it might take.

In combination, these powers carry a considerable potential for making the agency into a potent force. At a minimum it would appear to assure that casual oversight of the environmental by-products of conventional industrial activities is no longer permitted. Whether it achieves the further end of laying the basis for concerted environmental planning will be indicated over the next several years, as it: (a) becomes identified as a superintending body acting in an overriding public interest (as Section 102 implies), or (b) is relegated to acting as tribune within the executive branch, advancing its position and defending its cause in the manner of any other agency, e.g., the National Highway Administration or the Corps of Army Engineers.

Although enjoying consideration autonomy, the agency is an arm of the president's Executive Office with a quasi-cabinet status somewhere between a department and an independent commission. Its members, for example, serve at the president's pleasure. The upshot is that the EPA is highly susceptible to fluctuations in the political climate. Without the discretionary powers of a regulatory body, its authority is not secured against shifts in executive and/or legislative attitudes. And lacking the kinds of well-organized constituencies enjoyed by bureaucratic competitors, the EPA more than most executive agencies depends on the president's direct backing. Being so dependent, there likely are circumstances in which it will find it expedient to restrain its interpretative and discretionary powers in enforcing regulations and to bend to political winds. One explicit case of the EPA caving in under pressures generated by a powerful lobby was the hasty withdrawal of a proposed order to strictly curtail "clear-cutting" by logging companies. The lumber industry, acting through the National Forest Products Association, successfully mobilized its forces to force the change. More serious charges have been made in Congress that "the White House Office of Management and the Budget, responding to industry pressure, had repeatedly forced the agency to temper its enforcement of the Clean Air Act."[3] The EPA's guidelines to assist states in meeting national air quality standards, are mandated by law to include emissions limitations on industrial plants. Apparently, this stipulation was amended at the last moment so as to relieve industry of their full obligations under the act.

Anxiety to the agency's vulnerability to this kind of influence has led critics to seek means by which "citizen suits," such as provided in the Clean Air Act, can be extended in order to make them applicable to the EPA itself. The law as it now stands prohibits citizens from filing suits against actions taken by federal administrators charged with setting pollution standards. In other words, the discretionary powers with which the Environmental Protection Agency is vested to determine the tolerable levels of certain pollutants are not open to the same citizen action that other governmental activities are.[b]

---

[b]Environmentalists recently won a landmark decision when the U.S. Court of Appeals ruled that the EPA must act by a stipulated date to show cause why DDT should not be

Addressing himself to a bill introduced by Senators Hart and McGovern that would remove the agency's immunity to judicial oversight, the spokesman for the Council on Environmental Quality opposed the measure on the grounds that the courts have neither the competence nor the time to write, in effect, environmental legislation. The critics of the present restriction feel, however, that the agency might yield to the lobbying of economic interests or other government departments in determining feasible and acceptable levels of contamination.[5] The implication is that under some conditions, and in some instances, the agencies in question might find themselves constrained to interpret as "tolerable" pollution levels considered dangerous by environmentalists but clouded by the ambiguity of current standards. Thus the proposal for extending the scope for citizen suits.

The other answer to this problem (apart from the unlikely alternative of legislating specific standards) would be to transfer responsibilities to an independent regulatory commission, or to pare off that section of the Environmental Protection Agency responsible for setting standards and give its members secure tenure. The regulatory-agency approach itself is by no means free of complication. Although it does place the commissioners beyond the reach of the president (once appointed), it also places them beyond the reach of congressional or presidential oversight. The agency in effect becomes a judicial body open only to those pressures and ideas they choose to recognize. The experience of regulatory agencies is that they all too readily become the captives of groups they are intended to regulate, e.g., the Federal Communications Commission and the broadcasting industry; the Interstate Commerce Commission and the railroads; or, the Federal Trade Commission and the abuse of the consumer. Indeed, presidents have been known to select as commissioners individuals who serve as virtual representatives of the interests concerned.[c] The regulatory commission, though, remains a useful tool for ensuring compliance with legislated controls (as discussed in chapter 12).

---

completely banished. The legal relationship between the courts and the agency is still unclear, though.[4]

[c]The reasons for this are well known and are neatly summarized by Aaron Wildavsky. As he writes, "With the best of motives, the original regulatory passion begins to wane. The people whose interests are most directly affected maintain constant vigilance, while the rest of us turn to other pursuits. The regulatory agency is surrounded by the interests it is supposed to regulate. The inevitable accommodations may leave little regulation intact. Moreover, the existence of friendly regulatory bodies is used as a rationale for avoiding the necessity of other and possibly more stringent measures."[6] Vivid evidence that the environmental field is not impervious to this kind of abuse has been provided by the experience of state and local antipollution boards. As copiously documented by the *New York Times* in an extensive study, the overwhelming majority of these bodies are "heavily weighted with representatives of the principal sources of pollution."[7] The not unexpected effect is to cripple whatever pollution control laws are on the books. Abatement could hardly succeed when "the roster of corporations with employees on such boards reads like an abbreviated blue book of polluting industries of American industry, particularly the most pollution-troubled segments of industry." The report elicited a swift response from the head of the Environmental Protection Agency, William D. Ruckelshaus, who deplored the situation and called upon the states to review their practices.

The regulatory commission alternative is also implicit in another controversy generated by the new legislative initiatives. It concerns the implementation of the Section 102 requirement that all federal agencies submit "environmental impact" statements to the Council on Environmental Quality. The section states that when proposing legislation and "other major . . . actions significantly affecting the quality of the human environment," the agency in question should provide a public statement that includes recommendations for alternative courses of action. Ecology groups have effectively used this provision to thwart projects such as construction of nuclear power facilities by seeking and receiving court injunctions where impact statements have not been filed.[d] Many executive departments have routinely not complied and there is a mounting campaign to free themselves of this obligation by amendment to the NEPA.

The most grievous, and controversy-generating case is the Transportation Department's refusal to release the study of the SST's potentially adverse effects on the environment at the height of the congressional debate over funding for the project. With reference to the SST, it is important, and discouraging to note that EPA head Ruckelshaus, properly esteemed as a conscientious defender of environmental interests, testified publicly in favor of the project. The fact that on this issue his loyalty to the administration apparently was greater than his obligation to the environmental cause underscores the problem of independence. Unfortunately, there is no avoiding the paradox that political ties buy both influence *and* partiality. Other departments with "environmental impact" projects have been equally reticent. In its defense the council claims inadequate staff to process reports, the lack of legal power to overrule or to delay projects, uncertainty even as to its right to demand such statements, and ambiguity as to what constitutes major environmental effects. The problem though is not just one of "more teeth in the law and more money to enforce it."[9]

Even if endowed with larger staff and clearly defined powers of oversight, the council as presently constituted would not be able to escape the realities of bureaucratic politics. Every executive department acts according to the rules of bureaucratic life to preserve as much autonomy and independence of action as possible. It strives to achieve goals of organizational self-extension while resisting encroachments by other agencies. Controls such as those implicit in the impact statement procedure threaten every other administrative department. Not only are its plans and proposals open to review by a rival agency (and all agencies are perceived as enemies); but the review is of such a nature as to introduce criteria deemed extraneous to the fulfillment of the initiating department's organizational mission. That mission normally is defined specifically and narrowly: for the Department of Transportation to construct roads as expeditiously as possible; for the Army Corps of Engineers to build bridges and other public works in as many places as there are streams to be forded and congressional

---

[d]In the face of controversy about its responsibilities in this area, the EPA has developed elaborate procedures of meeting the requirements.[8]

friends to be gratified; for the Atomic Energy Commission to meet the nation's need for electric power through the construction of nuclear reactors. When considering new programs or ways of implementing old programs, these organizations have not routinely placed their actions in the broad context of overall national policy, nor automatically taken into account externalities like environmental pollution. In this respect they are, as we have noted before, similar to the technostructure of private industry. Functionally defined tasks combine to accomplish restricted organizational purposes. Executive departments are "public agencies" but each has only certain select tasks to perform in the "public interest."

The formal powers now enjoyed by the agency are an addition to presidential will, not a substitute for it. They can serve as the weapons with which the overseeing agency fights the battle of bureaucratic politics. Among these weapons are the power to set pollution standards for federal departments, as well as for private corporations and municipalities. If, along with the requirement of impact reports, the National Environmental Act were amended to augment the agency's powers to fix pollution standards, the strength of the environmental forces would be appreciably increased. And if those powers were coupled with the provision now in force permitting citizen action suits against government departments (even if excluding discretionary decision of the council itself), the controlling agency would constantly feel the pressure of being upstaged by private initiatives. It then could have a further incentive to use its control powers whatever the tangled state of bureaucratic politics. Failing the power to curb government polluters, however, and without a clear presidential mandate to do so, the agency is fated to lose many a bureaucratic contest, and to achieve very imperfectly its objective of cleansing the environment.[e]

An even more difficult achievement will be the active coordination of policy among federal departments to assure compliance with air and water quality standards. Controlling the governmental polluters entails establishing the principle of primacy intragovernmentally; meeting standards nationally focuses our attention on the planning dilemma.

By provision of the Clean Air Act, the Environmental Protection Agency is given the authority to set limits to six specified air pollutants. In May of 1971, it did so. The announcement by Director Ruckelshaus was accompanied by an extensive report analyzing the steps that states and municipalities would have to take in order to meet the standards by the mid-1975 compliance date

---

[e]A number of local administrations already have codes permitting individual citizens to prosecute alleged violators of legal pollution standards. The New York City law goes so far as to compensate the complainant by awarding him up to 50 percent of any fine decreed by the adjudicatory agency. The law's uniqueness lies in the monetary inducement and in its reversion to the mode of citizen action reminiscent of the participatory democracy of an earlier period in American history. Whether it succeeds in inculcating a sense of community consciousness among the jaded citizens of New York remains to be seen. Whether the fine schedules are severe enough to clamp down on pollution is equally open to question.

(subsequently moved back to 1976) as set by law. The report was anything but optimistic about the prospects for meeting the new requirements. Its rundown of the cities which today experience conditions defined as hazardous to the health (in one, or usually more of the six categories of pollutants) notes present levels so far above stipulated standards that many municipalities will fail to meet them even under the most favorable circumstances and with the best of intentions. Carbon monoxide, nitrogen oxides and sulfur oxides are three particularly difficult pollutants to eradicate. The former is caused largely by emissions from automobile exhausts. The last mentioned is produced by autos and waste generated by electric power plants. Of the seven cities where carbon monoxide pollution is now a major problem on the testimony of the Ruckelshaus report, only Cincinnati would "come close" to meeting the standard by 1975. Even that forecast assumes compliance by the automobile manufacturers with the 1975 deadline set in the Clean Air Act for producing engines that minimize polluting emissions. The outlook for curtailing nitrogen and sulfur oxides is described simply as "bleak."[10]

The answer, as Ruckelshaus outlined it, is to undertake more drastic changes in our modes of transportation, in the way we generate power (e.g., substituting nuclear plants for those dependent on fossil fuels—oil and coal) and in the uses to which power is put.[f] To bring down levels of sulfur oxides, similarly generated by the use of fossil fuels for power production as well as for heating, the use of natural gas as a replacement for coal and oil would have to rise about 15 percent. To curb auto emissions, even more dramatic action is envisaged. In some cities, according to the EPA, that means restricting the use of cars in the inner city during certain periods of the day, staggering commuter hours, and developing mass transit lines to reduce dependence on the automobiles.

The administrative commitment of one agency to the implementation of quality standards is not adequate to assure their achievement. Even with the cooperation of other departments, and with the most rigorous enforcement provisions, success depends on providing the appropriate options and choices at the level of overall national policy. Without coordinated planning they will not be offered. Piecemeal action in the characteristic mode of disjointed incrementalism is a recipe for frenetic irresolution. Only by moving with measured boldness to lay out the full dimensions of the problems, to take the interlocking decisions conditions warrant, can we avoid spasmatic responses to these problems.

Energy policy provides the most glaring example of inadequate, segmental policy-making. Whatever the inherent difficulty of reconciling power needs with environmental well-being, there is no excusing the failure to anticipate the drastic increase in the power demand and the price of meeting it. A simple

---

[f]A measure now contradicted by the president's call for greater reliance on coal to meet the energy crisis.

extrapolation of growth rates at least could have made clear the threat of shortage and indicated its possible consequences. The first sign that public officials were even aware of the saliency, if not the complexity of the problem, was the "plan" offered in the spring of 1971 by President Nixon for the development of clean nuclear power. It was more a statement of good intentions than a detailed action program. Moreover, it was linked in the most casual fashion with pollution standards of the administration's own EPA, and in no sense part of a systematic review of transportation and other major users of energy.

Only two years later, in the spring of 1973, in the wake of a winter of fuel shortages and the unprecedented resort to gasoline rationing (and coincidental with widespread publicity about the "energy crisis"), did a second message introduce a serious review of the situation.[11] It offered a broadstroke assessment of available energy resources, and those under development, in conjunction with a series of specific proposals to encourage their more intensive exploitation. A landmark in its official acknowledgement that a problem indeed existed, the report nonetheless has been properly criticized as "too little, too late."

There are three grounds for declaring the effort inadequate, and in some important respects misconceived. First, it continues to make the overly optimistic assumption that tinkering with the present policies for energy development and distribution will permit uninterrupted industrial growth and profligate consumption. Second, in the tradeoff of environmental purity with energy use, it clearly relegates the former to the status of a marginal consideration. Third, the policies it enunciates accept all the economic orthodoxies about the suitability of the fictitious market for satisfying energy requirements without raising fundamental questions of effectiveness and equity.

The message proposes a twofold strategy for meeting power requirements that are extrapolated from present consumption. Except for a hortatory proclamation of a national energy conservation ethic, presented seemingly almost as an afterthought, there is no overall examination of the present use pattern or consideration of the possible desirability of controlling augmented demand.

For the shortrun, it is recommended that more extensive use be made of coal reserves, that more investment should go into the exploitation of natural gas deposits, that public lands and the continental shelf be opened to exploration, and controls on oil imports be lifted. Development of nuclear energy (fast-breeder reactors, and perhaps fusion power in the more distant future) is seen the key to satisfying abundantly all foreseeable needs to the end of the century and beyond. (A crash research program into the exploitation of solar energy is also proposed).

A number of these measures threaten environmental damage, and danger (as with nuclear reactors). In response to these acknowledged difficulties, the report expresses optimism about safety technology, while downgrading environmental objectives. The possibility of oil spills and blowouts is denigrated, anxiety is voiced about "unnecessary delays in the development facilities," and, most strikingly, the second phase clean air standards scheduled to come into force by 1975 are postponed for "the duration of current shortages."[12] This last step in effect obviates the Ruckelshaus strategy for cleansing the urban atmosphere, e.g., the extensive use of high-sulfur coal prescribed for major metropolitan areas in the guidelines is urged on local and state authorities by the president. Disingenuously declaring economic prosperity the paramount component of the general welfare which the more stringent secondary standards are intended to achieve, the report in effect misinterprets the legislation for its own convenience. Listing the several ways in which rigorous enforcement would impede maximum resource utilization, the president simply asserts that environmental considerations must give way. Incrementalism once again demonstrates its potency as the protector of the *status quo,* and expediency is indulged to the detriment of the environment.

The report is as remarkable for its confidence in the ability of the market to solve the problem of energy shortages, as for its subordination of environmental goals. One of its key provisions is that the already generous investment tax credits for oil and gas exploration should be increased. It makes the curious assumption that the ample opportunities now available for amassing great wealth somehow provide insufficient incentive to entrepreneurs. It is difficult to imagine what enticement to gain is sufficient spur to enterprise under these conditions. Apart from the questions of reward and equity involved, the recommendation also overlooks the dominant position of the large petroleum companies and their power to manipulate the market. They now are able powerfully to influence supply and demand, and have been accused, apparently with some justification, of managing the recent crisis to their own advantage.[13] Further inducements to increase output would be in effect a bribe to curb their monopoly practices and to ameliorate the immediate shortage with no assurance that the same logic would not manifest itself at a somewhat higher level of production.

The report's companion assertion that regulation of natural gas prices by the federal government "has produced a serious and increasing shortage of this fuel" is open to the same skeptical comment.[14] The awareness that these energy reserves are finite also raises a fundamental question as to the reward structure for those conceded access to it. A rise in the price of a scarce commodity is a proper and long avoided reminder of its limited availability over time. It also promises windfall profits. There is both an ethical and practical argument for extending government regulation, rather than slackening it. Allowing prices to float upwards can indicate the economy's dependence on a diminishing energy supply without providing alternative sources or a rational policy for use. These tasks are primarily the responsibility of government. Thus the "profits" anticipated from raising the price of energy might preferably take the form of a consumption tax. Its proceeds could be directed into an "energy fund" analogous to the Highway Trust Fund, and used to finance research and development of new energy sources and less wasteful mechanical processes in manufacturing, transportation, and so forth. There is little point in directing vast sums into the private hands of the monopoly oil and gas industry when no amount of encouragement will conjure nonexistent resources, and where development of the only reasonable alternative, nuclear fuel, is essentially a public matter.

The systemic character of environmental conditions, and the need for embracing solutions that carefully link the several elements of each problem, is most clearly evinced by the proposal to substitute nuclear energy for that produced by the conventional fossil fueled power plant with its generous pollution index. Although there is pollution control technology that would considerably reduce emissions from oil or coal-burning generators (e.g., the installation of electrostatic precipitators to contain ash particles), it is expensive and only partially successful. Nuclear power harnessed to peaceful uses would seem to be the reasonable alternative. It is economically feasible, the technology is developing, the need is clear.

Nuclear reactors, of course, create their own pollution hazards. The most obvious and unique threat being that of explosion or radiation leakage. Although, evidence on these scores appears to be mounting that the dangers have been overestimated and the risk slight, there remain major engineering and design problems to be overcome before the safe operation of reactors can be assured.[15] It is, however, a more mundane problem than is the greatest source of concern, e.g., thermal pollution. Thermal reactors require vast quantities of water to circulate and cool the reactor. For this reason, reactors must be located on the shores of fresh-water lakes or rivers (salt water also can be used, but geography often militates against oceanside locations). The water it returns is some tens of degrees warmer than at the time of intake. The consequence of this dramatic rise in the water temperature is: (a) eutrophication—within a relatively short time, the body of water is ecologically "killed", i.e., its capacity to serve normal environmental functions destroyed;[16] and (b) a destabilization of temperature balance upon which aquatic life depends.

The alternative means for releasing the enormous surplus heat produced by a nuclear generator raise as many difficulties as they solve. "Cooling towers" are the option most discussed. These are vast grids, extending some hundreds of feet in height, that release the heat directly into the atmosphere. They have been used with technical success in the Ruhr, and one is under construction in Michigan in the wake of a successful ecology fight led by defenders of Lake Michigan. Their liability is that they are extremely unsightly, create potential navigational hazards for planes and migrating birds, and can modify local weather conditions. Their construction costs are also considerably in excess of a water-cooled plant.

Why not build the reactor, and its cooling tower, on sites far removed from population centers? A nuclear plant need not avail itself of raw materials and transportation. Apart from the expense of long-distance transmission, the problem is that long-distance power lines, though, would have to be constructed to carry the power to user centers. A promenade of pylons criss-crossing the countryside is hardly a desirable environmental solution, while to bury the lines would skyrocket the costs of power beyond any reasonable level. There is no escaping the truism that "technology will get you in the end."

So long as society pursues a lifestyle that requires regular increases in available power, we face undesirable side effects. Some means for providing it are preferable to others; but some adverse effects are unavoidable. In this respect the pollution issue is inseparable from the question of amenities. For most Americans clean air and water, visually salubrious surroundings, and quiet, are not so highly prized that they are willing to forego these conveniences that are dependent on energy consumption. Here we are running up against the same deep-seated cultural resistances that are at the heart of any discussion of a steady-state or low-growth economy.[g] Movements for social equality, the strong residuum of acquisitiveness in the society at large, and the ongoing process of technological self-generation, heighten the dilemma of how to create a livable environment.

Of course, before one reaches the point of direct value confrontation, there are significant steps that can be taken to alleviate the most deleterious pollution problems. There are also means to reduce the extraneous use of power and to diminish superfluous manufacture: e.g., the refinement of industrial processes to reduce waste, and the greater utilization of heat generated; the imposition of quality control standards for durable goods; the levying of heavy taxes on luxury goods that raise the costs, and thereby lower the use of those items; and the cutback in economically unproductive products.[18] The pruning of waste production could reduce the need for expansion while only marginally restricting the wealth available for assuring material well-being. Ultimately, however, a critical examination of the way we define material well-being will be a prerequisite for preventing a dangerous encroachment on environmental stability and health. At some point growth must be far more carefully modulated than it is at present.

The lesson of the EPA's air quality standards is rudimentary and essential.

---

[g]In a *New York Times Magazine* article entitled "The Economics of Pollution," Edwin L. Dale, Jr., offers further evidence of that enrichment philosophy which propels our society.[17] His implicit definition of material well-being does approach the open-ended. "By any fair test," as he says, "we are not really affluent, half of our households earn less than $8,500 a year." The poverty-line is thus raised $3,000 in a single jump. It is not clear to what criteria of human need for food, clothing, shelter, entertainment and comforting artifacts this figure is pegged. In fact, today "affluence" in America is not a condition measurable in physical terms. It is a psychological condition, dependent on the special circumstances of abundance and one that will rise with the availability of economic goods. Thus it is the culture that equates status with acquisition (and thereby builds into itself strong neurotic impulses) that is at issue, not basic welfare.

Each of the suggestions to meet agency criteria followed logically from the definition of the problem. Each entailed major planning initiatives that were not then underway, and which in most instances were unlikely to be launched in the near future. The failure to integrate pollution management with these other related areas of public policy says a good deal about the shortcomings and incapacities of our present manner of policy-making.[h]

<hr>

[h]The contradiction between the EPA's standard sitting authority and its limited power to provide the means and to determine the programs for meeting the standards devalues the whole process. Thus, in January 1973, the agency was placed under court order by a Los Angeles federal district judge to stipulate measures the county must take to meet Clean Air Act criteria. In doing so, it listed rationing of gasoline and severe restriction on the movement of automobiles. Since Los Angeles cannot live, economically, without vehicular transportation, and alternatives are not available, all parties concerned acknowledged the futility of the gesture. Whatever the shock value, the episode demonstrates how disjointed policy-making makes standard-setting an empty exercise.

6 Transportation

The inherent need for congruent planning in dealing with environment problems is most clearly seen in the recommendation for actions in the transportation field deemed preconditions for meeting the new air quality standards. Noting that the internal combustion engine is the major source of three of the six designated pollutants, Ruckelshaus made clear that effective control meant changing transportation habits. The development of commuter mass transit systems along with organizational innovations such as staggered work hours and greater reliance on motor pools were seen as central to resolution of the pollution problem. On strictly economic grounds there is a powerful case to be made for emphasizing mass transit and rail transit in general: the cost (in resources and undesirable side effects) of moving people by subway is lower per person-mile than by automobile—even more so when time now squandered in traffic delays is added. Yet nowhere in the statement did the agency chief offer proposals for how that critical mass transit was going to get built.[a] It is jejune to present alternatives that the states and municipalities cannot create for themselves (and that are not now available). It is a striking example of public policy-making that is unsatisfactory as technical congruence. (And once again we have evidence of the interplay between pollution control and environmental amenities.)

No public issue underscores the inadequacies of our approach to environmental problems, the biases of our political system, and the distortions of dominant economic theories than that of mass transportation. The derelict condition of present transit facilities in the cities (where they exist at all) and the infirm state of interurban railroads stand in striking contrast to the remarkable technological accomplishments in the more alluring domains of aerospace and military engineering, and in equally sharp contrast to the rapacious march of the highway across the American landscape. Just as pollution is permitted to reach crisis proportions before becoming the object of remedial attention, so does the loss of basic amenities proceed with negligent disregard by public authorities to the point of breakdown and sometimes beyond that point.

The causes are multiple, and not least among them is that Americans have

---

[a]Disregard for transportation needs continues. The *Second Annual Report of the Council on Environmental Quality*, a much more extensive and detailed review of environmental problems than the *First Report*, manages only a casual, general reference to transit needs. There was a total lack of any serious discussion of environmentally sound technologies and government's role in promoting them.

exhibited an infatuation with the individual automobile as a personalized mode of transportation. It has performed several psychological and cultural functions: serving as a symbol of achievement in a status anxious society, as an expression of power, as a sex fetish, as a basis for simultaneous differentiation and acceptance of uniform standards. There are, though, other reasons, some structural and some in the domain of political doctrine, for the neglect of public amenities. They are becoming increasingly apparent as the sheen wears off the auto's craven image and the need for mass transit becomes overwhelming.

The Market Myth

Among the articles of faith held with fervent irrationality by a sizable number of academics and public officials alike is that all choices as to how we might spend our wealth are somehow provided by the market mechanism. If we do not have mass transit, the argument goes, it is because not enough people have expressed a preference for it and have not been prepared to incur the costs. This line of reasoning is heard on the lips of legislators, corporation executives, and even, as we have noted, economists. The rejoinder is to reiterate the simple point that the individual is rarely presented with the opportunity to express a preference for efficient public transportation as opposed to the private automobile. He can take his car or use whatever sad imitation of mass transit is available; but there is no ready way for him to say in effect, "I would prefer a clean, efficient train service and would support expenditure for its construction." That is not market choice; it is a statement of political opinion directed at government, supporting a particular area of public expenditure. A market situation simply does not exist in the transportation field, nor does it with regard to any other public service. The relevant choice is between: (a) public expenditure or private consumption; and (b) public expenditure on one item (trains) or another (space exploration).

Let us consider the situation of a commuter. At the moment he steps out of his suburban door (or in New York City, his Queens, or his Brooklyn door) in the morning, the only options open to him are: (a) a shattering ride on the subway or a suburban train that is always overcrowded, liable to breakdown, and offers little assurance of safe transit; or (b) a stop-go, carbon monoxide inhaling ride in his private car on a traffic thronged highway (that carries with it the cost of parking). The fact that large numbers of persons choose the latter is often taken as buttressing the contention that the public would not forsake their motorized chariots for mass transit. It is a spurious line of argumentation. For the commuter, the choice is one of his individual marginal comfort. What with the pleasure of turning on his radio to hear last night's ball scores—even if it is for the second or third time—the commute by car is slightly less unpleasant and inconvenient than the commute by train. Of course, in so doing he is adding to the marginal discomfort of everyone else on the road, the *cumulative* inconvenience of which is enormous. What might make sense in terms of his individual options at the moment is senseless for the collectivity.[b]

Moreover, there is no opportunity for him to choose between that auto ride and the building of an efficient, reasonably uncrowded mass transit system. His election vote usually makes little impact since transportation is rarely a prominent issue, and at best would be only one of several in a campaign where candidate positions are less than crystal clear. As a consequence, there is no reason to see in his present preference principled opposition to expenditure on public transportation. More vivid testimony to the need is the enormous congestion of mass transit facilities presently available. If ever a system has reached the point of overload, it is American urban and commuter transportation networks. It is difficult to maintain, as some transportation people still insist on doing, that the public will not ride mass transit when at present every square foot now accessible is filled.[1]

That reluctance of congressional leaders and executive officials, including those in the Department of Transportation, to commit funds for mass transit often makes it necessary to resort to bond issues as sources of capital. The disinclination of states and municipalities to burden themselves with massive debts and amortization payments is then pointed to as evidence of public disinterest in systems of mass transit. This is a very ambiguous indicator, however. First, to defray the expense through bonding in itself relegates transportation to the category of a second-class public need. Most road construction and all space ventures are funded directly out of federal revenues. They are defined as a necessary public obligation and supported accordingly. Bonding not only increases the overall cost, but implies the optional nature of the undertaking. Second, transportation bond issues often lump mass transit programs with highway construction, as was recently the case in New York. This is the "trickle-around" approach to public expenditure; if enough money goes into concrete some will be made available for rails. In the event, an unconscious coalition of "antiroad" and "antirail" sentiment defeated the initiative narrowly.

A characteristic of the political alienation so pervasive today is the strong propensity to reject any proposal for new public spending with the increased taxes they imply. School construction, sewage systems, and dams suffer every bit as much as mass transportation in state and local elections. The reasons are varied and diffuse, and the negative attitudes toward government are powerful. However, since this attitude is *not* issue specific, the consequence of *selectively* choosing certain areas of public responsibility to be funded through the bonding route is to assure that they suffer disproportionately from antispending inclinations. While some programs are arbitrarily given protection from these

---

[b]It is also pertinent to note that the commuter is being offered options technically weighted in favor of automobiles. Today's auto, and the roads it uses, represent the latest in technical development. Rail facilities remain in conception and design unchanged for a half century; and in many cases a good portion of the equipment itself dates from that epoch.

direct expressions of popular skepticism, others are just as arbitrarily thrown to the wolves of disaffection. (A further liability of presenting transportation as a bond issue is that it becomes a referendum wherein the power of vested interests to exploit alienation is maximized. A classic example was provided in California in 1971 where the oil industry led an expensive and mendacious campaign against an initiative permitting the funneling of Highway Trust Fund moneys to mass transportation).

Pluralist Politics

The policy-making process tends to move in reference to what exists and responds to those interests that have organized themselves. What is established is a mammoth, self-perpetuating programmatic commitment to highway construction; what are organized are the administrative agencies whose missions are advanced by building roads, the legislative committees that take a proprietary interest in their programmatic offspring, and the private groups that gain economic advantage from autos. The Department of Transportation, and Congress, are inclined to take for granted the National Highway Trust Fund as inviolate and routinely extend the program while adding further direct allocations.[c] Even as mild a departure as President Nixon's recent proposal, incorporated in his beguiling revenue sharing for transportation, that local authorities be permitted to transfer funds at their discretion to other transportation projects met keen opposition. Quite apart from the doctrinal reasons for opposition to any diminution or restriction of the road-building programs, resistance reflects a common disinclination to change a good thing. Many people have a tangible stake in keeping things as they are. The highway complex comprising contractors and oil companies, teamster unions, state highway authorities, the executive administrators of the trust fund, local officials and pork barrel-minded congressmen is one of the most powerful in Washington.[2] (Recent confirmation of the highway lobby's prominence was appointment of Union Oil's head, Claude Brinegar, as Secretary of Transportation. The company has passionately opposed initiatives to support mass transportation with gasoline taxes.) Only a considerable exercise of political will can overcome it. The motivation for exercising that latent authority could come from a recognition of vital need impelled by a massive expression of popular concern sufficient to overcome the systematic bias against diffuse public causes. (The practical requirements for the success of such a movement are discussed in chapter 12.)

---

[c]It is striking that despite widespread expressions of concern about present transportation priorities, 1969 recorded a new high in the sum of Highway construction contracts nationwide, $6.6 billion.

Aversion to Public Expenditures

In the United States, the public sector allocates a smaller percentage of the gross national product than in any other Western nation with the possible exception of Switzerland.[3] Improving the environmental conditions of life requires large sums of money. However generous we are with finances for prestige ventures, the ingrained mistrust of public expenditure resists equivalent allocation on urban amenities and other environmental needs. Ironically, an issue of broad public concern can be, and is, handicapped for the very reason that it grows out of a condition common to a broad spectrum of the society. Short of an undeniable challenge to national survival that supersedes all other public business, as occurs in wartime, our democratic politics is more attentive to demands and needs of particular interests than it is to collective needs. For strictly structural reasons, leaving aside for the moment the consumer compulsions of the culture, greater total desire is required to satisfy public demands than private ones.

For example, let us assume a situation in which public demand for large federal expenditure on mass transit grows to the point where 60 percent of the electorate positively favors such a program. For two-thirds of these people it is second on their list of preferred areas of public expenditure, third for 10 percent, fourth for 5 percent, and so forth. Assigning preferences and values to each program, the overall score nationwide would be considerable, and the environmentalist mass transit issue would stand rather high in any ranking of desired public programs. Yet under our system of interest representation it would have less likelihood of being acted upon than several other proposals with a lower score, e.g., federal price supports for agricultural products. That is because people organize around primary interests, government departments with leverage on budgeting decisions respond to these organizations, and the dominant criterion of representation remains one of economic interest. More extensive organization by the pro-mass transit consituency and active lobbying would help; but given the rules of the game they would by no means be assured of more than limited success.

Transportation is the most striking case in point. The sad history of Amtrax, the public corporation created in 1971 to coordinate and to consolidate a national rail network is only the most recent example of this tendency to denigrate collective needs. Advertised as a major departure in federal support for public transportation, it has from the outset been a mockery of a railroad program. Its initial allocation of $48 million was ludicrous when placed against needs, and equally absurd when compared to airline subsidies, much less road construction funds. Even more discouraging, the 1970 federal expenditure on urban mass transit was $106 million. Partly in response to this derisive sum, and partly in sheer embarrassment at this long-standing neglect of a major urban need, Congress passed the Urban Mass Transportation Assistance Act that represented an authorization of $10 billion to be spent over a twelve-year period. At a per annum average of approximately $850 million, it is hardly going to revolutionize mass transportation. That conclusion is made clearer when we realize that political realities will dictate a very wide dispersal of the funds. Moreover, a sizable portion of the gross sum takes the form of loans, as opposed to grants, thereby adding a financial obligation to the commitments of recipient local governments.[4] By comparison, federal expenditures on highway construction were $4.5 billion in 1970 and $4.9 billion in 1972.[d]

The sums proposed for mass transit development by the Nixon administration would, if concentrated in two metropolitan areas, be barely sufficient to provide facilities on a scale permitting a significant shift from autos to commuter trains. To put it somewhat differently, present allocations are so paltry that were all the transportation districts in the nation prepared to deny themselves any federal assistance for four years, the cumulative resources thus made available would assist but two selected cities to cut auto pollution to meet EPA standards. (Unable to upgrade their services, the others would fail to meet the federal standards by 1976 even more egregiously than now predicted.) Under present arrangements for dispersing funds in dribs and drabs across the board, all of the problem cities receive such limited amounts that they can barely maintain present services.

The question of spending levels, and the public sector's proper share of the national income, can lead to some strangely convoluted reasoning. It is popular nowadays to say that government at all levels cannot meet its obligations because of severe financial constraints. State and local authorities in particular are said to be on the verge of bankruptcy—the federal government presumably being the receiver. On the face of it, the situation is absurd. It is difficult to accept a judgment that a nation with a trillion dollar economy cannot provide basic services for its citizens. What these statements really mean is: (a) that the citizenry is unwilling to forego regular increments in disposable private income to meet communal needs and their leaders do not have the courage to lay matters on the line and declare bluntly that private consumption is at the expense of health, comfort, and beauty; and/or (b) that the costs of creating a livable society are so inordinately high in our advanced industrial society (or at least in the urban portions of it) that they pose an unprecedented burden, the meeting of which would drastically alter the income level and lifestyle of our people. If the latter is true, (that for every increment in GNP we are poorer, in both discomfort and in the balance of wealth created and costs incurred) then

---

[d]Principled opposition to government initiative and control is starkly seen in the readiness to subsidize the corrupt private management of the Penn Central to the tune of several hundreds of millions of dollars, while denying Amtrak of Congress's own creation minimal operating funds. The fear of government direction is so strong that it inspired the chief lobbyist for the private railroads, former Senator John Smathers, to urge a further subsidy of $600 million spread over eleven years for the Penn Central as the way that the government could avoid the ultimate sin of nationalization.

the price of economic growth exceeds the benefits and we have been chasing our tail. If this proposition is not accepted, then the financial crisis simply means that our affluent citizens selfishly do not want to pay taxes. Economists who see no answer to government penury but retrenchment are stating political preferences and making political judgments. Economists—some of the same—who reduce environmental effects to the limbo of externalities can hardly be permitted to do so when adjustment for these amenities will cost us more than the growth implied by industrial expansion. (A cousin to this sort of analysis is the argument that increases in wealth, i.e., GNP, are necessary to pay for the costs of pollution abatement. It, too, takes for granted the present maldistribution of funds and the scarcity it creates for environment programs. It adds the major complication of leaving unspecified whether the new pollution generated by growth will not outweigh the investment in control it is intended to permit. Although these calculations nowhere have been systematically made, the postwar evidence of environmental degradation as increasing disproportionately to growth in GNP suggest that, in fact, after further economic growth we will have lost environmental ground. In a sense, the argument in favor of continued expansion to pay for present needs is reminiscent of a classic Donald Duck cartoon. Gettting to work on building a picket fence, Donald finds his dwindling supply of available slats inadequate to complete the job. Faced with this dilemma, he begins feverishly to speed up his effort so as to finish before supplies run out).

Revenue-sharing and the Bankruptcy of Incrementalism

The strong distaste of making public choices with regard to public priorities has given new expression in President Nixon's infatuation with revenue sharing. As applied to the transportation field, and to most others as well, it is less an innovation than an admission of intellectual bankruptcy. The administration's proposal would have permitted state and local government to determine according to their own definition of need the transportation program into which they want to put federal moneys previously obligated to specific federal programs. Even the previously sacrosanct Highway Trust Fund could be tapped. These provisions had a superficial attraction. A closer look at the proposals, though, reveals: (a) that the transfer of funds from the HTF could be made only for one year; (b) they would be of limited amounts; (c) that there would be no increase in the gross sums available above present allocations. Local authorities are thus offered the opportunity to divert already hard-pressed funds from preestablished programs to undertake feasibility studies and some design work on mass transit projects for which there would be no expectation of further support. *Revenue-sharing is the avoidance strategy* of federal leaders who are unprepared to make the hard choices entailed in reapportioning the national product away from consumption and into public programs.[5] It is an escape route for stymied incrementalists. Faced with a major crisis of social organization that is not readily intelligible in the framework of present patterns of expenditure and government program, they remain true to their disdain for rational planning and initiating leadership (as well as their dislike for making fundamental choices) by transferring responsibility—if not very much money—to local authorities.

Furthermore, revenue-sharing would have the effect of reinforcing the exclusive power of local jurisdictions which, in their multitude, are impediments to the rational, regional planning that is necessary to deal with the kind of metropolitan problem that transportation is. At present, political jurisdictions do not coincide with the boundaries of the problem area. Where such a discrepancy exists between structure and function, only outside initiative and leverage can produce necessary coordination. Revenue sharing denies the national government the tool to accomplish that end. Were the Congress at some future date to vote large sums for mass transit, the administrative agency allocating the funds might reasonably be expected to require the creation of regional authorities as a precondition for receipt of federal funds. Under the terms of revenue-sharing, the federal government has no means for enforcing this provision.

Complicating the public debate about the assumption by government of major new responsibilities in areas of social amentiy like mass transit (and indirectly encouraging ideas like revenue-sharing) is the pervasive discontent with government programs in general, and disillusionment with grand federal schemes in particular. There is a crisis of confidence in public authority that feeds the disposition to avoid difficult choices. Accepting the blanket condemnation of government means an abdication by public officials of responsibility for deciding among national objectives and for exercising the leadership that will make these choices understandable. There is a strong element of self-confirming analysis in the disparagement of national programs. Whether couched in the academic phraseology of the "End of Liberalism" or in strident know-nothing attacks on Washington bureaucrats, the vocal rejection of the federal government as the instrument for social accomplishment tends to create the very pessimism and disaffection that is given as one evidence of its ineffectualness.[6] In fact, for all its faults, the federal government has a far greater administrative and intellectual capacity than do most local bodies of government. Its ability to execute is clearly seen in a program like NASA. However we assess the desirability of its objectives, that program nevertheless has been run efficiently and successfully. Much of the recent attack on federal authorities has the poverty program as its point of reference. The War on Poverty, however, is the least characteristic of federal programs. In design and implementation, the OEO bears little ressemblance to the classic New Deal program that today is the object of so much denigration. A conjectured national mass transit program obviously would have more in common—with respect to organization—with NASA than with OEO. (The problem of policy management is discussed at greater length in chapter 12).

Incrementalism and Environmental Planning

Our digression into the field of transportation was intended: (a) to establish the inability of present programs to change materially present conditions of either pollution or disamenity; (b) to underscore the futility of stating environmental goals without a consonant readiness to undertake the programs necessary for their realization; and (c) to point up the liabilities of relying on the procedures of incremental policy-making.

We have argued that without proper attention to the automobile and to power demands even present unencouraging estimates for pollution abatement by 1975 are overly optimistic. The possibility remains that the heightened attention to the requisites for reducing pollution levels will generate new pressures for expanding mass transit. No doubt Mr. Ruckelshaus so intended them.

The course of public policy over the next few years will provide a definitive test for the incrementalist analysis. According to its precepts, the marginalist reaction to the new manifest obligation to comply with federal standards will be to search around for means to meet them. The searchers in this case are likely to be state and municipal officials, congressmen from these areas, and officials of the Environmental Protection Agency. One avenue of approach already outlined is expansion of mass transit. The incrementalist estimate is that effort will move in that direction, not because of any systematic analysis of environmental amenities, nor as part of an integrated program for improving the nation's transportation networks, but through a process of marginal adjustment. If we look more carefully at the incrementalist model, skepticism would appear in order as to whether this response, pragmatically and disjointedly made, in fact will be forthcoming.

The model does not presume incremental logic for the governmental system as a *corporate entity*. It presumes that each executive or legislative organization will respond to its changing needs and constituencies incrementally. As the administrative body that sets pollution standards and is responsible for assuring compliance with them, the EPA will have a bureaucratic incentive to advance programs that will further that end. These are not the obligations of the Department of Transportation, the Treasury Department, the Department of Commerce, their legislative collaborators on Capitol Hill, or the powerful lobbies that serve as their constituency. The only place in the system where systemic connections can be made is the White House.

If the president recognizes the overwhelming logic linking mass transit to pollution abatement, if he himself perceives the importance of action, and/or of the political advantages to be gained from making the program work, and is prepared to exercise his leadership, complementary mass transit development is much more likely to be forthcoming. Otherwise, the outcome will be determined by the relative strengths and tactical skills of these organizational actors who play the game of bureaucratic politics under our system of dissociated powers and incremental policy-making.[e] Given the biases in the system militating against support for mass transit, the outlook is not very bright. Incrementalism under those circumstances would have failed, again, to produce the systemically logical response.

---

[e]The principle of dissociated powers, of course, extends into the president's Executive Office itself. Environmentalist sentiment has no priority claim on presidential attention or support. Evidence of this was abundant even at the height of the Nixon administration's public infatuation with the environment. Just a few weeks before Mr. Ruckelshaus made front page news with his announcement of pollution standards, a member of the Council of Economic Advisors was attacking environmentalists for their "extremism" and, declaiming that any air standard is only a "value judgment" which should be left to local option.[7] Some months later former Commerce Secretary Maurice Stans was ominously noting the perilous plight of businessmen subjected to the public and political torment of environmentalist assault.[8] The president himself has shown a responsiveness to pressures contrary to environmentalist causes and has been a staunch advocate of environmentally degrading projects, e.g., the SST. In that case, he also exhibited the mania for a new technique for its own sake that is the environmentalist's bugbear. There is, therefore, reason for skepticism about the use of presidential power to compensate for the drawbacks of incrementalist decision-making.

7 Planning, PPBS, and Environmental Policy

In arguing the case for congruent policy-making, we are suggesting a planning approach that emphasizes expanding the scope and perspective of government action. We are concerned not only with planning as a technique, as a more rational way of ordering a problem and proceeding to its resolution. It is the basis for recognizing and defining problems that is most critical. Sophisticated systems analysis, or Planning and Program Budgeting Systems (PPBS) is only a partial answer.

In his admirable work, the *Politics and Economics of Public Spending,* former Budget Director Charles L. Schultze, neatly lays out the ingredients of what he calls *strategic planning.* He defines it as "programming the use of resources to carry out an approved set of activities in an efficient manner."[1] Ideally, "it is planning for establishing and specifying objectives, choosing among alternative programs to achieve these objectives, and allocating resources among those programs."[2] In contrast to disjointed incrementalism, which serves in his analysis as the critical point of reference and about which he has some properly scathing remarks, his concept of strategic planning attempts "to specify objectives systematically arrived at in such a way as to strengthen the hand of the upper levels of the executive."[3] So conceived, it encourages public officials to reflect on fundamental aims of current programs, to analyze consciously the output of a given program, to engage in multiyear planning, and to allocate resources on a multiyear basis to match scheduled programmatic goals. This is exactly the approach that is required if environmental policy is to mean more than desultory initiatives, uncoordinated in range and timespan. It outlines the antithesis to the largely incremental way in which government now makes policy.

PPBS though, is not in itself an answer to disjunctures in national policy. If applied at a sufficiently high level of authority, from whose vantage point the coordinate relationships that bear on an issue are observable, these techniques are extraordinarily helpful. They allow the policymaker to act with efficiency and with logical consistency. If, however, they are restricted within the confines of administratively bounded departments, they serve only to render more orderly the functioning of partial programs which cumulatively do not represent a systemic rationality and might well provide systematically absurd results.[a] For example, the introduction of PPBS could assist the AEC to locate nuclear power

---

[a] A companion technique, "cost-benefit analysis," has shared a similar popularity as an administrative instrument for rationalizing budgetary decisions. It also matches PPBS's limited capacity to calculate externalities, assimilate welfare considerations, or reconcile divergent purposes without determinations of political preference.[4]

reactors where they are most central to markets and to schedule development of nuclear energy to match needs extrapolated from present demands. It could assist the Department of Transportation to plan its national highway network in such a way as to extend road utilization. It could enable the Environmental Protection Agency to devise elaborate guidelines for the retrofitting of industrial plants with pollution control devices that would be pegged to a system of tax write-offs and penalties. It could do all of these things without assuring that those interlocking elements of public policy are so coordinated as to achieve the environmental objective of allowing states to meet pollution standards. Increased efficiency in each of these areas can make sense in its own programmatic terms without making collective sense. The key is in *defining the goal* toward which technique is applied. PPBS as a technique would be invaluable for integrating governmental efforts to achieve the objective of a healthy environment. It is neutral, though, as to the formulation of that objective and in the determination of its importance, and it says nothing with regard to the will of national leaders to meet it.

PPBS is an administrative *methodology*. It is of consequence only in relation to ends in the same manner that social science methodology takes on meaning only in reference to theory. The technique of scientific analysis is employed to establish the validity of certain theoretical propositions that purport to explain some element of discernible reality. Those propositions might or might not be correct; they might apply to a limited sector of society or to a broad phenomenon. The "efficiency" of the method of analysis, as technique, does not depend on the consequence of the problem or on the correctness of the proposition. It is simply a tool; some methodological tools are more refined and of greater utility than others. Similarly, PPBS is a tool—an instrument for structuring programs to achieve policy objectives. Its effectiveness exists independent of the desirability or comprehensiveness of those policies.[b]

PPBS has only been utilized in limited areas of public policy; particularly in certain fields of defense management in the Pentagon under Robert McNamara (and even there it succeeded only partially in overcoming the bureaucratic propensities that dictate defense spending). It has yet to become the *modus operandi* in any major domain of domestic policy that *cuts across* existing departmental boundaries. Certainly the approach sketched by Schultze did not prevail in the Bureau of the Budget when under his direction, however strenuous his exertions to extend the scope of coordinated planning and to force attention to spending priorities.

---

[b]The reliance on the technique itself is misleading. The belief that more efficient methods will overcome shortsighted policy-making misconstrues the issue. To carry our analogy with scholarly method one step further, that approach is equivalent to perfecting a computer program to collate responses to a questionnaire when we have no adequate theory from which to derive the questions. Without explicit statement of purpose, the refinement of means is of uncertain significance and overall effect.

To achieve that kind of systemic logic, more fundamental changes would have to occur over time in what we expect our government to accomplish, and the ends it is intended to serve. The first step would be to recognize the failure of present methods to manage a problem of such central importance to the survival of the society that there is engendered a readiness to try new approaches. The second is the commensurate growth in communal sentiment that in its political expression inspires public officials to concert government policy toward remedying the problem. It is by no means clear that the environmental issue is so acute as to produce these changes in political attitude. Ecological disaster does not appear to be in the offing. Whatever the potential dangers of proceeding along the courses of unrestrained industrial expansion and population growth, present levels of concern would seem to assure that remedial action sufficient to ward off catastrophe will be taken—at least in the near future with regard to the health hazards of pollution. It is perhaps just these reformist efforts that, by preventing a more critical problem from developing, also preclude a more drastic change in our overall public approach toward the environment. The "better" is the enemy of the "best." Without a pervasive sense of crisis, it is unlikely that we shall see that keen sense of collective destiny requisite for dramatic transformation in the way men organize their society. Lacking the solidarity fashioned by adversity, and the will forged of clear purpose, our innovations and inventions are prone to be remedial in goal and marginal in effect.

Planning, Nonplanning and Antiplanning

From one vantage point, the debate over the feasibility or advantages of planning—i.e., conscious, rational policy-making that seeks systematically to achieve well-defined objectives—is misdirected. The question is not whether to plan but what kind of planning we engage in. Governmental behavior does not take the form of existential response to unconsidered circumstances. It entails judgments about ends and about the effective means for attaining them. It involves the purposeful use of organizational and administrative technique.[c]

The differences we have noted between incrementalism and a more orderly approach have to do with: (a) the policymaker's explicitness about his objectives; (b) the range of pertinent concerns and ramifying effects that he takes into account; and (c) the time-span encompassed. In nearly all instances, however, the calculus itself is logically rational within its own temporal and

---

[c]Whereas the overt purpose of bureaucracy is consciously defined and formalistically perceived, its mode of functioning is such that most of its members tend to act without explicit reference to its institutional purposes. The resultant mechanical mode of operation, pursuing purely organizational ends rather than substantive ones, has a decidedly conservative effect. Thus the resistance to change of a highly bureaucratized political system.

latitudinal bounds. The behavior of officials is rarely instinctual or compulsive, although it is often habitual, reflecting the conditioning of institutional circumstances and the absorption of conventional wisdom.

But the distinctive mode remains volitional behavior—the application of intelligence. What is striking about our public institutions—and paradoxical in the present situation—is that they combine unique elements of formal rationality with a great capacity to generate, and to tolerate, gross systemic irrationalities. The whole web of highly interdependent institutions that constitutes a modern society represents an extraordinarily intricate, functionally rational interlocking of diverse persons and organizations. Elaborate rationality is also exhibited in the various, specific domains of administrative operation. The Treasury or the Transportation Department (if we speak of public agencies); General Motors or U.S. Steel (if we speak of private corporations); Oak Ridge Nuclear Laboratory or NASA (if we speak of technical organizations); accomplish tasks of coordination that must appear remarkable from any historically comparative vantage point.[5]

Irrationality and illogicality are by-products of the very forms and practices to which these other achievements can be attributed. We already have noted the causes of this systemic irrationality: the dissociation of governmental powers, the plural pattern of representation, the selectively narrow criteria of political participation, the pragmatic culture that disdains that kind of explicit, embracing view of the whole that would enable public authority to anticipate communal problems and would allow for their appraisal. The overall effect is extreme self-consciousness about the immediate institutional framework of action, and a decided lack of self-consciousness about essential purposes. It is highly rational problem-solving that relies on custom and conventional wisdom to define the problem to be solved.

If we consider planning in the abstract as a form of technique, i.e., "a systematic disciplined approach to objectives,"[6] we can see that a good portion of what both public and private organizations do is planning. What is at issue is the comprehensiveness of the planning and the designation of appropriate objects for planning. The planning impulse is just another manifestation of the technical orientation of modern society. Aron, for example, defines technical as: "The logical use of means, whether material or human, to achieve ends or to create objects conceived in advance."[7] The desired capacity to act with formalistic assurance is a trait of most contemporary institutions, be they industrial corporations or government bureaucracies. It is this disposition that leads to planning. Planning as a technique is both an expression of the broader rationalizing propensity, and a means for organizing mechanical technology.

Galbraith affirms that "all technology leads to planning, i.e., application of organized knowledge to practical tasks."[8] However, a practical task is not self-defining. Practical tasks that are commonly recognized, and to which technique is applied, are those associated with: (a) mechanical innovation and its application to industry; (b) the coordination of the economic infrastructure of society; and (c) adjustment of the interplay of economic interests in the industrial system. Conditions generated as side effects of this whole system of interlocking areas of planned activity are not readily recognized or acknowledged as tasks requireing the application of technique planning. Thus the apparent neglect of environmental problems.

We perhaps can facilitate this inquiry into the "planning issue" by cataloguing three types of planning. Loosely defined they are *planning as technical exploitation, planning as technical congruence,* and *planning for human use.* Planning as technical exploitation implies the organization for development, application, and utilization of mechanical devices. Industry routinely engages in this kind of planning as it progressively rationalizes its production, refines new products, and markets them. Planning as technical congruence is what governmental activity represents for the most part. It coordinates the routine innovation of our technologically prolific society so that it fits present patterns of social organization, as well as preexisting technology. Occasionally it innovates in this respect (as in the space program); more often it responds to the ramifying impact of new industries, new products, new techniques appearing at various points in our society. Planning for human use is of a different order than the first two. It does not make the same implicit assumption as to the inherent virtue of technology, nor does it equate progress, technical innovation, and general welfare with industrial expansion. Having as its reference point some notion of "the good society," planning for human use monitors innovations to assess their overall effects on society. Indeed, it intelligently uses rationality to carve out areas insulated from, or deemed unamenable to, rational techniques. (As an example, restraint in dictating the organization of work in a factory or the exact arrangement of living quarters in new buildings.)[d]

Referring to the transportation issue once again, we might say that planning

---

[d]For a society that proclaims a principled dislike for planning and affirms the virtues of the unhampered market in allocating resources, we exhibit rich examples of elaborate, government schemes that run directly counter to market indications. Consider the expensive subsidies that the federal (and state) government provides for residents of cities in the Southwest: e.g., Los Angeles. Climatic and topographical conditions are such that southern California is endowed with water resources sufficient only to support a small fraction of the present population. The balance has been provided courtesy of the Colorado River dams, constructed along with aquaducts in the 1930s and 1940s. Further infusions recently have come via the multibillion dollar project to transport northern California water to the South. The adverse environmental effects are considerable: the salination of the Lower Colorado, possible serious disturbances of the ecology of San Francisco Bay, and Los Angeles' air pollution,

Such lavish public outlays could be defended were their strategic resources in southern California critical to a major national industry. In fact, the area's greatest resource is sunshine, attracting mobile industries, e.g., aerospace, that depend primarily on skilled personnel. By providing the requirements for life in this sunny, but arid region (only a small portion of whose cost is assumed by its consumers), government is subsidizing a "convenience" for a select segment of the population.

as technical exploitation is building private automobiles that move as fast as possible, at as little cost as possible. Planning as technical congruence is the construction of new, safer highways for the use of autos. Planning for human use, as yet only rarely discernible, would be to decide whether society benefits from a given volume of cars considering the automobile industry's place in the economy, pollution effects, congestion created, alternative means of transportation available, and so on. Planning for human use, then, would judge the conditions favorable for the use of automobiles so as to maximize benefit derived from vehicular technology.

As is only too evident, nearly all of our planning is of the first two types. They coincide with the pragmatic, growth maximizing inclination of the society. By contrast, planning for human use depends on some explicit conception of communal good, of a desirable social condition. Environmental planning rejects the notion that "meaning is to be found in the becoming," that change for its own sake is a valid way of proceeding, that participation in the current of progress is to be equated with the good life itself.[e] Modern man is taught to believe that life is movement; any self-contained state, therefore, can only be equated with death. Where purpose and meaning are to be found only in the act of striving, then the routinized change associated with industrial development becomes seen as a requisite for survival. There being no objectifiable point of attainment, we do not seek to construct an enduring condition embodying preferred social values.

The urban environment provides only the most vivid evidence of our failure, if not inability to plan for human use. Our society is replete with examples of assertive, complex planning instituted to make technology work while even the most rudimentary apparatus is lacking for managing its environmental effects. Virtually every large city in the United States offers examples of mindless initiatives, destructive of basic urban amenities, that pass as planning. The neglect of planning for human use is all the more disheartening because of the nominal presence in every municipality of persons designated as city planners. Presumably trained and employed to design the urban environment, by far the greatest part of their activity seems to be devoted to technically congruent tasks in alleviating the most damaging effects of the city's random growth and

---

[e]The readiness to act without apparent reference to ultimate objective is not uncharacteristic of modern behavior patterns and standards of normality. Psychologists of individual behavior like the social analyst operate without any clear idea of the positive norm. Health is defined negatively as freedom from debilitating symptoms. It is a narrowly clinical interpretation of well-being. As a consequence, the analyst is able only to recognize certain disabling symptoms and treats them so that the organism will continue to function. Survival here, too, becomes the standard of achievement.

Rather than using intelligent judgment based on some theory of human behavior and confirmed by the evidence of experience, laissez faire is installed in the place of professional responsibility. Straining our analogy somewhat, the resistance of the social analyst to the idea of questioning the givens of the system whose functioning they describe is attributable to the system-dependent character of the theories themselves. When conditions appear that are not made comprehensible by available conceptual tools, social analysis becomes stymied.

consequent deterioration. What commonly passes for planning in our cities, is often from the perspective of urban design, nonplanning.

New York City provides two outstanding examples of an allied species of concerted technical exploitation that might properly be called "antiplanning." The first proposal, ultimately rejected in a rare show of good sense, was to tax automobiles entering Manhattan Island so as to restrict the number of vehicles in the traffic choked streets of midtown. It was aimed primarily at commuters. On the surface it seemed logical to expect that the imposition of monetary cost on the use of the private auto would have the desired effect of curtailing its movements into the center of the city. The strategy could only be expected to work, though, were there an alternative mode of transportation available whose use would entail costs—monetary and psychic—less than those incurred by paying the commuter tax on autos. In fact, the only alternatives were the intolerably crowded, increasingly dangerous rail facilities. Not only would the cost for the individual commuter be considerable, these additional loads could break down the system entirely—even assuming that there was physically space available for the new hordes. In pursuit of the commendable end of alleviating traffic congestion, a gimmicky device was contemplated that lacked even the logic of technical congruence behind it.

The second glaring instance of antiplanning is the construction of the World Trade Center. Encompassing two huge office towers, each well over 100 stories, the project's completion will bring to the thronged tip of Manhattan some tens of thousands of employees. Transportation, sidewalk space available, public facilities, will remain constant, and the overall effect will be a sharp decline of the amenity level of the area. Here planning once again does not even reach the level of technical congruence. The motivation to build the monstrosity in the first place was a desire to expand the city's tax base. Given the functionally illogical administrative boundaries in the metropolitan area, the city authorities are compelled to solicit business, and to urge relocation within the confines of the city, regardless of the site's suitability. Thus the inducement to the Port Authority to construct the Trade Center. Modern construction technology permits buildings of enormous height; thus, their inordinate size. Given the city's perilous financial health that inspired the project, the municipality lacks the funds for expanding the public facilities in the area of construction; thus the enormous congestion that results. Planning as technical exploitation in this way reaches the nadir of environmental irrationality even as the Trade Center reaches new heights.[f]

---

[f]It should be noted that even the economic gain expected from locating large office complexes in central areas has been called into question. A number of recent analyses suggest that the financial costs incurred providing necessary service for the building's upkeep exceed the tax revenue they generate. Ironically, if property tax schedules were adjusted to remove the present inequities, which favor commercial real estate, tax yield might increase to the point where high-rise construction would be feasible—at least in narrow economic terms.

Part 3
Ways and Means

8

Legislative and Administrative Procedures: Costs

There are two questions to be asked about the economics of cleaning up the environment and the provision of amenities: (a) what is the most feasible means to proceed with remedial measures; and (b) who should incur the costs? There are no issues more controversial and pregnant with potential conflict, or more illuminating of the profound challenge environmental issues pose for public authorities.

Certainly it is not going to be a financially painless operation. Whereas it costs nothing for people to refrain from throwing beer cans out of car windows, it will cost a great deal to purify the air and water of the industrial and municipal wastes that now corrupt them, or to find alternative, economical and safe means for their disposal.[a] The Council on Environmental Quality (CEQ) estimates that the cumulative public and private expenditures for air and water pollution control in the period 1970-80 necessary for effective prevention and cleanup, i.e., to meet the EPA's air and water pollution standards, would be $201 billion. That figure rises to $287.1 billion if solid wastes are included.[3] The price of mass transit and urban services will be even greater; although no reliable figures exist for amenity costs. Nor do these sums include costs of controlling new pollution generated by economic growth during the period.

There are some sources of pollution on which the government can act directly, federal agencies and local municipalities are among the most active polluters (e.g., sewage disposal). The simplest approach is for controls to be imposed legislatively or through executive orders. Costs would appear as increases in departmental budgets. The Environmental Protection Agency, whose statutory power to require environmental impact reports from federal departments is, as we observed, a subject of debate, is endowed with uncertain enforcement powers over other agencies of government.[4] Given the resistance, if

---

[a]President Nixon has upon occasion given the impression that the environmental problem can be solved in the manner of a Boy Scout crusade. He properly has been called to task for implying that "the transition can be smooth or effortless."[1] It is understandable that reassuring remarks to this effect should be forthcoming before an audience of business and industrial leaders. For it is very likely that unless there is a swift reconciliation of the industrial ethic and profit motive on the one hand, and the conservationist impulse on the other, businessmen, government officials, and environmentalists likely will find themselves in more and more open and bitter clashes. The extent of sentiment unsympathetic to the environmental cause within the administration is considerable and by no means veiled. Former Secretary of Commerce Maurice Stans was fond of saying that "business is 99.44 per cent pure."[2] Hendric S. Hontakker, a member of the Council of Economic Advisors, has been equally flippant in his reduction of environmental problems to "a value judgment."

not imperviousness of administrative bureaucracies to well-intentioned persuasion from without, further congressional actions would seem desirable. It might consider specific prohibitions where there is undeniable environmental damage, as with radioactivity from nuclear power facilities or disposal of biological and chemical weapons. Once a specific class of actions are declared illegal, the way is open for private suits against noncompliant agencies. In this way, compliance could be enforced through the courts rather than left to the indeterminate processes of intragovernmental regulation. (Outright prohibitions and fixed standards have drawbacks. They do not permit environmental administrators to make discretionary judgments, adjusting rules to accord with new technologies, changing conditions of scarcity, and overall planning needs. Moreover, the criteria by which compulsory control or prohibitions are based, might come to be viewed as definitive and thereby work against more subtle, and perhaps more far-reaching forms of environmental management).

Some forms of *pollution by industry* as well have become the object of blanket prohibitions, as with those federal and state regulations controlling automobile emissions. Normally such prohibitions to bring social behavior into line with a legislatively defined preferred condition poses an administrative nightmare of enforcing the rules on millions of potential violators. The massive noncompliance, violation of statute, and corruption of enforcement agencies that ensues is daily witnessed with regard to gambling, drug, and vice laws. However, in this instance, enforcement is vastly simplified by imposing responsibility directly on the manufacturer.

The arduous chore of enforcing them on tens of millions of automobile owners is avoided through legislative prescriptions that are imposed on the auto companies. The Clean Air Act of 1970 simply requires that all automobiles sold in the US meet federal emission standards; by 1975 (the deadline has now been moved back to 1976 under industry pressure) a 90 percent reduction of hydrocarbons and carbon monoxide, and a similar standard for nitrogen oxides. The limited number of firms in the field simplifies the problem of ensuring compliance.

Complications arise in other ways, namely the unaccommodating attitude of the auto industry. Manufacturers seemed resigned to nominal compliance. The engine modifications they plan do not entail basic redesign, but rather the attachment of elaborate devices to present engines. This approach has two undesirable consequences. One, in order to maintain power output, horsepower is being increased, mileage reduced, and accordingly greater demands placed on petroleum resources just at the time when proper anxiety is being felt about the energy crisis. Two, this cumbersome equipment requires periodic tuning if it is to continue to meet emission standards once outside the factory gates. Present legislation does not provide for further checks. Acknowledging this shortcoming, amendments have been proposed to provide regular inspection and to make car owners liable to penalties for failure to meet standards. This latter provision, of course, raises the difficult issues of enforcement seemingly overcome by focusing on manufacture. The apparent need is for more basic research and development of a modified internal combustion engine, or an entirely new steam or electric engine, which is more efficient than contemplated designs. Auto companies have been slow to move in this direction. They might be encouraged to act with a keener sense of urgency were Washington to be more stringent in prescription of emission requirements, and perhaps prepared to enter into a cost-sharing agreement on research and development. (Some indirect technical benefits might also be expected from the National Science Foundation's RANN—Research Aimed at National Needs—program of research support.)[b]

Even more difficult enforcement problems are faced in attempting to devise effective and just policies for other industrial polluters. There are a number of possible administrative approaches each with its own complications, advantages, and shortcomings.

One much discussed and popular approach is to impose a polluter's tax, or effluent charge. A fee could be set per quantum of matter released, or a fee imposed on the quantity of effluent or emission. In this way, air and water would cease to be "free" goods and their degradation no longer could be considered costless externalities. Such fees would, in effect, be fines intended to induce the polluter to reduce his pollution. If there is a general failure to do so in a particular region, the fines collected could be applied to public authorities to the construction, in the case of waterways, of common facilities. (Indeed, there might be an initial policy of collecting fees for just such an undertaking.)[5] Although there are difficulties in assuring precise measurement, reasonable estimates could be made as our knowledge of pollution improves (especially with regard to streams where there is considerable difficulty in differentiating among several contributors) and our instruments for detecting it perfected. The assumption is that the costs incurred would motivate the polluter to install the

---

[b]The setting of air quality standards is a more striking attempt at general level to use gross measures to produce a series of ramifying changes in present practices. By stipulating levels of acceptable pollution, the EPA has transferred responsibility to local authorities for devising the specific means by which to bring their areas of jurisdiction in conformity with federal standards. We already have described the failure to formulate programs that would permit compliance by opening necessary options in the transportation and power fields. New Yorkers, in their unending urban agony, were presented with the concrete dilemma of having to choose between clean air and adequate power in the fall of 1970. Thanks to inefficient planning (as technical congruence) in anticipating the growing demand for power, the city has suffered chronic shortages and brown-outs. The maintenance of minimal service depended on the inauguration of a massive new plant (Ravenshead) which, in fact, had the glaring shortcoming of lacking any effective devices for controlling emissions. It threatened to become a major contributor to New York's already aggrieved pollution situation. Installation of the devices would put back the plan's starting date by a good year. The city fathers were up against it. Having failed to engage in planning (for human use) to coordinate power needs with environmental ones, they were now faced with very unattractive tradeoffs. After much agonized soul-searching, they made a qualified choice for more pollution and fewer brown-outs. This not unexpected choice, needless to say, will hardly ease their task in trying to meet the recently promulgated federal air quality standards.

necessary control technology or otherwise alter his activities so as to prevent extensive discharges.

Advocates of the effluent charge approach see the market system as generating strong pressures on manufacturers to avoid the additional costs resulting from noncompliance. The price advantage of compliant firms freed from the financial burden of fees or fines (an advantage that would increase as costs of abatement are met) is seen as creating a strain to reach stipulated levels of acceptable emission. Two conditions would have to be met for this analysis cum prescription to be valid. First, fees must be set high enough as to impose a greater cost than the price of installing controls. Second, the field of commerce in question must be characterized by genuine competition rather than oligopolistic manipulation of the market. The former raises the issue of initial legislative purpose and the integrity of administrative enforcement; the latter returns our attention to the earlier discussed imperfections of the market.

Supporters of effluent charges offer various elaborations of their analysis to deal with these difficulties and imperfections. It has been suggested that were an entire industry, or a large segment of it, to connive in resisting remedial action, absorbing the cost of fees and passing them on to consumers, powerful incentives would be created to substitute other items (and for other manufac-turers to provide them). With regard to building materials, for example, if large lumber mills in a region conspired to act in concert to blunt the intention of the law, an advantage would be given suppliers of bricks, prestressed concrete, and so forth. The first problem with this reasoning is that it makes too facile assumptions about the ease of substitutability. Some items cannot readily be supplanted, e.g., metals of various kinds (or the flexibility of consumer tastes taken for granted). Alternatives, in some instances, might be developed over time and market opportunities encourage production. But pollution would continue during the interval and cost the polluters little if anything under ologopolistic conditions. Furthermore, the initial price advantage of a particular industry might be so great that even with the increase in production costs from charges and fines, it conceivably could maintain the upper hand over established or new potential competitors (e.g., lumber as a building material compared to brick in parts of the western US).

Perhaps the greatest weakness of the effluent charge approach is apparent in the transportation field. The imposition by the federal government of emission standards on the auto industry is a case in point. Some opponents of this initiative argue the preferability of levying "a tax on each make of new automobile, graduated according to the amount of pollution it emits and to the length of the warranty it provides. Each year the tax could become higher. Rather than a once and for all showdown, characterized by claims and counterclaims as to what the automakers can and cannot produce, the tax would provide a steadily increasing incentive for the manufacturers to reduce pollution."[6] (The same logic, it is asserted, could be applied to the oil industry, by placing a tax on lead in gasoline).

The immediate criticism is the one made above—monopolistic tendencies neutralize competitive pressures. Proponents of pollution charges anticipate this argument by ingeniously fusing the market situation to the market of political representation. They suggest that were the costs of cars and/or gasoline to become onerously high as the price absorbed emission fees, the owners' discontent would translate itself into massive pressure on government to provide an alternative, e.g., mass transportation. In this way, both a "free" economy and the purity of the system of interest politics would be preserved, the latter being called in to redress the inadequacies of the former.

There is, however, no assurance that the pieces would fit neatly together as sketeched in the scenario. It is not at all clear what represents intolerable cost for the consumer, or whether the critical point of discontent would be reached before unabated pollution attains crisis proportions. Second, our system of representation impedes easy translation of diffuse, if widely-felt needs into clear statements of legislative preference (see chapter 6). Moreover, the whole process envisaged is so convoluted and uncertain in final result as hardly to constitute a preferred method for meeting environmental needs and defraying the costs. Only a doctrinaire commitment to the fictitious market and deep distrust of governmental initiative makes its advocacy at all plausible. It would appear more in keeping with both the spirit of community action and the conditions for successful environmental management for public authorities to respond to manifest problems by asserting the proper powers of government to satisfy collective needs.

There is yet another drawback to a system of control build around pollution fees. Where there is no compulsory compliance, there are a variety of circumstances in which the guilty party might find it expedient to pay the charges rather than check the effluent. Although it is true that firms as a rule do not pass up opportunities to cut production costs, there are important exceptions. A marginal firm, in perilous financial health and with limited reserves, could find it easier to limp along from year to year paying the costs of pollution in increments rather than incurring the full expense of installing the necessary machinery. Even more strikingly, a local plant maintained as a tax loss by a parent company would have an interest in increasing operation expenses and would feel no motivation to control its industrial discharges. Furthermore, in many cases there are organizational costs that a large corporation entails in undertaking these remedial steps that could offset the monetary gains associated with avoiding fines. For many large firms, the inertial force of doing business as usual might militate against compliance.[c]

---

[c]As we noted, there is counterpart drawback to compulsory federal standards, i.e., they leave little flexibility for establishing variable standards in accordance with local conditions. An emission level that in one area is environmentally damaging might in another have less deleterious effect and/or produce effects, that given low population densities, are acceptable by any reasonable criteria of benefits denied and costs of amelioration. The prevailing approach in the EPA is to combine standard setting with pollution charges responsive to local conditions, as described in the CEQ report: "Regulatory authority can be used to

All of these complications pertain as well, in varying ways, to other tax arrangments that could be devised: e.g., rebates for industrial investment in pollution devices, or federally guaranteeed state and local loans.[d] The success of the last-mentioned approach is further threatened by the inevitable inconsistency of pollution codes enacted by a multiplicity of local jurisdictions. If a company deems the costs of pollution abatement are onerously high, and fines are at an equally intolerable level, it could decide simply to shift location. Just as industry has been attracted south by cheap labor and a preferential tax structure, it might be attracted to any region which is prepared to accept pollution as the price for economic growth. The transfer would spare the first community a polluter, but it would also work havoc on its financial structure. In addition, the pollution would not have been contained, but simply redistributed. Communities might freely be accorded the right to exercise this local option were it not for two other considerations. One, the pollution caused is usually not restricted to the place of release. It spreads far beyond municipal or even state boundaries. Los Angeles's smog, for example, is now clearly visible half-way across the Mohave Desert and is chemically detectable as far away as Colorado and New Mexico. (The construction of the enormous fossil-fueled Four Corners power plant in New Mexico to meet burgeoning Southern Californian needs literally shifts the pollution to a remote, but scenic area). The citizens of locales in between should be granted the same options as the residents of Los Angeles, who, for their own reasons, have chosen to suffer the discomfort and threat to health of massive pollution. Similarly, our increasing knowledge of the fragile ecological balance of the environment underscores the interdependence of all its component elements. The ramifying effects of pollution are not only widespread in the first degree. They also are expressed in a chain reaction of environmental changes. These changes are often unpredictable and of major consequence.

There is also the question of environmental rights. We might ask what constitutes community choice and whether a majority of a city (if indeed it is a majority) should be permitted to take action that threatens the well-being of those citizens who are not prepared to make the tradeoff between the environment and prosperity. Are clean air and water corporate property to be

---

establish ambient standards and back-up enforcement, while pollution charges provide the economic incentive to achieve these standards."[7]

[d]Tax incentives for installation of environmentally sound technology are discussed in the *Second Annual Report*. The EPA estimates that "if the best presently available technology were applied to all existing sources of particulate emissions, they would drop by 95 percent."[8] However, present rates of investment are low. According to the generous estimates of the EPA, only $3.3 billion of $103 billion invested in infrastructure went for environmental facilities.[9] The report is peculiarly lacking in discussion of the government's role in promoting environmentally sound technologies. This neglect is further evidence of continuing shortcomings in congruent planning. Much discussion was engendered by the announcement by the administration of a broad plan for coordinating federal support for research and technological development.[10] The particulars suggest, though, that the motivation is concern about the competitiveness of US industries and that consequently the program stressed commercial needs rather than being environmentally oriented.[11]

disposed of by officials acting in the name of the community, or does each individual have an inalienable right to those goods in their untainted form? As Mishan argues, there is sound, logical reason to define pollution as theft, and on that basis to permit the individual to file suit if his access to clean air and water is impeded.[12] As matters now stand, he can be victimized without recourse to judicial action. Thus, by leaving the power of pollution control in local hands, we would both exacerbate the problems of ensuring compliance and leave many persons liable to gross infringement on their right to a clean environment. National standards imposed uniformly are a precondition to effective control, whatever the particular administrative mode of enforcing compliance. The unity of the problem should be matched by the comprehensiveness of the remedy.

Restrictive laws, whether they involve financial levies or other penalties, do share a liability of a different order. To be applied with any degree of effect, they would entail an enormous enforcement apparatus and place a heavy burden on the courts. Our legal system is already so overburdened as to leave itself open to charges of dereliction. Tightly written laws will be of little positive use if justice is not swift and efficient. The effectiveness of all law depends on habitual compliance. Where violation is the rule rather than the exception, no legal mechanism will succeed in assuring the desired behavior. In the case of pollution codes, moreover, the tens of thousands of potential violators are being asked to take new actions, e.g., install control devices, and not merely to avoid certain prohibited actions. (Normally, the higher the penalty the greater the spur to action. However, in the cases of marginal or tax-loss firms, there might be an inverse relationship between the size of the costs and the readiness to comply.) Initiation of change, therefore, should have its own appeal and attraction, rather than being just compelled. Ideally, a broadly diffused sensitivity to environmental problems would inspire corporate managers, shareholders, and other responsible members of the technostructure actively to support compliance with abatement regulations. The predisposition to conform with antipollution laws is a necessary ingredient to their successful implementation.

Admittedly, dramatic conversions on a mass scale are not likely to occur. However strong the growing tide of environmental concern, there remains a contradiction between the common economic standard of profitability and corporate good-citizenship. Only over time will broad shifts in cultural values produce redefinition of institutional and professional role for the businessman. Until that happy day arrives, the threat of coercive legal action is a necessary spur to compliance with the requirements for a clean environment, whatever the administrative and judicial difficulties.

The Stockholder Movement

One unconventional avenue of approach is the campaign to enlist large institutional stockholders in the environmentalist and consumer cause. This technique, actively pursued by Ralph Nader's Center for the Study of Responsive Law, has already been employed with some early successes.[e] The idea is to win pledges of support from those institutions which are disposed to acknowledge some broad public responsibilities. Universities and foundations are the most obvious targets of persuasive effort. Other potential participants are retirement funds, cooperatives, insurance companies, and even investment banks. The likelihood of success in gaining the commitment of these institutional shareholders is increased where the members of the institution are susceptible to environmental appeals and can be formed into an active pressure group working within the organization, e.g., college professors and students in private universities, or school teachers and other professionals who belong to equity trusts. Investment in corporate shares is normally made on strictly financial grounds to obtain a secure holding that will show a return on capital. Profitability has been as much a concern of the institutional investor as of the private individual who commits his capital. Qualification of this pecuniary motivation depends on a shift in the group's perception of its investment's ultimate purposes, and a readiness to trade some margin of financial advantage for the satisfaction of exercising a wider public responsibility. If the contributors to a retirement fund are genuinely concerned with the pollution caused by a manufacturing firm in which they hold a block of stock, they might be prepared to join with other shareholders, similarly motivated, to impose on the corporation's management a policy of abatement. They would also have to accept the possibility that profits will be cut as a consequence. Were the constituencies of a sufficiently large number of investors disposed to make this exchange, the firm would be compelled to move against pollution.

The corporate end of the institutional shareholder is often functionally different from the commercial enterprise. Its interest in profitability is not an expression of its central purpose; monetary gain is not its reason for being. Rather, its investment in stock is intended to permit it to perform its organizational tasks: of teaching and supporting research in the case of the university; or providing the means for the good life of its members in the case of the retirement fund. When "the good life" is seen as threatened by the corporation's single-minded pursuit of profit, or the university's humanitarian

---

[e]There are perhaps alternative strategies as well for influencing corporate behavior from within. These include various proposals for introducing into the decision-making structure representatives of the community business services, on whose support it relies for its economic success. If we take the functional view of the modern corporation that sees it as a complex organization enmeshed in a web of interdependent relationships within the industrial system, then its public character is accentuated. No longer the personalized domain that it was in an earlier entrepreneurial period, increasingly dependent on government assistance of different sorts, run by a technostructure rather than by self-willed manager-owners, the large capitalist structure today is *private* business only by courtesy of nomenclature. Its behavior is properly the concern of all those who deal with it: workers, stockholders, consumers, and the broad constituency of its pollution. It remains to devise the means by which this public identity can be given practical expression.

goals contradicted by such single-mindedness, these institutions will consider using the power derived from their financial holdings to influence corporate behavior.

The strategies of stockholder movements can be directed at two objectives: (a) to require a specific corporate action, e.g., to install antipollution equipment on smokestacks; and/or (b) to place a representative of environmental interests on the board of directors. The former approach has the advantage of imposing an explicit course of action, but suffers from the danger of being a one-shot affair. Stockholder oversight in the particular instance is difficult, and a refractory management might require periodic campaigns to mobilize the votes on recurrent issues. The business executive conventionally measures professional achievement in profits, and his security of tenure normally is also a function of profits. An environmental-oriented campaign on the part of stockholders compels him partially to redefine his criteria of both. In this way, the standard of performance is, to some degree, defined for the manager by his constituency of enviroment-minded institutional stockholders. Permanent representation gives formal, institutional expression to the corporation's environmental commitment and assures that a voice will be on hand to raise those issues routinely. The danger here is that of co-optation. Token representation might be simply the most expedient means of neutralizing pressure and fostering a more responsive image.

To date, neither approach has clearly established itself. The strength marshalled by stockholder movements has as yet been insufficient to permit environmentalists to force substantial changes in business practices. Environmental concerns are still not salient enough to motivate institutional investors in large enough numbers to unite against the negligent practices of the corporations they collectively own. The arithmetic of corporate ownership is also against them since only in rare instances do these organizations susceptible to environmental action have the potential for constituting a majority bloc.

A variation on the Nader approach is that offered in theory by Robert Dahl in his speculative work, *After the Revolution*.[13] As a founding and highly influential member of the pluralist school of democracy, he not surprisingly is attracted to what he calls interest-group management. Taking the "public nature" of the contemporary corporation as his point of departure, he develops the logic of granting not only workers, but other importantly affected interests such as consumers and governments the right to a direct say in management—for example, through representatives on the board of directors of an enterprise. By whatever instrumentality, it is desirable to carve out a place for the corporation's public constituency. Although there is no denying the need for direct governmental regulations, ultimately the environmental problem can only be resolved, and its healthy condition assured, when our economic institutions give proper account to externalities *as a matter of course*. Under those circumstances, the formidable forces of organizational inertia would be working on the side of the angels.

Who Pays the Costs

The different approaches to regulation of private polluters leave open the question of who pays the costs. (The economic issues we refer to here are not those we discussed with reference to allocations of national resources to provide urban amenities, or those connected with doctrines of steady-state economy, although they do overlap in certain respects.) Some impose the *immediate* cost on the polluter, e.g., discharges fees or investment in pollution control equipment, as could be decreed by law (the automobile industry's necessary compliance with the Clean Air Act's provisions is a case in point), or dictated by stockholders. But the bearer of the *ultimate* cost is not clear. In most instances it can be predicted that the firm will simply pass on the costs to the consumer in the form of higher prices. Pollution control will be viewed as just another operating expense to be included in the calculus of profit or loss. Unless the firm is compelled to absorb the additional costs, this is the logical course of action. It means that the users of power, or the purchasers of automobiles, will pay for reduction in carbon monoxide and nitric oxide emissions. The corporation maintains profit margins intact and merely administers and oversees the change in manufacture.

Where tax rebates are available to offset the costs of pollution control, there is no doubt who foots the bill. (The tax incentive approach was incorporated in a provision of the Tax Reform Act of 1969 that allows firms to deduct the costs of installing waste treatment facilities.) It is the public at large, as represented by the government. Under either approach, the private corporation will have escaped financial responsibility. It is hardly the most equitable arrangement for a number of reasons. First, a massive program to abate pollution would mean the direction of considerable industrial resources into a "nonproducer" area. In other words, expenditure will be in infrastructure (control equipment) that does not itself generate wealth (conventionally defined). As a consequence, growth rates of the GNP could tend to be lowered and/or disposable public income reduced. Yet the firm which installs the equipment can maintain its policy of profit maximization since investment costs of the equipment are covered by either the state (tax rebates) or the consumer (through higher prices). Second, under none of these schemes would the corporation be obliged to defray the costs of cleaning up the pollution it created during all the years of its laissez faire operations when environmental effects were considered externalitites. The atmosphere and many bodies of water will purify themselves over time if no new pollutants are introduced. Other conditions will not be as easily remedied. Euthrophied lakes are permanently lost as recreation areas; and the accumulation of urban grime will be very expensive to remove. It is as unrealistic to expect that reparations will be collected for pure air and water lost as it was that steel mills in the 19th century would be compelled to pay reparations for the tuberculosis caused by the pollution of their belching smokestacks. However, it is not entirely unreasonable for them to be held responsible for some portion of the costs met in cleaning up the mess they caused. The responsibility is in one sense public, since all those who earned a livelihood as employees of the business, or as users of its products, benefited from its operations. The sin has also been collective in terms of the social values that encouraged indiscriminate industrial activity, and in the cultural norms that blinded us to its consequences. But the owners (including institutional owners) profited disproportionately and they might equitably be required to assume a special burden, rather than diffusing all the cost among the tax-paying and product-buying public. Therefore, attentive interest in the modalities of pollution regulation should be forhtcoming so that some percentage of the costs should be directly borne by the corporation.

If we were forced to choose between tax rebates that burden the public treasury with the costs of pollution control and policies that permit them to be passed on to the consumer, the former would appear more equitable. Taxes, especially federal ones, are collected according to a progressive schedule; price increases are in effect regressive sales taxes. Even if the immediate consumer is another commercial firm, ultimately the costs will be passed on to the consumer. The intermediary might, in fact, take advantage of the built-in pollution escalator to tack on a little extra, as is often done in periods of rising prices.[14]

9

Technology Assessment and Political Choice

There is no more appropriate way to consider the practical meaning of speculations about the direction of industrial society than by critically applying them to the subject of technology assessment. It is a topic of central theoretical as well as policy significance, entailing all the fundamental questions about technology's place in modern society; the neutrality of invention and the determination of priorities in research; the desirablity and efficacy of making critical technical evaluations based on preferred social objectives; and the mechanisms for concerting policy to achieve those objectives.

Among the proposals for institutional change that have burgeoned with the ecology movement, the idea of "Technology Assessment Boards" stands out as one of the most germane. In concept, it would provide society with the mechanism for systematically anticipating the effects, beneficial and adverse, that might flow from technological innovations. Our readiness uncritically to attribute virtue to invention until recently has permitted technology to dictate its place in our lives. The pace of innovation has accelerated so rapidly that effects have long outstripped our present capacity to manage them. Today the question whether man or machine is the master in their increasingly symbiotic relationship is more than rhetorical. However remarkable our technical achievements, they have not been matched by equivalent diligence and intelligent attention to where their outcomes were leading. In fact, the industrial system does not monitor its technology except with reference to its specific applications to equally technical tasks. Technology assessment is meant to overcome that deficiency.

As a public undertaking it implies two functions: monitoring and evaluation. The former emphasizes review of new mechanical techniques as they are generated by our technologically fecund civilization. It operates at the stages of development and application—denoting properties, probable routes of effect, and ramifications. So defined, technology assessment also attempts to anticipate unintended externalities, to note alternative technical means to accomplish a specified task, and to estimate their relative practicality. *Assessment as evaluation* is a more broadly conceived policy tool. Based on an explicit set of objectives, it formulates standards by which to judge critically the overall desirability of innovative technologies, managing their development and regulating their spread. It is prepared to reach conclusions in estimating the tradeoffs between a technology's positive worth (measured by ascribing values to the task it performs and the expected increase in efficiency) against its negative effects (requiring a similar ascription of values). It has the further attribute of being prepared to offer advice as to the relative merits of financially competitive research and development efforts.

"Technology Assessment I," as a self-limiting monitoring concept, raises the question of its adequacy as a tool for dealing with the technological abuses of our industrial system. The latter, more ambitious formulation as an instrument for logically consistent policy-making underscores the difficulties we face in setting standards of social utility and for systematizing programs so as to achieve them. The various proposals now under consideration for constituting official technology assessment bodies all accept the first set of purposes while disagreeing over the feasibility of inaugurating controls of the latter type. Both challenge us to consider critically how we might proceed to render liable to skeptical judgement what have been the givens for the policymaker and analyst alike.

The most publicized and lucid of these proposals is that contained in the report of the National Academy of Sciences, prepared on request of the Congressional Committee on Science and Astronautics, *Technology: Processes of Assessment and Choice.*[1] Composed largely of distinguished scientist/statesmen, the academy panel defined its task broadly. Acknowledging the damage that has resulted from unconsidered technological change, its members admitted the responsibility of those who create knowledge to provide considered estimates of its potential social meaning. The choice, as they stated it, is "between technological advance that proceeds without adequate consideration of its consequences and technological change that is influenced by a deeper concern for the interaction between man's tools and the human environment in which they do their work."[2] Their preference is to reject the orthodox laissez innover faith.

As for the means, the panel suggests establishing a *series* of technology assessment boards located at various levels of government, and in both the congressional and executive domains. The goal is to provide multiple sources of capability available to the coordinate branches of government. Whereas concentrating responsibility in one organization would strengthen its claim to definitive expertise, the authors are anxious lest it become isolated within the labyrinth of public agencies. By creating a plurality of assessment boards, associated with the different facets of public authority, it is hoped that the technology assessment function will come to permeate all of official policy-making. In this way, intelligent analysis of technology will inform political decisions *routinely*. The voice of expert counsel under those circumstances would not appear to be coming from without, intruding, as it were, upon the governmental bodies pursuing their normal activities. Rather, the voice in its several modulations would be integrated into the process of governance.

The executive component, as advocated by the academy panel, would take the form of an expanded Office of Science and Technology. That body, which served under the President's Science Advisory Council (until the latter was abolished in 1972 by President Nixon) was domiciled within the Executive Office of the President but had greater independence and was politically more distant than the National Security Council or Council of Economic Advisors. Under the proposed arrangement, a division for Technology Assessment would have been set up in the office with a considerable expansion of functions and responsibilities. (Most of these functions overlap those now perfromed by the Council on Environmental Quality, which it would largely supplant. The emphasis is on an apolitical body that stands further removed from executive power than the council.) Close cooperation was envisaged between the board housed in the Office of Science and Technology and the National Science Foundation. The latter would be encouraged to expand its own assessment activities and to develop its extensive grants program to promote pertinent research and practical studies.

The proposed congressional component would have taken one of two forms: a "Joint Committee on Technology Assessment" or a separate "Technology Assessment Office" serving the Congress. The latter alternative has now been chosen with the creation in 1972 of an Office of Technology Assessment. It will not undertake studies of its own but rather would contract them to research institutes or universities. The idea is for a research service to provide Congress with an informed assessment of the implications of legislation dealing with technological matters.

By contrast the Joint Committee idea was patterned after the Joint Committee on Atomic Energy. Equipped with a select, highly specialized staff, the committee would "be entrusted with important powers and duties of investigation and systematic review."[3] Its legislative responsibilities were not specified. This in effect was the format conceived in the ill-fated proposal of Rep. Emilio Daddario, former Chairman of the House Committee on Science and Aeronautics. His somewhat more far-reaching vision of the panel idea would have constituted a larger and more powerful technology assessment unit that would parallel the panel's proposed Executive Office. Its own staff, or researchers working on contract, were intended to assess new technologies, explore possible damaging aspects, and suggest remedies. It also would have operated a similar early-warning system. The Daddario proposal died aborning, preempted by the Legislative Reorganization Act of 1970, that designated the Congressional Research Service to do the same job in more restricted compass and in more muted style. (The disinclination of Congress to create a full-blown Office of Technology Assessment or to establish a Joint Committee is partly due to the potential for partisan conflict it carries. The more powerful the office, the sharper the competition to control its staffing; the more powerful committee, the greater the reluctance to hand it over to a potential rival, e.g., Senator Muskie, at the time of its consideration the likeliest Democratic candidate for president).[4]

As conceived by the academy panel, this medley of boards would be restricted to analysis and survey. Their monitoring would not entail judging the merits of particular developments and projects, but rather would take the form of indicating lines of development and outlining probable impacts. The authors make clear that "any new mechanism [they] propose must be carefully insulated from direct policy-making powers and responsibilities . . . ." Above all, it must be given no authority to screen or "clear" new technological undertaking.[5] In contrast to a regulatory commission, like the FCC or SEC, that uses discretionary powers in administering codes so as to approve or to prohibit specific actions, the Technology Assessment Board would lack powers to dictate outcomes.

The panel's reluctance to go the regulatory agency route is understandable. Commissions are prone to become the prisoners of the interests they are intended to regulate. The "public guardian" role changes gradually into that of running interference against the public. Commissions often end up seeing the industry's problems before those of the public. This syndrome is most fully developed in those areas where the official agency has dual responsibility for both regulation and promotion, e.g., the AEC or the FAA. The AEC's close working relationship with manufacturers of reactors and power companies has forged a partnership of bureaucratic interest that often is impervious to direction and insulated from political influence. Until recent revisions were made in its operating procedures, the commission's uncritical oversight of power plant location and its damaging environmental effects was one direct result. Similarly, as the academy report explains, "there is ample evidence . . . that the Federal Aviation Agency, assigned the tasks of promoting the SST, cannot be fully trusted to evaluate the sonic boom objectively."[6] In that instance, a regulatory agency in effect "monopolized" a particular technology and acted as its protector.

The Technology Assessment Board, therefore, would not be an "action" organization with a programmatic mission. Its supporters believe that without any axes to grind, it would do better the job of delineating our technological futures and serving as a source of technical guidance. It must be close to the political process, but not *that* close. It must consider important problems, but not ones of urgency demanding immediate political decision. To use a simple example, the kind of problem it typically could anticipate, and assist in the resolution of, is that of controlling the emissions created by jet planes in takeoff. Modification of jet engines to remove pollutants is technically rather simple, and is inexpensive if done at the time of engine installation. However, the equipment is relatively expensive to install once the plane is in service. A Technology Assessment Board might have been expected to consider the potential polluting effects of jet engines, analyze the technical difficulties and offer courses of action to overcome them. With the problem thus publicized and solutions made available, proper regulations would likely have been forthcoming. This is the type of function envisaged for the board by its advocates. And they want to be clear on the point: "It is easy to misconceive the role of technology *forecasting* as a means of *controlling* technological development."[7] Neutral as to policy decisions, it would inform and assess *only*.

Limitations of Monitoring

To use the much-discussed case of the SST, if a monitoring agency had been in place some years ago, it is very likely that the aircraft's drawbacks would have been noted much earlier than in fact they were. Its noise level, pollution potential , and *perhaps* some of its total financial cost would have been revealed—allowing for more knowledgeable judgments about its benefits and liabilities. Other, more basic considerations, though, probably would not have been included in the assessment process: its functionality compared to different types of transportation systems; the worth of improved long-distance transport relative to urban mass transit needs; and the jobs at stake. By awaiting the appearance of new technology before assessing it, we in effect would be accepting as given the bias built into present structural arrangements for exploiting technical skills. The concentration of available engineering skills in the aircraft industry itself favors federal support for that facet of transportation R & D. In the manner of interlocking bureaucratic structures, and in accordance with the rules of organizational inertia, new technologies will be generated to a great extent without any explicit decision as to need. As one consequence of taking the sources of technological innovation for granted, attention remains fixed on existing arrangements rather than seeking answers to the basic question of whom we want to move, by what means, where, and with what sense of need? Thus it also can detract from the obligation to consider promoting technologies in associated fields that might be of greater overall social utility.

The academy panel affirms that it has given "primary attention to assessment endeavors that use technology as a starting point."[8] It appears to assume that new technologies appear in random fashion, any effort to curb them being both doomed to failure and threatening to impose dangerous restrictions on invention. Regulation, however humanely inspired, poses the spectre of censorship and control over free endeavor. As the authors state their purpose, it "is not to conceive ways to curb or restrain or otherwise 'fix' technology but rather to discover and repair the deficiencies in the processes and institutions by which society puts the tools of science and technology to work."[9] The board, therefore, would operate without any measure for detecting a problem, as well as without firm criteria for expressing approval or disapproval.

Only an arbitrary analytical division can separate technology assessment from the exercise of broader government responsibilities of management and control. The appearance of new technologies is not entirely random, cast up by the free play of the scientific mind and the innovative spirit. Public authority encouraged and channeled these impulses in certain preferred directions. The number of aerospace engineers and nuclear physicists in the country is not attributable to the natural inclinations of talent. It has taken concerted, expensive governmental programs to train them, provide outlets for their application, and support for their work. Governmental oversight of their technological progeny is, therefore, not just the prudent exercise of political authority to protect the public interest, but a proper assumption of responsibility for the social effects of what it has fostered. There is, then, an ethical and practical case for an assumption of powers congruent with the impact of science and technology on our collective existence.

Where certain conditions are self-evidentially "problems," e.g., emissions from automobile or jet engines, a monitoring board could make a vital contribution. It is in the gray areas such as the *social amenity* aspect of the transportation problem that the assessment of technology, unless guided by a broader and more clearly developed conception of the pertinent considerations, can readily overlook latent, undesirable effects. Without such a framework, each potential problem would have to be discovered and responded to on an *ad hoc* basis. The significance or meaning of information is not self-explanatory. Where the terms of reference are limited to the immediate effects of technologies already in being, we cannot effectively anticipate and avoid gross abuse. Rather, we would rely on a confident faith that piecemeal adjustment to a technologically determined future will produce rational policy. To do otherwise would involve technology assessment in a constant process of evaluation. It is this task that the academy panel shies away from.

Implicit in the panel's report is abundant, if no longer unqualified, faith in the virtue of scientific research and technical innovation. The commonsensical proposition that pollution (and some areas of amenity, e.g., high speed mass transit) will require the invention of new mechanical means, is often used to reassert the conviction that a clear line of beneficence runs from research through development to human good. That doyen of scientific statesmen, Sir Solly Zuckerman, recently offered the ringing declaration that "all environmental improvement depends upon scientific and technical progress."[10] He continued, "the growth of human knowledge—exponentially"—is the great compensating factor to be placed against population rise, pollution increase, and resource depletion.

A skeptical critic would wonder whether this affirmation represents a reasoned judgment as to the severity of an environmental condition and the most feasible means for its alleviation or a weakness of science to avail itself of the outstanding social problem of the moment to affirm the virtues of the scientific and technological enterprise. It also raises the more profound issue as to whether highly formalized, very specialized knowlege is sufficient to our needs. Such confidence in our intellectual competencies would be more reassuring were we to demonstrate as much sagacity with regard to the requirements for the good society as we do brilliance in mechanical invention and scientific discovery. Zucherman asked rhetorically, "can we seriously imagine that we would not find ways inhibiting the uses of such an aircraft (the SST-Concorde) as we become aware of possibly harmful side effects?" Our entire environmental experience would advise such cautious doubts, as well as query why it would not be wiser to inhibit development of an idle and expensive technological indulgence in the first place.

Political Choice

Somewhere along the way public choices have to be made as to whether a particular technology is beneficial or pernicious, important or insignificant, worth the cost or not. Depending on the extent and manner of government responsibility, that decision can come at any one of several stages: in the contribution of research and then development funds; in the technology's purchase or deployment; or in the regulation of its use. The dilemma of how to make those determinations according to what standards, without thwarting innovation or abusing the power of control, is not easy to solve. And, certainly, there is good reason to question whether initiatives of that magnitude could or should be the responsibility of boards such as those outlined by the academy panel. They are properly matters of an elected political authority. Nevertheless, it would appear that the more restricted technology assessment function cannot readily remain in its narrowly drawn boundaries if political leaders take up their proper responsibilities. For then the analytical act of outlining the connections between innovation and social impact becomes a necessary prelude to the political act of passing judgments; and the deliberations of such a body, whether desired or not, would become integral to the policy process. As such, technology assessment could not avoid constant evaluation.

Upon leaving the realm of scientific knowledge and technological competence, we enter the domain of policy options where assessment and evaluation, as the panel acknowledges, become the responsibility of public officials. It follows that in this setting the scientist is just one expert among other specialists. Nonscientific specialists have an equally, and perhaps more, critical role to play in recognizing and defining problems arising from the social impact of technology. The planning of environmental futures, the estimation of environment needs, the drawing of options that balance the costs and benefits of development, all are issues that are not characteristically formulated in a way intellectually accessible to the theoretical constructs of the scientist or susceptible to resolution through application of his research method. The panel members gingerly avoided the issue of possible competition between natural scientists and other specialists by conveniently restricting membership on the proposed "Technology Board" to scientists. This restriction nicely coincides with their belief that assessment of technologies already well along in the development pipeline ought to be the board's only function. If it were to concern itself with social consequences, or even more daringly, state preferences as to courses of development, the services of nonscientists could not be so easily dispensed with.

Scientists who are very leery of control on research might well feel threatened by a board composed of professional strangers that makes judgments on the desirability of new technologies. Judgment implies a standard of the good; that standard must include social and cultural considerations. These might place a lessened importance on certain areas of scientific research as opposed to others, or even downgrade basic science itself. The result would not be censorship but a limitation of scientific work. At a time when scientists are speaking portentously of the damage being done by the cutbacks in research already made, such an eventuality looms as an unmitigated disaster. To channel money out of the physical sciences and related areas of applied research is to threaten the scientific estate. It follows that they should experience some queasiness about associating technology assessment with the task of establishing national priorities.

Collateral to the incrementalist approach that the academy panel advocates is the disposition to see the problem as that of strengthening the environmentalist position *as another interest* among several. Thus they write that "the very essence of the panel's concern about the narrowness of the critieria that presently dominate technological choices is a conviction that *the present system fails to give all affected interests effective representation in the crucial processes of decision.*"[11] But the paramount issue is the difference between a *heightened sense of collective interest* and public policy as the outcome of *competition among partial interests*. It is the underplaying of this distinction that leads the panel toward advocating a pressure-group approach to making technological choices on basic environmental issues. Incrementalism as policy process and interest politics as the basis for formulating issues once again join hands. The authors of the academy report take for granted as a property of the system "a political process that responds only to relatively proximate and demonstrable difficulties." They therefore believe that "any effort to design a truly anticipatory assessment structure would almost surely fail to provide a realistic link between such a structure and the making of policy."[12]

The board's neutrality then is absolutely genuine. It would feed information and expert analyses into the process and let the strongest interest win. Proceduralism prevails once again. But the procedures as we noted are not neutral. So that except in those instances where knowledge itself can be expected to produce meliorative action (revelations about mercury poisoning), the neutralism of the Assessment Board will only lower the ignorance level in selective areas defined by incremental criteria.[a]

---

[a]The panel's addiction to the pluralist model is even more clearly established in the listing

Technology Assessment As Evaluation

A number of these critical themes about the necessity of making technology assessment an instrument for achieving explicitly defined (and by implication now undefined) national priorities have recently been taken up by Harvey Brooks, an author of the academy report. As chairman of the OECD study on future directions of science policy, he is largely responsible for their provocative report, *Science, Growth and Society.*[14] Reviewing the history of public support for R & D, he notes that industrial expansion "has required particular kinds of scientific knowledge and specialized training. Thus, the form and mix of science and technology as developed in the education system and industry has been molded around these requirements."[15] Individual and collective enrichment no longer are the exclusive goal of modern societies. "We now find ourselves in a situation where the marginal utility of collective needs is increasing."[16] In the process of formulating these needs and devising the means for achieving them, science policy will be more closely scrutinized to assay how it fits into an overall policy for the satisfaction of those collective needs. The aim, in Brooks's words, "cannot be solely the expression of science and technology but must include the management and direction of technological programs for the securing of other ends."[17]

The whole of the OECD study is a lucid exposition of, and trenchant attack on, our single-minded pursuit of industrial expansion and technical virtuosity for their own sakes. Such awareness of the abuses that result from laissez innover ideas, and the social needs unmet by policies so tailored, is a precondition for intelligent direction of public policy. But Brooks's statement poses as many dilemmas about the manner in which we conduct our public business as it resolves doubts about the desirability in principle of managing our technological environment.

First, by what indicators do we adduce that "the marginal utility of collective needs is increasing?" If we are speaking of expressions of popular preference, it is pertinent to inquire how such sentiment is gauged. Are the forms of representation and the structure of government as responsive to diffuse support for public effort to meet out communal wants, like the environment, as they are attentive to meeting the particular claims of interests definded by productive function? If we are speaking of an objectively definable condition that calls for priority action, then we must ask: (a) as to the disposition of political leaders to assert their discretionary powers in initiating innovative programs; (b) about the

---

(among possible abuses of a system of technology assessment) of excessive restrictions on new technology imposed by well-organized and influential opponents. In their view, everyone and every cause should have its fair crack at getting their way. "For this reason it is particularly important to couple improved assessment with improved methods of representing weak and poorly organized interest groups."[13] The only unambiguous indicator of strength is legislative or administrative victories. Do we accept the logical conclusion that were the aerospace lobby to suffer a series of budgetary reverses, fair play dictates remedial efforts to compensate for the technologies they were denied?

institutional restraints that bear on their manner of defining and acting upon public issues; and (c) whether the issue between private consumption and public expenditure in the allocation of national product has been drawn in such a way as to permit rational choice, and how aware of the issue are our political leaders who frame public problems and formulate national programs? (See Part 5 for an assessment of specific proposals to meet these needs.)

Part 4
Ecology Politics

10 Welfarists and Environmentalists: Another Liberal Dilemma

The final requirement for effective environmental action is votes. The essence of a democratic system of politics is electing candidates sympathetic to your views and pressuring officials to implement them. The course we take will largely be determined by "ecology politics." The environment, though, is not an issue whose impact is easy to estimate.[1]

Ecology, which until recently was a nonissue, has become a popular issue. There is no certainty, though, as to its ultimate success in precipitating a major overhaul of public policy. The long, pervasive disregard for our surroundings allowed a condition of such drastic proportions to develop that the eventual reaction could not have failed to set off a general clamor. Today's faddish preoccupation with ecology combines expressions of deep-seated guilt for generations of neglect and genuine interest in reform with a widely felt desire to get in on a popular cause of unquestioned virtue. Despite a number of useful initiatives, verbiage and cosmetic gestures outweigh concrete achievement to date. The difficulty of assuring accomplishment commensurate with the problem is not surprising. As we have noted, the set of conditions we call the environmental problem are necessary by-products of the industrial system, not coincidental ones. They represent the logical outgrowth of our unqualified societal commitment to economic growth and technological change. To alter drastically the present state of environmental affairs implies a renovation of the way we manage our public business and conduct our private lives. Societies never change that fast or that completely. A qualified pessimism, therefore, would appear appropriate in assessing the prospects for the future.

Up to a few years ago, ecology was marginal to the political process, and environmentalists had little, if any influence on public policy. The change in the magnitude of environmentalist sentiment and the backing for environmental causes is striking; organizationally, though, the movement remains weak. As a consequence, expressions of concern and desultory motion are out of proportion to programmatic action. The appropriation of ecological symbolism and the use of its appeals by a president who has been temperamentally and ideologically as unsympathetic to the environmental cause as Richard Nixon shows how persuasive is its positive image. The tokenism of most policies initiated by the administration (and only partially expanded by the Congress), is sobering evidence of how inadequate are ritual genuflexions to a noble ideal. Moreover, our system of political representation continues to diminish the impact of certain kinds of interest and to disadvantage certain causes. So long as most individuals act politically first as producers and consumers, so long as economic associations and political parties monitor government policy so that it meets partial claims rather than comprehensive needs, environmental problems will receive less attention than popular concern warrants. As that concern mounts, as environmental sentiment spreads in the country at large and is diffused through the political system, positive governmental response will grow. However, the discrepancy between popular desire and programmatic achievement probably will remain. Awareness and sympathetic attention are preconditions for effective remedial action. They are not sufficient ones. The depth of popular concern, the pressure felt by legislators, and their own sense of need will dictate whether we overcome systemic biases and get basic change rather than marginal reform. Although it is unlikely that we will revert back to the old contemptuous attitude toward the environment, the scope and exact character of the reform defy prediction. We can, however, discern those features of ecology politics that will influence the outcome.

Questions of pollution and amenity in the human habitat are characteristically "style" issues—involving matters of preferred social value rather than material interest. A *style issue* is one that tends to move large numbers of people widely dispersed and often is a subject of intense feeling for only a relatively small percentage of them. Support for a style issue typically builds behind a movement that cuts across, and occasionally transcends party formations and interest coalitions. It draws members from points all along the political spectrum, although normally there is a concentration among persons with certain backgrounds and political orientations. That is its strength and its weakness.

The scope of environmentalist feeling ranging across the political spectrum in the manner of a style issue can be an asset. When a program acquires backing from disparate political forces, it avoids being labelled as preferential legislation or a partisan ploy. Normally, the very fact that Congressman A from Faction F sponsored a piece of legislation means that Congressman C from Faction D will instinctively oppose it. By drawing support broadly, an environmental issue can partially overcome these built-in counterbalances. In this way, it does indeed appear as public action in the "national interest." But a cross-cutting issue is not necessarily a transcendent one. It must reach that "critical mass" point of support where most are favorably disposed and many are active supporters. Without the activists, the issue can remain in the background—enjoying a great deal of distant sympathy and little close attention. It becomes another of those noble causes everyone adheres to in principle and does little about in practice. With active supporters, but without broad backing, it will face a different problem. Under those circumstances, it can lose that aura of universal good which could permit it to slide through the minefield of legislative politics intact. It will have become just another contentious issue, with its friends *and* enemies. As a relatively new issue with few powerful organizational backers (and few legislators who have built their careers on it), it suffers from major handicaps. Successes when they occur are irregular and of limited impact.

That is the liability, and the other side of the coin, for an issue unattached to the established constellations of power and interest. There is a very thin line between everyone's child and no one's. The key is saliency. If an issue like the environment is to succeed, it will win big. The level of support required for a style issue to cross that line between being the object of good intentions and becoming a concern that moves a wide band of legislators to action is so high as to assume wide-ranging programs when reached. Thus, although the location of that critical mass point, is by no means clear, there should be abundant evidence when it is reached.

The future of the environment as a political issue, and its fate in the arena of public policy, depends in large measure on the staying power of the ecology movement. If it is, indeed, a fad, its meteoric flight across the political horizon will leave little in the way of enduring policy and lasting effect. Certainly, ecology will have been ensconced as a field of study, the environment will have been added to the array of public concerns and worries, and some remedial steps taken; but concerted programs to manage our natural and communal environment will be lacking.

The prime requirement for political success is the organizational capability matching popular support that permits sustained effort. To date, organizational development has been slow and spotty, built around individual causes rather than to advance environmental interests generally. This might be expected from a movement that has blossomed as a cultural reaction against the rigid structure of our industrial system as well as the dangerous fruits of its workings. Although the growth of savvy political organizations would not necessarily be the surest sign that the movement has taken root, it will be a harbinger of its practical effectiveness. Then the cause's freshness, range of support, and fervor would make its more conventional, organizational efforts all the more potent.

All facets of the environment movement will not fare equally. Efforts aimed at alleviating pollution are favored by the tangability of the danger; in the new circumstance of heightened awareness, it calls forth governmental action to cure and to prevent. Social amenities will be less affected. The former requires response to a perceived negative; the latter would entail a constructive vision of a more desirable future. Action to deal with pollution can be inspired by little more than dim consciousness of life's survival requisites. The conception of a more commodious society can only be inspired by an explicit ideal of the good society; and one which departs from the prevailing image of the good society as a stable, if artless, arrangement of acquisitive appetites. The procedures for alleviating pollution fit the political conventions and administrative means of our public institutions. Planning for social amenity would place demands on the political process which, given its incrementalist orientation and pluralist construction, it could not easily manage. Pollution abatement implies no direct conflict with the dominant values of the industrial system, just their expedient modification. It is a form of planning as technical congruence. Creating an amenable urban environment by contrast means upsetting the established priorities that place consumer prerogatives above communal well-being. A concerted attack on environmental disamenity, by directly challenging "consumption-as-usual," also threatens the established pattern of interest politics, and with it the payoffs in disposable income that are the system's lubricant. Whatever the costs of pollution control (and whatever the pattern of their distribution), the direction of economic activity might escape with only marginal alteration. The financial costs of constructing livable cities and of providing for amenities on a national scale promise to be greater. Moreover, they require a mix of skills and talents different from those now available (although these often could be applied to programs of pollution control).

If we were to predict the future, we would envision an American whose air and water is cleaner, but whose cities are further degenerated, and whose traffic is probably more congested. It would be an American that assured its nominal survival, out of danger from asphyxiation or eutrophication; but failed to build on a fuller vision of what our abundance in means and skills could provide.[a]

Environmental Commitment and Political Loyalties

Perhaps the most distinctive feature of the environment as a political issue is the breadth and variety of support it enjoys, as well as of the opposition it has created. Its backers are a mixed assortment by any standard social or political indicator. Proenvironmentalists are found on the right and on the left of the political spectrum; they are Consciousness I people, Consciousness III people and, occasionally, even Consciousness II people.[2] It is not self-evidently a Republican or Democratic cause, a liberal or conservative one. Each of the orthodox political groupings is divided on the issue.

On the conservative side of the spectrum, the split occurs along several faces. Traditional conservatives living in small towns or rural areas have a conservationist bent as is found among those who experience nature directly. Moreover,

---

[a]We can expect appreciably different levels of support for remedial problems as among kinds of pollution as well. For example, Congress has shown itself generous in funding programs for construction of municipal sewage facilities (witness its overriding a presidential veto to pass the $24 billion Water Quality Bill in 1972). Measures to control industrial sources of pollution fare less well. The former is more in the traditional category of public works: it gratifies constituents, meets a clear local need, is financed out of general tax funds, and implies no curbs on other designated activities. The latter could alienate business interests, disturb those who stand to lose their jobs if a plant closes, and in general underscores the necessary tradeoff between economic growth and environmental goods.

for them protection of the environment tends to be associated with preservation of those surroundings in which the unique American virtues of independence and self-reliance were nurtured. Urbanites, of whatever political orientation, ordinarily are less atune to ecological appeals. The image of their America is of one great industrial artifact, which they view as both the source of our largess and visible expression of our unique accomplishments.

A second division among conservatives is discernible between "old" and "new" wealth. It is not unexpected that the environmentalist strain diminishes to the vanishing point among those for whom conservatism means the protection of vested interest in commercial ventures. Oil tycoons, timber companies and mine operators are not numbered among the ecology forces; neither are regions dominated by such industries known as hotbeds of environmental action, e.g., Texas. Wealth and privilege themselves, however, are not necessarily the determinants of environmental attitudes. Rather it is the source of wealth, i.e., whether the commercial activity is itself environmentally damaging, and the strength of entrepreneurial laissez faire attitudes that are determining influences. The members of the established upper class do not derive their status and sense of accomplishment from business initiatives. They are secure in their social position, pillars of society, who can afford to cultivate an image of public service. However rapacious their forebears might have been in creating the family fortune, they are now free to act as environmental statesmen. Thus ecology is a topic more likely to elicit positive sentiments in the boardrooms of a large eastern banking establishment whose commercial activities are widely diffused and a few levels removed from direct management responsibilities than in a Houston or Dallas country club among oil millionaires, or in real estate circles where land developers predominate. Today's entrepreneur still has his mark to make and is prepared to do so with cavalier disregard for environmental consequences.

At the liberal end of the spectrum, there are equally noticeable differences between working-class liberals and liberal middle-class professionals in the priority they accord environmental issues. Union officials and congressional representatives from blue-collar districts are rarely found among the activists of the movement. The reasons are evident. Concern with the comforts of one's surroundings is in direct relationship to one's economic well-being. It is positively correlated with education and leisure. The worker preoccupied with job security and the wage increments that move him another notch above the subsistence level tends to be less attentive to the style issues and less responsive to appeals on its behalf. Moreover, there is an understandable disinclination to trade some portion of industrial growth for a cleaner or more amenable environment so long as "basic" wants are unmet, present distribution patterns remained fixed, and until environmental degradation reaches the point of tangible danger.

"Environmentalists" and "Welfarists": Another
Liberal Dilemma

The cleavages cut in liberal ranks by environmental advocacy are worthy of closer examination. Liberalism has been the dominant political philosophy of recent American life. Its progressive principles of enlightened social policy embody the faith of a democratic culture, and at the same time it has been bound to the notion of economic expansion as an unmitigated good. Most of the academic doctrines we have skeptically examined in this essay are the work of self-avowed liberals; their critics also pronounce themselves liberals. The liberal's convulsive struggling, at the plane of both intellectual discourse and practical politics, is the most vivid expression of the general scrutiny of its values and purposes our society is undergoing.

Already suffering the trials and tribulations of deeply divisive conflicts over race and radicalism, the community of American liberalism has rather suddenly been confronted with yet another contentious issue—the environment. A recent arrival in the arena of political debate and intellectual discussion, the environment nevertheless has swiftly succeeded in generating a level of antagonism worthy of more veteran causes. Hardly a day passes without the *New York Times* (that rich lode of all kinds of social indicators) reporting upon or lending its pages to more or less informed opinion either: (a) grieving as to how ecology freaks are relegating ghetto children to a bleak, energy-deprived future; or (b) despairing over the resiliency of the "salvation though satiation" faith and its imperviousness to environmental truth.[3] The imprecision in defining environmental problems and in elaborating themes undoubtedly has contributed to these rhetorical excesses. There are, though, unavoidable points of contention that reflect the issue's profoundly disturbing effects on all varieties of cultural value and social doctrine.

For liberals, it is not fully intelligible as either the classic "bread and butter" issue or the classic style issue dealing with human rights. Environmental concerns are so intricately woven into the fabric of modern industrialism that they touch nearly every aspect of social organization. Practical programs and academic analyses alike are finding themselves required to unravel a good portion of our public life and governmental policy in order to make sense of, and to act on, newly recognized environmental conditions. The environment's dramatic emergence, consequently, has caught liberals with their theoretical pants down. (Of course, newly awakened environmental awareness has caught most other intellectuals—not to mention politicians—in an equally embarrassing position.) It also has complicated the unresolved split between the white working-class liberals concerned primarily with the traditional economic issues and the advocates of radical reform to deal with questions of poverty and racism. The result has been a complex array of attitudes. Without pretending to chart all the permutations of the middle class—trade union—"poor"—white professional—

ethnic—black liberal world, and in full awareness of the dangers of neat categorization, some clarification of the multiple perspectives might be gained from a simple pairing of environmentalists with those we shall loosely refer to as "welfarists" (a category that subsumes both orthodox and more militant social reformers).

There are important differences in perspective between the two groups that, while surfacing only intermittently, are deeply rooted in basically divergent attitudes toward the centrality of the "growth ethic" in social thinking. Rather than being interested in controlling industrial expansion, the welfarist (academic analyst or sympathetic public official) takes economic expansion to be a highly desirable objective, and accepts material enrichment as the legitimate and often paramount goal of individual and group effort. Social critics who see in poverty and discrimination the priority problem of contemporary America tend to look upon "environmentalists" as misguided, lacking in proportion, and as elitists who seek to make their lives comfortable while denigrating the more basic needs of the underprivileged.[4] Whatever their sympathies for environmental ideals, in practical terms they believe that a curtailment of growth and/or the inauguration of comprehensive, expensive programs to clean up pollution and to improve amenities would greatly complicate the tasks of raising the private incomes of the poor and of increasing public expenditure for programs aimed at remedying conditions of social injustice. Redistribution of resources, they believe, can take two forms: (a) direct changes in income allocation through manipulation of tax schedules and income maintenance programs; and (b) indirectly, a redistribution of public funds through large-scale programs, for the most part federal, to improve housing, education, health facilities, and so forth, among the disadvantaged. Were a policy of zero or marginal economic growth to prevail, either approach to social spending—or some combination of the two—would depend on an appreciable lowering of the disposable income of groups in the upper tax brackets. In addition, were large sums to be spent on environmental programs with the size of the pie fixed, the competition for the public dollar would be further sharpened and pressures to restrict private consumption by the well-to-do accentuated.

Most welfarists believe it is politically unrealistic to expect elected officials to implement a strategy of income levelling. In their view, an overtly redistributive policy is discouraged by the progressive dissipation of populist sentiments that might be tapped in a campaign against the extravagantly wealthy, especially when the claimants are minorities. The judgment is undeniably correct. The most cursory review of the American political scene reveals how little force populist appeals have had when aimed at those comfortably ensconced in the upper reaches of the tax brackets. The abortive attempt in the 90th Congress to introduce tax reform (with a few minor exceptions such as reduction in the oil depletion allowance from 27 to 21 percent) demonstrated the weakness of economic populism.[5] (Liberal politicians share some of the responsibility since their near total abandonment of the issue, until their interest was rekindled by the electoral successes of George Wallace, could not but have dimmed public awareness.)

Populism as the little man's cry of outrage against the vested interest, the overly compensated rich, and traditionally the anonymous power manipulators, has been replaced by the populism of the Middle American berating the poor and the minorities for their seemingly unjustified demands. Among the skilled workers, and the lower middle class in general, it is now more likely directed downwards at welfare recipients of unearned rewards. Indeed, to the extent that populist grievance is directed upwards, it focuses on the upper-class advocates of minority causes who are seen as encouraging unwarranted demands. This transmogrification of populism leads to the presumption on the part of welfarists that the resources for implementing their programs are far more likely to be forthcoming in an expanding economy. They, therefore, look skeptically at the environmentalists and fear their competition for the finite federal dollar.[b]

Environmentalists agree that the portion of national product arrogated by the government to meet collective need is crucial to any assessment of societal purpose. It is one of their contentions that the spending required to create a suitable human environment demands an appreciable redirection of national economic resources away from private consumption and into areas of public activity, e.g., modern interurban or urban mass transit systems, urban construction, developing and installing pollution control technologies. (The costs of pollution abatement alone as we observed are estimated at tens of billions of dollars.) To meet these expenses, without curtailing obligations in other areas of public expenditure, means permitting government to spend a larger share of the national wealth. They differ from the welfarists in acknowledging and accepting the reality that the considerably augmented public expenditure such programs entail necessarily implies a modification of many social habits associated with neurotic consumption. The almost routine expectation of ever-higher incomes that prevails today presages sharp conflicts over dramatic increases in environmental programs and potentially major cultural stress as a result of consumer deprivation. They recognize that consumption in our society often represents the displacement of frustration, an attempt to assuage anxiety, the opportunity

---

[b]One would have expected both environmentalists and welfarists to have been outraged by the terms of President Nixon's new economic policies announced with great éclat in August 1971. With the automobile as its heraldic symbol, the policy proclaims that prosperity equals private consumption. Technically, the economy can be stimulated by increasing public expenditure or by cutting taxes. The effects are very different. Taking the latter route, we increase our stock of hardtops, color TV sets, and cosmetics. Taking the former, we can endow the community with hospitals, schools, housing and/or mass transit, cleaner surroundings and so forth. The liberals' near universal acceptance of the Nixon logic is striking evidence of how pervasive is the residual distrust and/or doubts about the political feasibility of large-scale public enterprise where national prestige or defense are not involved. The upshot is the intriguing "trickle-up" theory: large incrases in disposable private income generating small increases (through taxes) in disposable public funds.

for acquiring status; that it is more psychological than utilitarian in nature; and that these cultural impulses, therefore, are a very real impediment to the kinds of policy initiatives necessary to achieve the end of a livable environment. At the same time the redirection of public effort and money is itself viewed as a precondition for creating at least the physical amenities and surroundings that would be less likely to induce the kind of neurotic behavior which demands an economy based upon compulsive buying.

As things now stand, conflict among economic strata is muted by the provision of increments out of growth. Were growth curtailed, long-standing expectations of routine increases in disposable income would greatly sharpen the antagonisms between the blue-collar worker and the black apprentice, the public employee and the self-employed, the rich and the not-so-rich. Given the interdependence of wealth and status in our society, particularly the dependence on income rises as symbols of accomplishment and as the basis for individual and group differentiation, heightened tension throughout the society could result from economic equilibrium unless meliorative initiatives are taken in anticipation. It is just that tension and the threat it poses to both social stability and proper attention to the legitimate demands of the poor that so concerns welfarists and heightens their anxiety about the environmental movement.

The conflict takes on an immediacy that the debate otherwise lacks when there is discussion of new areas for public expenditure. The welfarist talks of money for programs aimed at improving conditions of the underprivileged, the environmentalist talks about collective community need. (These positions, of course, are not logically exclusive; and, indeed, many persons engaged in the reformist efforts evince concern about both domains. John Gardner's *Common Cause,* for example, ranges broadly over the whole gamut of social issues from racism and poverty to military spending, consumer protection, and pollution. Nevertheless, there are emphases and accents that do have important, practical implications). There is also little reluctance on the part of the welfarists to move against those cases of air and water pollution where the costs of abatement are not excessive. Some pollution problems pose so obvious a danger (and in numerous instances affect the poor disproportionately) that there is an unquestioned desire to deal with them. Even in those select areas, though, the common belief that the level of expenditure involved is relatively low is mistaken. It might be taken as a convenient rule of thumb that the financial costs for remedying even the most obvious pollution problems normally are underestimated as grossly as are Pentagon procurement contracts.[6]

Social amenities are a different matter altogether. They clearly demand major expenditures and as such are a direct rival to the welfarists program. Striking evidence of the divergence in outlook and preference is to be found in the extensive *Counter Budget* prepared by the Urban Coalition released in 1971.[7] It might be taken as an affirmative statement of welfarist thinking. On tax policy, it urges initiatives to fill the most glaring loopholes but it is not optimistic about, nor pushes very hard for substantial redistribution through revision of income tax schedules. The proposed budget is severely critical of present levels of military expenditure and looks to a fine paring of the defense budget to provide approximately $28 billion in new money. Its major programmatic innovations are in the welfare field where it proposes increased outlays of some tens of billions of dollars for manpower training, health, education, and, particularly, income maintenance. In sharp contrast to these increases, the *Counter Budget* is disparaging of environmental amenity needs. Looking at its proposals for transportation, we note a carefully reasoned opposition to any substantial increase in expenditures whatsoever. It is hardest on interurban rail transit, which it deems worthy of only a cut in the present miniscule budget of a few hundred million dollars. Admiring of our present facilities, the authors say: "the case for public subsidy of a truly national railway passenger system appears dubious *in view of the existence of other effective competing transportation modes: airplanes, buses, and private automobiles."* (Italics Urban Coalition.)[8]

They envisage an annual expenditure for the next five years of $119 million in gradually diminishing sums and anticipate a phasing out of support for anything but maintenance of existing facilities. Commuter railroads fare no better. Disregarding the grotesque, pollution-generating, and wasteful congestion that results from moving hundred of thousands of people by auto, the *Counter Budget* proposes gradually reducing financing to an anticipated 1976 level of $61 million—a sum inadequate to more than research the depths of the problem.

Urban mass transit is treated with somewhat more solicitude. Recognizing the desirability of improving present services, the report nevertheless assigns the task a relatively low priority compared to other social needs. The budget advocates mass transit expenditures rising to a figure of $1.4 billion in 1976. This represents only a marginal increase over present authorizations (in a budget which carries the burden of $80 billion defense expenditure). Since the average cost of installing an urban rail system is estimated to be in the order of $1.5 billion, it is clear that the authors do not feel that an early, concerted effort at upgrading transportation in our cities is a matter of immediate concern.

The *Counter Budget*'s conclusion on "Pollution Control" is even more discouraging to environmentalists, stating as its objective:

To bring under control these pollutants that are recognized to be an immediate threat to personal health; to provide adequate surveillance and control to ensure that conditions do not *worsen* to the extent that they will be uncontrollable five or ten years hence. (Italics mine)

The *Counter Budget*, therefore, recommends total outlays of $1.02 billion, a figure that is $341 million *less* than that proposed by the Nixon administration for 1972 (a sum that was augmented by the Congress). The reason is clear:

In view of the many other unmet needs also competing for federal resources we have serious reservations about spending large sums on pollution control at this time.[9]

So when the crunch comes there is in fact a strong current of disagreement between the welfarists and the environmentalists. The disagreement would seem to entail more than just practical judgment as to what are the most pressing social problems and how we act on them even with limited resources. The welfarist's apparent insensitivity to the deleterious and demeaning effects of environmental degradation on the urban poor is not entirely explicable in terms of the imperative to make harsh, realistic choices. For it is also hard realism that a lack of urban transportation in Los Angeles relegates the unemployed black to economic imprisonment in Watts. It is hard realism that blacks suffer disproportionately from pollution aggravated illnesses, e.g., emphysema. It is hard realism that the poor and disadvantaged live in the most congested sections of our cities where noxious emissions are most intense, dirt and noise most concentrated and physical comforts in scant supply.[10]

The disagreement is deeper than pragmatic assessment of need. However sharp their attack on inequity and discrimination, the welfarist's view of the world seems to reflect conventional images as to how modern society operates. His belief in progress measured by material indicators in an interminably expansionist economy is basically the same; his faith in technology as the instrument of growth and as a source of benefit is unqualified; overt environmental consequences are deemed externalities that can be remedied by the left hand of the body politic while attention is paid the more important business of expanding wealth; politics indeed is a matter of who gets what, when, how much; a reformist's objectives are exclusively to influence the process of allocation to assure a more equitable distribution of wealth; the quality of life is not the proper subject of political debate except insofar as it touches on racial issues or threatens impending disaster. The welfarists are bread and butter activists. They are enlightened specialists in the nitty-gritty. The nitty-gritty by their definition does not include the movement of people (the majority poor) from one part of the city to another without enduring massive delay and discomfort. It does not include the defilement of air and water (which the poor are more likely to breathe and drink than the wealthy suburbanite); nor the destruction of recreation sites (on which the less affluent and less mobile poor most depend).

Both their acceptance of the dominant progress myth of the society, and their readiness to perpetuate pluralist politics so long as the sides are evened up, is confirmed by the *Counter Budget*'s authors' accommodating attitude toward the space program. They, in effect, agree with the expenditure level anticipated by the 1972 budget and are prepared to allocate $2.8 billion annually on the space shuttle and related projects. That is $500 million more than the proposed budget for mass transit—hardly a radical revision of priorities. The exact thinking that led to these conclusions is not available to us and open to scrutiny. But from the tone and the thrust of the *Counter Budget* as a whole, we can distill two sets of attitudes that seem pertinent. One is simply the pervasive feeling, a resistant residue of our technological compulsion, that space exploration and development of advanced technology are elements of progress worthy of support, even if our practical needs on earth do not permit indulgence of our more Olympian impulses. Two, pluralist politics dictate that everybody—or almost everybody—should get a piece of the action. Since the *Counter Budget* foresees drastic curtailment of military expenditures, there is need to console the aerospace industries and to assuage the angry chagrin of grandeur-minded patriots. Space programs go a way toward accomplishing these ends.

The overall impact of the *Counter Budget,* if it were to become agenda for the nation, would be positive. The burden of exorbitant, redundant defense spending would be lightened; steps would be taken to deal with economic deprivation among the poor; the shameful system of health services would be remedied; and, hopefully, racial strife moderated. Equally striking is what it would not change. Cities would be more congested—thanks to progressive deterioration over time, travel in and around them nightmarish, the abuses of the automobile only partially relieved, effective resource and land planning (as urged by the *Counter Budget*) severely restricted by the pressure of unrestrained industrial growth, air at least as polluted as it is now, and water no less impure. The America inspired by the *Counter Budget* might be more just; it certainly will be no more comfortable.

That the future will reflect welfarist thinking is at best problematical. But its compelling strength among liberals is undeniable, as is its challenge to the environmentalist cause. It is equally clear that to the extent that the costs of pollution control and of providing amenities are not borne by those who are the prime beneficiaries of industrial affluence, and to the extent that there is inadequate planning to make these relationships intelligible and the case for public expenditure persuasive, resistance among all shades of bread and butter liberals to enlistment in the environmental cause will continue. Many of the attitudes toward public policy expressed by the welfarists coincide with those held by less reform-minded social analysts (and occasional actors). From an environmental perspective, there is relatively little to distinguish the authors of the *Counter Budget* from the less *outré* liberalism of the conventional pluralists. Only the drasticness of the former's attack on military spending, and in the details of their prescription for programs like income maintenance, carry the seeds of disagreement. But they are more judgments about political practicality than basic disagreements of objective and principle.

There is, though, one area, muted in the *Counter Budget* but otherwise prominent in welfarist thinking, that is an object of conflict between the keen social reformer and the old-style liberal pragmatists. It is the issue of "participation" "community control," "direct democracy," and related notions.

The search for alternatives to hierarchy, formal organization, and central administration is pervasive among the former and innovators of means by which those who today are recipients of governmental programs might actively participate in them, rather than serve as mere objects of attention. These innovations meet with little sympathy on the part of the liberal reformers who still adhere to a more conventional idea of what is feasible in the implementation of social reform measures. These differences are beyond the scope of this book, but it might well be kept in mind as a further complicating factor in the arena of public policy.

It is perhaps useful to schematize some of the cross-cutting elements in the interplay among environmentalists, welfarists, and liberal pluralists (see Table 10-1).

Table 10-1
Attitudes of Environmentalists, Welfarists, and Liberal Pluralists

	Attitude Toward Econ. Growth & Technology	Pollution Control	Income Redistribution	Expenditure on Environ. II	Policy Process	Structure of Power	Participation
Environmentalist	Skeptical	Acute concern	Ambivalent	Strongly favor	Systematic rationality; Communal perspective	Accentuate coordinating mechanisms; Mild elitism	Policy based on *broad* communal basis
Welfarist	Positive	Mild interest	Positive	Indifferent	Incremental-ism after shift in weighting of priorities	Pluralist with change in weighting of forces Mild elitism	Participation at all levels
Plural Liberalism	Positive	Mild interest	Ambivalent	Indifferent	Incremental-ism	Pluralist	Organiza-tional

11 Radical Doctrine and the Environment

After a period of relative quiescence in which it seemed relegated to minor status on the political and intellectual margins of Western societies, Marxism is striving to reestablish itself as a major doctrinal force. It is doing so at a time when civil order in the industrial democracies is undergoing its severest strains in more than a generation. Only a few years ago, the prevailing (indeed, near universal) outlook emphasized the dissipation of ideological fervor, the muting of class conflict, the functional harmony created by the industrial system, and the community of value that at once sustained and was confirmed by the institutional workings of liberal democracy.[1] The present manifestations of widespread political estrangement, organizational alienation, and renewed ideological engagement have called into question many of the precepts about the political role of democratic man in an industrial setting that had been propounded by the optimistic theorists of postindustrial politics. Those theorists were correct to stress the interdependencies of structure and interest, and the mechanical mode of operation characteristic of contemporary societies.

Radical doctrine with a Marxist orientation is reasserting itself in association with just these shortcomings. Technology, and its impact on both our physical and institutional environment, has become a subject with irresistible attraction for social theorists of all stripes. The dominant criticism in the field has come from those who, while rejecting the conventional pluralistic faith that we live in the best of all possible industrial-democratic worlds, have defined the problem in terms of situational logic and unintended consequence rather than calcualted excess or exploitation. They have stressed the systemic nature of the adverse conditions, the communality of their effects, and the undirected movement of the industrial order. John Kenneth Galbraith is the most articulate expositor of this position and Lewis Mumford its philosophical progenitor.[2] The emergence of a radical critique of the contemporary malaise now provides an intriguing counterpoise and challenge to the former analysis, as well as a test of how pertinent neo-Marxist doctrine is to this package of intellectual concerns and personal complaints.

Neo-Marxism, as movement and as doctrine, is witness to the extent and intensity of the grievances felt about these conditions and is evidence that a significant portion of the aggrieved, particularly among the young, reject the idea that industrial democracies can adjust themselves to manage these problems. It also confirms the durability of the Marxist tradition and its irresistible appeal to the radical consciousness. Marxist terms, concepts, and symbolisms dominate today's revolutionary dialogue; its partisans think in a world of Marxist imagery. One reason for this extraordinary longevity is the comfort offered by its rich tradition. With a claim to historical legitimacy, Marxism adds continuity to a movement born of cultural and political complaints markedly different from those that have inspired more orthodox radical causes. The rediscovery of the early Marx's preoccupation with alienation is a powerful inducement, suggesting that something akin to the phenomenon experienced by today's middle-class student served as the reference point for the great revolutionary's philosophical system and revolutionary ideology. Alienation is the conceptual opening through which classic Marxism is suffused with existential and communalist ideas of more recent vintage. (Cohn-Bendit's revealing restatement of the revolutionary battle cry, "The problem is organization, the enemy is the ruling class," is seen less as a reformulation than a reversion to a more authentic Marxism.)[3]

In order to maintain this doctrinal affiliation, and to draw intellectual substance from it, the newly rekindled radicalism felt obliged to make more explicit theoretical applications to contemporary circumstance. The attempt to establish Marxism's cogency has focused on that most elusive, and most central concept, "class." It is the linchpin of a neo-Marxist doctrine that views the pernicious environmental and organizational effects of industrialism as neither inevitable or coincidental. Instead, they are attributed to the callous self-interestedness of those ruling groups who oversee, derive disproportionate benefit from, and suffer least inconvenience from the workings of the industrial system.

The radical, neo-Marxist view is given expression by a medley of writers, in particular, Norman Birnbaum, Herbert Marcuse, and John McDermott.[4] They carry the attack with verve and force but ultimately, I believe, fail to make their case. Let us see why.

The essence of their analysis is, as McDermott asserts, that "technology is creating the basis for a new and sharp class conflict in our society."[5] To his mind, technology, its attendant cultural values, organizational structures, and environmental effects, cannot properly be viewed apart from the pattern of social stratification it creates. Technology is by no means neutral with respect to the hierarchy of reward and privilege in society. The earlier class structure of a nascent industrialism was based on strict differences in political rights, productive function, and economic remuneration. The maturing of capitalism, it is acknowledged, did serve to remove some of these distinctions, thanks to the acceptance of universal suffrage, mass education, and the growth of meritocratic standards of achievement and status. But as we move into the stage of high technology, "the direction has been reversed and we now observe evidence of a growing separation between ruling and lower class culture in America, a separation that is particularly enhanced by the rapid growth of technology."[6]

This new distinction is not based primarily on differences in monetary return, or vocation *as conventionally defined.* Rather, the cleavage is between those who enjoy the opportunity to play a "creative role in the social processes consequent on technological changes [as] is reserved for a scientific and technical elite, the elite which presumably discovers and organizes that knowledge; [and those] in the lower and, I think, middle levels of American society [who] now seem cut off from those experiences in which near social means and distant social ends are balanced and adjusted."[7] Not only do the "experiences of the higher managers tend to separate and isolate themselves in ideology as well as in reality and appearance from those of the managed, . . ." but it represents a calculated attempt "systematically [to deny] to the general population experiences which are analogous to those of higher management."[8]

Having striven imaginatively to revive a class-focused conflict model with which to analyze critically the industrial system, the neo-Marxists provide a superficially attractive overview. We are offered once again "the class enemy" and the "ruling elite" whose disappearance as central objects of attack in social criticism had been keenly felt as a dramatic loss. If valid, this perspective affords the radical the comfort of long-lost antagonists, minimizes the disturbing element of paradox and irony, and cuts through the latent fatalism of the Galbraithian vision. But reality is unaccommodating, however ravishing these doctrinal temptations. Every argument in the position suffers from insufficient substantiation. Its credibility depends on a generous rendering of sociological concepts that often leaves them a bare shadow of their normal epistomological selves; and on attributions of motivation that are as lacking in evidence as they are daring.

Three propositions need the most careful scrutiny: (1) that there is a discernible point of division between the "managers" and the "managed"; (2) that occupational activity of one stratum is self-evidently more creative and gratifying than another; (3) that there is a conscious awareness of belonging to one or the other that leads to concerted social and political efforts on the part of the elite to maintain its advantageous position. Looking at the first of these, one is hard pressed to discern where the class breakpoint is located. A modern industrial society obviously does have hierarchy, but it is characteristically the hierarchy of a status system rather than of a class system. In a class pattern of stratification, there are a few broad and distinct horizontal layers wherein the members of each perform characteristic economic functions and have a commonly recognized position in the social order. In a status pattern of stratification there exist manifold graded positions that, however categorically defined, are (a) structured horizontally as well as vertically, and (b) offer their holders perquisites more difficult to translate into political power than a superior class position. Bureaucratic organization, the model social institution in McDermott's analysis, is one classic type of status institution. Everyone who is part of the organization has someone above him and someone below him and many laterally related to him. The rungs on the ladder may be more or less accommodating, but compared to a class structure, they are very narrow indeed.

Consonant with the specialization of functions and the specific denotation of responsibilities at each level, steps are carefully graded (except, theoretically, for the man at the very top who, as we shall argue, is restricted by the institutionally defined obligations of the organization he heads). Blue-collar workers in industry might readily be classified among the "managed." But what of white-collar workers—the veritable host of office personnel whose rapid expansion in commerce, service enterprises, as well as manufacturing firms have made them numerically the largest category of jobholders in the United States? McDermott correctly claims that in modern corporations they often suffer most acutely from regimentation and routinization. The trick is to separate the "managers" among the white-collar personnel (with the opportunity to fulfill themselves vocationally) from those—professional as well as clerical—who are the "underclass," cut off from opportunities to express themselves. Anyone with experience of either a governmental or industrial bureaucracy is aware of, and sensitive to, a myriad of fine gradations. However, it would be arbitrary to draw a line on the organization chart dividing the "creators" from the "raw material." The tasks, skills, and job responsibilities subtly shade into each other so as to defy the most strenuous efforts of the class-oriented theorist. Thus, whereas it is possible to specify who has authority over whom with reference to a particular set of responsibilities, there is no definable stratum of authorities to be contrasted with the subjects of authority, unless one's vision is restricted to the very top and very bottom of the ladder, i.e., the board of directors (or agency heads) and the washer women. Again, the phenomenon of nuanced gradation does not permit the kind of crisp distinctions on which a class model might be built.

The second difficulty with the neo-Marxist class-oriented thesis is its failure to provide a viable standard of creativity. If we assume that vocational gratification depends on using one's skills and talents in an imaginative way, with reference to tasks that tap an individual's potential and apply it to personally meaningful social objectives, then there are few discernible occupational roles at any level that qualify.

Let us take the example of an engineer employed by one of our automobile firms, e.g., the head of a department, not an apprentice draftsman. How wide is his latitude for creative innovation, how broad are his discretionary powers? Is he free to use fully his craft and intelligence to design a functionally elegant automobile? He certainly is not. His range of choice is narrowly bounded by the company's need to be profitable, by the restrictions on mechanical innovation that aim to keep down production costs entailed in design changes, by the market pressures generated by competitive manufacturers similarly structured and motivated. What of the executive leadership itself? Leaving aside the junior vice-presidents (already a bare fraction of the managerial class) who are administrative assistants free only to implement orders as expeditiously as possible, how creative does the system permit the top brass to be?

The corporation is not a self-contained political system whose leaders enjoy wide discretion in determining objectives and means to attain them. Its executives and directors are themselves accountable to stockholders, a diffuse group almost all of whom nevertheless share an interest in seeking maximum return on investment. Indeed, the most influential are large, institutional shareholders (investment funds, insurance companies, etc.) that, in turn, are structured very much like the corporation itself with their institutional imperatives and bureaucratic structures. Just as our political system, organized on pluralist principles and following the ethic of incrementalism within governmental bureaucracies, restricts vision and limits the scope for imaginative initiative, so does an industrial system, built around interlocking techno-structures, minimize opportunities for creativity. Tasks of managerial administration might entail institutional power; they rarely entail personal self-realization. Of course, corporation executives do have more prerogatives and responsibility for business policy than their self-serving claims of impotence suggest. Auto company leaders could have taken the lead in installing safety devices or supported development of pollution free engines. Potentially, there is room for creativity in the form of decisions to pursue policies of broader social benefit. It is not just material self-interest and organizational status that encourages them to do otherwise. More potent factors are their sharing in the definition of cultural good motivating the society at large, and their socialization into technostructures inhibiting any propensity to reformulate purpose.

The arbitrariness of the distinction between "managers" and "managed," and its bluntness as a tool for understanding the abuses of the industrial system, is clearly indicated by a case such as that of the Boeing Company and the SST. The most striking aspect of the single-minded commitment to the dev="lopment of this aeronautic extravagance (and the unyielding support of Washington officials and auxiliary contractors), is not that it represents the willfulness of a managerial elite, or that "the creative stratum" sought an unprecedented opportunity for vocational gratification that would be denied the "underclass." Rather, it was that everyone involved derived his sustenance and occupational status from building the aircraft. The workers whose jobs were at stake, the engineers, technicians, and craftsmen whose sense of accomplishment was threatened (along with *their* jobs) supported the project from the first gleaming of the idea to the bitter end with just as much intensity as did the management. They were all enmeshed in the industrial system that had structured choices for them in a special sort of way. Objectively, it would have been far preferable, and viable in every aspect, if those people were at work on developing high-speed rail transit. But that is not an option that casually can be taken up by the Boeing management. There is not the government support or the contracts available for high-speed trains that there are for aircraft. In its advertising, corporate preferences, and research, Boeing undoubtedly adds to the bias built into the system. But its executives can hardly be burdened with exclusive responsibility and blame. The redirection of technical effort toward environmental needs presumes public choices which in turn depend on political action. In that domain again it is a combination of cultural bias common to the whole society and the system distortion that neglects collective need and communal interest that are the primary impediments.

Even more telling for the radical thesis is that even a change in the mission of the corporate process will not alter relationships within the corporation. Whether Boeing produces pollution control devices and high-speed locomotives or supersonic aircraft, the organizational plan and the definition of jobs will be essentially the same. To change those realities would require a basic reordering of industrial structure. Prescriptive formulas for accomplishing that ideal end are, whatever their merits and feasibility, not dependent on McDermott's resurrected class analysis.

Galbraith's view of industrial organization remains, by contrast, the more fruitful approach to conceptualizing institutional realities. The strength of Galbraith's analysis, and the essential correctness of his position, grows out of his perceptive insight into the mechanical workings of the industrial system. He effectively argues that the distinctive feature of the environmental and organizational defects of our society is their inadvertent occurrence. Each member of the technostructure is obliged to act within the severely bounded framework of the formal organization. As a consequence, constraints are placed on his imagination, creativity, and initiative. Thus the problem of alienation and uncertain human purpose. He is also confined in his perception of systemic effects, and extraorganizational collective ends. Thus the neglect of environmental defects.

Galbraith by implication challenges the radicals image of the creative elite at the level of personal psychology as well. He supports the contention that the technostructure is as suppressive of individuality at all levels as McDermott vividly describes it among the managed. As the former puts it: "The real accomplishment of modern science and technology consists in taking ordinary men, informing them narrowly and deeply and then, through appropriate organizations, arranging to have their knowledge combined with that of other specialized but equally ordinary men. This dispenses with the need for genius. The resulting performance, though less inspiring, is far more predictable."[9] The mature corporation has a life of its own, fitting individuals to its organizational requirements. Given the pervasiveness of the "industrial ethos," individual dispositions are rarely out of line with the forms and objectives of the technostructure. Personal motivation, social value, and organizational function stand in direct relationship to each other. To use Galbraith's words again: "the goals of the mature corporation will be a reflection of the goals of the members of the technostructure. And the goals of the society will tend to be those of the corporation."[10] There is then no primacy of control in the interest of any calculating group that manipulates the whole.

One offshoot of the Galbraithian analysis is that the preeminent goal of the corporation becomes organizational survival. Even profitability is subordinate. In fact, of course, profitability normally creates the opportunity for expansion, which means growth of the technostructure as well. As such it is welcome as the requirement for corporate well-being. (Similarly, in the governmental domain, congressional support for heavy military expenditures is taken as the requirement for the Pentagon's institutional health, and augmented appropriations for HEW promise a bracing rise in promotions and status for members of that technostructure.) Profit from an organizational vantage point is as much an indicator of professional accomplishment as a source of personal wealth. Most members of the corporate technostructure share only indirectly in profits, even if their job tenure depends on a certain financial success for the corporation. What they do get is a greater range of ersatz standards of success, and a richer menu of status symbols, poor indicators of personal gratification or psychic contentment.[a]

The radical sociologist Birnbaum looks at this same reality and sees a political elite in the form of "state technicians," or technocrats, in ultimate alliance with the managers.[11] In his elaboration of this thesis, he cannot escape the intellectual cul-de-sac he enters by trying to reconcile a doctrinal principle assuming structure and conscious will with a reality of diffusion and implicit purpose. The managers turn out to be anyone who exercises *more* organizational authority and receives *more* in the way of material return than an unspecified someone else. Since nearly everyone has both more and less authority and/or salary than someone else, we are back to McDermott's dilemma of trying to find a logical breakpoint. Birnbaum's contribution to this effort is the notion that there exists a directive technocratic authority of permanent officials in government who coordinate the industrial system in the interest of the managerial strata. Whatever the rise in influence of highly placed civil servants, no Western society has as yet reached the stage of Saint Simon's administrative state. Everywhere they clearly are subordinate to politically elected authorities who in turn are open to the multiple pressures of enfranchised constituents. On this score the pluralist model, *as description*, remains more accurate than does one based on the idea of a self-conscious political class. Once again, we are thrown back to considering a revolution in industrial organization itself as the

---

[a]The airlines' attitude toward the SST is an interesting case in point. Purchase of the inordinately expensive supersonic transport was a risky venture for companies that were already financially overextended. Yet almost to a man, airline executives offered profuse expressions of support for the project. One suspects that hopes of profit maximization were not their sole motivation. The introduction of new technology is crucial to their self-esteem, sense of achievement, and institutional purpose. From whatever evidence we have, their employees felt no differently. In this instance the rote workings of the technostructure, spurred by the cultural bias in favor of technical virtuosity, lead toward an environmentally damaging course of action that does not even offer the prospects of increased efficiency and profitability.

answer both to personal alienation within the technostructure and to dissatisfaction with the policy outputs of private and public technostructure, economic and political.

Organizational Alienation, Participation, and the Environment

Undeniable from any theoretical vantage point are the alienating effects of modern organization and life patterns. As Aron has noted with his usual perspicasity: "Alienation is less an isolated aspect of the social order, or of collective psychology, than it is the product of the ever-present threat of rationalized techniques in complex organizations and in heavily populated societies."[12] Industrial efficiency, and its concommitant formal organization, depend on the routinization of selective aspects of human personality and require emotional neutrality in their functioning. Modern organization provides that network of standardized rules and procedures which assures that social behavior meets technological need. Rationalized organization has an extraordinary capacity to absorb variously motivated individuals and to so deploy them within the apparatus as to achieve systemic ends. These ends are the common social objectives of producing as much, as innovatively, and as efficiently as possible. Thus the world of formal organization and regulation with which we are all familiar.

The economic success of our society and its ability to live according to the rules of legal equity are functions of this structure. At the same time it suffers from three distinct shortcomings: it offers little in the way of communal loyalties, inducing a sense of individual meaninglessness; it neglects the nonproductive environment; and it restricts personal political involvement to formal, highly-structured channels. These conditions are interrelated and have common causes, but the answer to one need not answer the others. Private routes to happiness do not presume social changes; authoritarian government could do away with pollution; and a well-integrated association of fellows can be at the expense of any programmatic accomplishment.

Schemes for refashioning the instrumental, modern organization into something approximating a traditional kind of organic community have abounded since the inception of the modern industrial age. They have carried the encompassing hope of improving man's collective life and rendered more just its operations, while satisfying the individual's need for place and purpose. The Utopian communities of the early nineteenth century, the Guild Socialism of the English Fabians, the idealist communism of the early Marx, and, from a rightist perspective, the 'corporation' of Fascist design, all represent attempts at imparting a sense of belonging and communalism into the functionally specific industrial institution while mitigating class conflict. The theme waxes and wanes, but it is never entirely absent from the stream of discourse on the condition of modern man. More recently these ideas have resurfaced in new guises as part of the radical criticism of "postindustrial society."

Actual innovation, though, is as rare as talk is rife. It is probably corect to say that nowhere have the separate functions of labor and management been unified as was envisaged by revolutionary syndicalism. The one possible exception is the Yugoslav system of a "labor-managed economy."[13] It does exhibit many features characteristic of the "ideal-type" guild system. One, workers participate in the management of the enterprises through general meetings on overall policy as well as through representation on the councils that serve as the organization's executive committee. Two, income is shared according to distributive roles established by democratic procedures. Three, labor in its managerial capacity is free to qualify the standard conception of production optimization and efficiency, including elements other than profitability. The opportunity would seem to exist, therefore, for workers to exercise an appreciable degree of collective power to express their communal concerns. Since the individual member's involvement in the enterprise is not limited to his narrow task in the productive process, he should be in a position to take a broader view of his responsibilities and range of concerns. In theory, the system of worker participation could make it possible to include many more variables in his calculus of welfare and benefit. Simply by posing choices for the worker that he would not be presented with in his more restricted capacity as laborer alone, the system logically would appear to increase the prospects that questions of institutional purpose would be considered.

Although evidence based on the Yugoslav experience is scarce, it does suggest that the deleterious psychological effects of industrial labor are attenuated. If the physical tedium itself cannot be easily relieved (except through the lowering of norms where the value placed on productive efficiency, and, therefore, profit, is lessened), the worker's relation to his job is qualitatively affected. It is far more difficult, though, to estimate or to interpret the consequence of this pattern for systemic environmental effects.

Externalities would face fewer *structural* impediments to their being included in the calculation of the industrial enterprise under the Yugoslav system. But the cultural and doctrinal resistances are likely to be equally resistant. There is nothing irreconcilable between a worker-managed corporative structure and a stress on "profitability," i.e., efficiency, accumulation of wealth, and its enjoyment in a consumer economy. There *is* an unavoidable tradeoff between productivity and environmental amenity. Any economy would have to be prepared to make some choices along these lines if it were genuinely committed to achieving a more agreeable habitat. Whereas the community mindedness of the participatory system does less to preclude posing the choices, it does not presume an answer. The Yugoslav experience to date does not even suggest one. The country is still in the throes of an expansionist period, preoccupied with growth rates, and does not face immediate problems of pollution and physical degradation. It will be some years before we can assess whether their system anticipated these problems better than we did (although they certainly will have the advantage of being informed about the troubles of their predecessors), took measures to deal with them, and could more effectively use the industrial enterprise as a vehicle for self-regulation.

One key to the puzzle will be the degree to which communal attitudes within the individual enterprise are successfully translated into a broader sense of political community. Leaving aside the special features of the Yugoslav situation (positively, the shared revolutionary inheritance and its unitary political culture; negatively, residual and pernicious regional antagonisms), it is by no means clear that resolution of the problem of individual value in the industrial system through organizational restructuring implies a keener sense of communal identity beyond the confines of the organization.[b] A sense of belonging does not necessarily mean action to clean up pollution or to improve urban mass transit. Indeed, a renewed sense of intimacy in the narrower setting could be at the expense of larger loyalties and concerns (except perhaps rhetorically).

In a sense, this phenomenon is another expression of the paradoxical relationship between personal ends and social need as is always manifest in radical movements. Where the priority emphasis is placed on securing a setting conducive to the meeting of personal psychic needs, it often entails insulation rather than engagement. A modicum of success in achieving a tolerable private existence can compensate for the discomfort and unappealing quality of the general social condition. The intimate community is a shield and a nest. It serves a politically beneficial function in permitting the individual member to revert back to the communal womb for sustenance and inspiration. However, it can also buffer the individual against the necessity to become at all active "out there." Whereas alienation in isolation can be a spur to action, the personal gratifications of his own small community might attenuate a person's discontent in such a way as to make him more tolerant of the overall condition of his physical and social environment.

[b]On this score the experience of experimental colleges in this country is by no means encouraging. Innovative institutions founded on principles of participation, groupism, and free choice have appeared as alternatives to the formal structure of the conventional university. They have exhibited an unfortunate tendency to be less concerned with using their freedom to acquire a unique, yet substantive understanding of their society than with cultivating cloying, self-conscious communities of "precious" people. There is a strong disposition to sit around holding hands and talking about how nasty the rest of the world is rather than to acquire the knowledge and developing the means for effective action.

**Part 5
Some Tentative Suggestions for
Reform**

Our examination of the environmental issue has stressed the systemic properties of our industrial society. The distortion of our relationship to our surroundings is explainable by reference to both our values—cultural norms, political beliefs, economic doctrines—and our institutional structures. They are mutually reinforcing aspects of the same reality. Values legitimize established ways of conducting our affairs, and institutional arrangments perpetuate those conditions that confirm our purpose. It is appropriate, therefore, that we offer guidelines for change that encompass the two dimensions of our present dilemma.

12 Institutions and Public Policy

We have devoted the bulk of this essay to (a) a critical account of how our public institutions mishandle environmental problems; (b) an exposition of the thesis that misfeasance reflects logical features of our political system; and (c) a skeptical view of recent programmatic initiatives and policy innovations that emphasized their lack of primacy and comprehensiveness. Given the blind thrust (or more accurately, the dimly conscious progression) of our civilization, there is an intellectual temptation to accept with stark fatalism the inexorable consequences in environmental disarray. We are not that pessimistic. However strong the routine impulses of industrialism, they are not incontrovertible. Their qualification and redirection depend on skillfully devising the means to break the interlocking logic of enmeshed institutions structured to fulfill the mission of change, random invention, and enrichment suitable to an earlier epoch of industrialism. Some positive suggestions are in order.

There are two aspects to any strategy for improving the way in which we manage our collective environment. The first is the institutional structures through which we handle our public affairs; and the second is the pattern of representation through which popular sentiment is translated into official actions.

Political Structures

The overriding reforms dictated by environmental need are for (a) effective regulation of deleterious action taken by private industries or governmental bodies; and (b) mechanisms of planning and coordination.

In our discussions of technology assessment and the EPA, we considered the merits and liabilities of various formal arrangements for controlling industrial technologies and production so as to avoid their adverse environmental effects. The recommendation of assessment boards to perform essentially monitoring functions are well-taken, and their implementation would meet the important requirements for informed anticipation of new technologies' ramifying social effects. Similarly, the powers mandated to the EPA, and the legislation it is called upon to administer, can be expected to have an appreciable cleansing effect. As regulatory bodies, though, the shortcomings of both are just as apparent.

First, for the reasons outlined earlier, a more powerful, autonomous

121

commission is called for. The weakness of the regulatory commission is generally acknowledged and much publicized, i.e., its susceptibility for degenerating into a protector of the interests it is meant to oversee. On balance, though, it still seems an advantageous mode of approach for accomplishing the specific, critical task of enforcing compliance with prescriptive legislation. Given the undeniable danger of maladministration, it is imperative that measures be taken to maximize the half-life of effectiveness between inauguration and administrative senility (if not capture). There are two characteristic ways of safeguarding a regulatory agency's integrity: (a) sagacious initial appointments and (b) accentuating opportunities for judicial appeal.

It is, of course, not very original or imaginative to call for appointment of able, dedicated commissioners, and there is a temptation to disparage so facile a recommendation. Yet there is no avoiding the compelling truth that only by according power to individuals with a well-defined view of a more palatable environmental future will effective regulation be possible. To presume that some exquisitely subtle rearrangement of legal formats and administrative procedures, without changes in the thinking of those who work the system, can produce new policies is to fall prey to the blandishments of the "organizational fix." A new way of doing things is in itself no guarantee that the results will be any different from what they were in the past. Fresh ideas and the assertion of political will are the indispensable elements of reform.

However uninspiring the performance of regulatory agencies in the American government have been, in most cases, there is evidence that the caliber of appointeed does make a difference. It is hard to deny that if maverick FCC Commissioner Nicholas Johnson were joined by four like-minded men, radical changes would occur in the use of the airways and television circuits. Similarly, five dedicated environmentalists empowered to apply even existing legislation could profoundly alter the priority now given amenity and environmental purity and could thus lower our tolerance for environmental damage.

The effectiveness of an environmental regulatory commission would be reinforced and extended by a broad writing of its mandate. As we conceive it, the commission would have three essential purposes:

1. To initiate proceedings against violators of regulatory codes. These cases would be tried before the board sitting as an administrative court. This adjudicative role would be a function of its responsibility to regulate in accordance with the specifications of its legal mandates. As with all administrative courts, appeal to higher judicial authorities would be permitted.

2. To act on "class-action" suits. The commission would be free to support a suit initiated by private parties, on behalf of broad category of plaintiffs, i.e., "class-action," if it were to judge the claim to be a valid one. The commission then could enter the case as an interested party. No restriction would pertain

to suits directed at other federal agencies or local jurisdictions. Such a provision would have the salutary effects of: (a) reaffirming the primacy of environmental authority over other executive departments; (b) confirming the right of private citizens to appeal against, and thereby question, administrative rulings made on the basis of legislated statute; and (c) engage the commission in the broad range of environmental issues rather than limit itself to implementation of specific regulations pertinent only to particular categories of potential violators.

3. Serious consideration should also be given empowering it to investigate concrete problems of pollution. Conceivably, the commission could be endowed with its own expert staff that would initiate studies in the manner of an official "Nader's Raiders." To this extent it would complement functions now performed by the Council on Environmental Quality. (Some affiliation might be established with a semipublic "Environmental Institute" such as was planned by the council jointly with the Ford Foundation until the proposal apparently was killed by the Nixon administration in fear of its possible excessive zeal in pushing environmental causes).

Second, central planning mechanisms and coordinating bodies are even more difficult to design. There are two functions to be performed: the intellectual one of framing public needs comprehensively and formulating options that make the linkages among the several disparate pieces of policy; and the administrative one of assuring that the organizational parts for adopting and executing policy mesh—i.e., planning and operation.

Addressing itself to the planning deficiency in western societies, Brooks's OECD report recommends "creation of a governmental mechanism, operating under specific authorization and full support of the head of government, with responsibility for investigation of long-range policy issues."[1] It would be distinguished by freedom "from the pressures of short-range problems within the time periods of political terms in office."[2] The image is that of a "council of wise men," embody all the virtues attributed to sages. Presumably the membership would, like Galbraith's scientific-educational estate, combine philosophy, expertise, and intellectual detachment. The composite body would be knowledgeable as to the specialized skills on which the industrial system is dependent; it would act in full awareness of our society's premises, operative principles and purposes; and ideally it would possess a conception of "the good life" distilled from the cultural heritage and social ideals of our civilization.[a]

---

[a]The British government's Central Policy Review Unit, established in 1971 by the Conservatives, is in part inspired by the Brooks argument. A small body of approximately thirty-five, headed by Lord Rothschild and directly responsible to the Cabinet, its main functions are understood to be: (a) to review in depth, if not detail, broad issues of long-term effect such as the "energy crisis"; (b) to make known to the government its views as to the preferred course of action on those more immediate problems that could impinge

There is no denying the desirability of having such a council at the disposal of our political leaders. There is less certainty as to how it might be achieved. The availability of persons meeting the job requirements is in doubt. One characteristic of the modern industrial, democratic society is that it lacks a class or profession that serves as cynosure of its values and commands commensurate respect. Brooks's model seems to be a "Royal Commission" in permanent session and with an expanded mandate. Such a body constituted in the United States quite understandably would devolve into a Presidential Commission on National Goals, with just about as little practical effect. Where there is no acknowledged elite, the politically expedient standards for selection of members will dictate the commission's conclusions. And were agreement on these standards preexisting, the commission itself would be superfluous.

The answers to the planning lacuna must be prosaic. Looking first as to mechanisms for policy coordination, in the American system there would appear to be two candidates for this practical, if crucial task: the newly reconstituted Office of Management and Budget, and the cabinet. The former is better suited to perform the function of program integration, making the necessary tradeoffs among public goals and devising the concrete strategies for achieving them. The cabinet's potential role more appropriately could be that of administrative coordination, concentrating on the implementation of programs and policies.

The recently consolidated OMB was structured with the proclaimed objective of systematizing the process of establishing priorities and matching them to budgeting allocations. It absorbed those agencies in the executive branch with some responsibility for oversight or coordination and assumed their functions. The former Office of the Budget, though, served largely as the ultimate arena in which the contestants—private interests, government bureaucracies, congressional factions, and their favored programs—for the federal dollar bargained and fought. Whatever his powers of decision, the director was not empowered to make policy choices of a long-standing or far-reaching character. He was limited to determinations of marginal preference within bounds severely narrowed by the complex process of executive and legislative aggregation and compromise. The OMB was intended to introduce a larger component of programmatic structuring in the preparation of the budget and to institute more extensive procedures for reviewing programs already underway. In practice, though, there is little if any evidence that any drastic changes have occurred. Budgets, and

---

on longer-term considerations. The unit's operations are veiled in secrecy and its performance difficult to evaluate. Its activities have highlighted three obstacles to fulfilling its tasks successfully and completely: one, the resistance of the permanent civil service to making available necessary information; two, the competing demands on its time of policy advice and planning that poses a particular problem for a group of that limited size; and three, the lack of institutional means for bringing the work of the several ministries into line with the unit's forward-looking schemes. Although the British system is in some respects more susceptible to gentle steering of this sort than is the American, and small informal bodies can work effectively, the scale of the Rothschild operation still seems incommensurate with its responsibilities and potential influence on policy.

government policy in general, still reflect the plural bases of interest representation and the dissociation of executive organization.

There is, however, no necessary reason why the OMB could not serve as the prime instrument for operational planning. Budgetary allocations are expressions of public value and statements of social purpose, as well as an accounting of the monetary means to achieve them. The budgetary process is a method of determining who bears what fraction of the costs to achieve what governmentally defined end. For the most part, the values that guide budgetary decisions are implicit. We are suggesting that they be made explicit so as to serve as reference points for the overall formulation of federal government policy.

The notion of using the cabinet, perhaps with an accentuated vice-presidential role, as an administrative coordinating mechanism is logically simple and indicates what appears to be the most obvious institution to do the job. It comprises the heads of executive departments and agencies that implement government policy. As the de facto committee of government operations, it could be the body to assure that the coordinate elements of policy are implemented according to design and could monitor their effectiveness. Never in America's history, of course, has it functioned in that way. As every freshman student of government knows, its members' bases for selection, their historical role as intragovernmental representatives of their departmental interest, and the presidential aversion to collegial government militate against turning the cabinet into an instrument for concerting policy.

Yet there is no compelling reason why the cabinet could not serve to make national policy more coherent than it is now. Political debts can be paid in ways less damaging to the apparatus of government; the logic of bureaucratic politics could be attenuated by a firm presidential intention to employ department secretaries as collaborators in the formulation of overall administration policy; and the dependence of secretaries on expertise now filtered by departmental officialdom could be overcome by encouraging the formation of personal staffs (perhaps in the manner of the French cabinet) composed of men who share the executive's political orientation and sense of purpose, are knowledgeable in the appropriate policy areas, and are capable of adapting administrative tools to policy goals.

The prerequisite for reworking the cabinet as an institution is a chief executive convinced of the virtues of comprehensive policy-making, desirous of fashioning a coherent set of programs, and aware of the impediments that the present fragmented system poses to its achievement.[b]

---

[b]Our recommendations for institutional innovations to facilitate program planning and administrative coordination are limited to the executive branch of government. Our neglect of Congress does not imply disparagement of the legislature's very considerable powers of initiation and control. The executive, though, is the arm of government capable of conducting a comprehensive review of policy, designing cognate programs, and formulating a budget for their realization. As the only elected official with a national constituency, the president is mandated to act for the society as is no other public official. The political

The intellectual side of the planning function is prior to program formation and coordination. It is also perhaps the most vital, and least practised, governmental function. At the present time, primary responsibility for delineating environmental futures and making the connections among present programs, their extrapolated effects, and longer-term need, lies with the CEQ. Its statutory obligations include the charge "to analyze and interpret environmental trends and information of all kinds ... and to formulate and recommend national policies to promote the improvement of the quality of the environment." Its efforts to do so are presented in the annual Environmental Quality Reports. While these documents do constitute a wide-ranging overview of environmental problems and the existing means with which to deal with them, they are in no sense comprehensive assessments of environmental conditions or outlines to guide environmental planners. With recent legislation as the most common point of departure, and sensitive to the political interests of the incumbent administration, the CEQ staff provides a compendious statement of where we are, rather than an appraisal of where we are likely to wind up, much less a rigorous consideration of where we could be and guidelines for getting there.

Apart from uncertain political backing and imperfect agreement in the nature of its task, the CEQ suffers from two other related deficiencies. One, its own staff is of limited size, highly dependent on contract studies or the unsatisfactory parochial analyzes of other government departments. Two, whereas it is possible, with some difficulty, to tap experts with specialized knowledge of the several technical areas embraced by the environmental policy, there are very few, readily available environmental planners practiced in the act of analyzing the intricate interplay of natural, technical, and social factors and assessing their long-term impact on man and society (this is the problem of knowledge we discuss in chapter 13).

The case for endowing the CEQ with a more extensive planning staff (and/or creating an Environment Institute) is supported by the analysis of anomalies and disjointedness in environmentally related policy areas, e.g., transportation and energy. At the present time, each department of government is implicitly making environmental decisions without full understanding of their implications. The task of planning unit is to create a frame for policy that makes connections

paramountry thereby created is matched by his unique administrative responsibilities and powers to direct the operations of government.

Congress, by contrast, enjoys limited resources for the broad study of public policy or for the planning of integrated programs. Were "ecology politics" to result in keener awaremess of environmental needs and greater responsiveness to the requirements for intelligent environmental management, the legislative fate of new initiatives in the field would be favoured. But it remains ill-suited to do the intellectual job of fitting the pieces into a coherent whole. The recent Senate initiative to create a permanent, bipartisan unit for research and analysis of social policy is a welcome attempt to provide Congress with some means to assess long-term policy requirements. It should be viewed, though, as a legislative supplement to executive bodies.

explicit and to guide assessments of the ramifying effects a particular action is likely to have. This work could take the form of outlines for conjectured environmental futures that state in effect: if you do a, given circumstances we understand as x and y, then the likely consequences are b. Alternatively, given these same circumstances, initiatives d and e lead to result f. A series of such systematic outlines of policy areas would not be a definitive blueprint for government policy in every particular case but a necessary reference for intelligent planning that specifies elements of indeterminancy and points of decision. The process aims at a heightened consciousness about the elaborate intersections of means and ends, intended and inadvertent, over time. Systematic understanding and the formulation of alternatives does not presume extensive physical planning. Rather, it is a prelude to demarcating needs and the conditions for satisfying them (the thrust of the OECD argument).

This type of activity, which represents the analytical phase of the planning function, is nowhere done on a regular basis but would seem to be the prerequisite for policy-making that avoids the pitfalls of incrementalism. Whatever the political difficulties of strategic planning (administrative coordination and governmental continuity being two conditions not easily assured), policy by design is something for which public authorities have shown little inclination or aptitude. A skepticism as to the likelihood of success combines with anxieties over potential incursions on governmental freedom of action and group liberties to reinforce attachment to customary procedures. Given the prevailing compartmentalization of knowledge, academic and practical, the intellectual undertaking itself does represent a considerable challenge. Although it depends on a host of technical competencies, the outstanding need is for those who can fit the pieces together. The seeming inappropriateness of either the specialized expert or the traditional generalist is another expression of our dilemma. It is unlikely to be resolved so long as we deny the importance of the integral thinking we leave untutored in the academy and neglect in the chambers of power.[c]

Without the sort of strategic planning that imparts meaning to government policy, it is unrealistic to expect any institutional arrangement or rearrangement to solve the problem of disjointed policy-making. Procedural "quick-fixes" are no more valid than technological ones, and just as pernicious in creating the illusion of easy "outs." When we speak of setting priorities, establishing preferences and linking programs, it is only the president acting with support of

---

[c]As for fears about the pernicious effects of planning, many seem inspired by promiscuous use of the term to embrace everything from "think-tank" exercises to totalitarian regimentation. Substituting a term without these perjorative connotations might well assuage some anxieties and permit more reasonable discussion of how we make public policy. Planning entails judgments about what should not, as well as what should be done. Planning not to plan is a quite logical, and often desirable activity. Another of reason's paradoxes is that is can be used to determine when not to assert itself, and to hold in abeyance the architectonic impulse.

the Congress who can do these things. There is no purely institutional substitute for an administration that knows its mind and asserts itself to achieve carefully thought out objectives; or for the solicitous and informed Congress that supports them. From an environmental perspective, what is critical is a national leadership with a deep and reasoned commitment to dealing with pollution and disamenity. There is no mystery as to the means: (a) money—tens of billions of dollars for meliorative and prophylactic pollution technologies, mass transit, etc.; (b) research and development programs aimed at providing requisite skills and technologies; and (c) corresponding emphases in educational policy. Once there is the political will to act on the basis of new, explicit priorities, the planning potential of the OMB can be exploited, as could the latent capacity of the cabinet for coordination and oversight, and the appropriate supporting bodies established.

Third, effective implementation depends on compliance and efficient performance: (1) by federal agencies and (2) by local authorities. There is a growing and general awareness that bureaucratic inflexibility, if not recalcitrance is one of modern government's most resistant problems. It taxes the strength of executives and often frustrates political purpose. The same organizational routines that enable large-scale entities to function with regularity become liabilities when missions are changed and institutional purposes redirected.

The propensity of any technostructure's members to act on the basis of convention and socialized belief is strengthened by the intellectual supports that their organization provides. Every government bureaucracy possesses a collective set of ideas and dominant beliefs as to what they are supposed to achieve and the most advantageous ways of going about doing it. The institutional need to reduce internal friction and to facilitate communication combines with group conformity pressures to turn these common beliefs into orthodoxies that acquire the character of unquestioned and unquestionable received doctrine. The organization's dependence on established wisdom reflects the premiums placed on preserving its institutional coherence and capacity to perform smoothly tasks of policy implementation. The disposition of one well-socialized into the organization is to accept these conventional ideas as following incontrovertibly out of the natural order of things.

Under pressure to change, as when political directions are revised, the organizational forces of inertia and self-preservation strain the bureaucratic response toward incremental adjustment. In keeping with the parsimony principle of organizational continuity, the institution will change its thinking and amend its practices only to the extent necessary to assure its survival. There is an economy of intellectual effort whereby changes occur along a continuum from the particular preference to the general principle. It is matched by an economy of structural reform along an analogous continuum from the mundane procedure to the basic format.[d] A readiness of elected officials to allow

---

[d]Large organizations, as the embodiments of the industrial system's practical rationality, are

departmental bureaucracies to define the limits of practicality will thwart any attempt to escape the swamp of incremental policy-making. A tolerance for their conservative resistance to implementation of new policies can be as fatal.

Characteristically there are two ways of avoiding the latter difficulty. One is to bypass existing agencies and to create new, functionally specific bodies as was done in the case of NASA. This might well be the appropriate course to take in the transportation field where the Department of Transportation's phobic dislike for public transit, its infatuation with automobiles, and its intimate liaison with the highway lobby make it an awkward instrument for implementing a multibillion dollar mass transportation program. The other is to perfect means for political oversight. Where clear policy preferences have been established and departmental heads participate actively in presidential decisions, the chances for effective assertion of authority by the secretary and his assistants are increased.

To assist them it might be feasible to consider the formation of what, for want of a more descriptive term, we call "reverse ombudsmen." These would be associates of the president and/or his secretaries (in the latter instance, perhaps members of our proposed cabinet) whose responsibility would be to determine faulty administration of, or noncompliance with, executive acts and legislative programs. Preferably, their activities would be concerted with Congress' General Accounting Office that provides oversight of a more legalistic sort. Unlikely to be the most popular figures in government, they nevertheless would help to assure that government acts in reasonable approximation to its intentions. We do not conceive of them as "intendants" or a parallel government; their task simply would be to find out what is happening with the application of programs and report to their executive superiors who are responsible for monitoring the administrative domains in their charge. In an atmosphere of spirited dedication to programmatic success, (again, the space program is an appropriate example), more active and voluntary cooperation might be expected to mitigate the friction generated by these reverse ombudsmen.

Centralization and National Citizenship

Implementation by local authorities offers a still thornier problem that involves the nether jungle of our functionally irrational system of local jurisdictions, with their welter of contentious forces. Whatever the devices that could be conceived by the federal government for expediting cooperation with state, municipal, and

---

perhaps the most powerful agent of cultural conditioning in our society. Their norms of conduct have spilled over institutional boundaries to pervade the society at large: the subordination of substance to procedure; the ingrained skepticism of new and/or bold ideas combined with loyalty to conventional wisdom; the implicit belief that there are no alternatives to the means available and the ideas in force; the premiums placed on uniformity of thought and behavior. These dispositions are evident among elected officials, as well as bureaucrats among whom they inhibit innovative thinking, and put a brake on the initiation of new programs.

other local bodies, the inordinate convolution of the problem hardly permits summary exposition. So let us briefly note two ingredients of a reform approach.

First, initiative should be taken to endow program agencies with highly competent, specially-trained teams to assist in the adaptation and utilization of grant moneys. The provision of R & D services in this form could facilitate the task of local officials in planning construction of a transportation network, or relating their power requirements, and provision, to pollution restrictions. Such expertise is today strikingly lacking in even the largest urban centers. Availing itself of what hopefully will be new programs for applied technical research, the federal government could be in a position to make available that expertise.

Second, it is incumbent on federal authorities to specify guidelines and to oversee their compliance. Technically, this responsiblity is built into most present programs. In fact, uncertainty of original intention and inadequate means of supervision often combine to permit excessive leeway in the use or misuse of funds as local officials choose, or as they are compelled to do so by local political forces and economic interests. Admittedly, the impetus recently has been in the opposite direction, i.e., toward unrestricted grants. But schemes such as revenue-sharing are more a statement of federal authorities' inability to establish preferred social needs than realization of a political principle. Where well-conceived programs aimed at meeting clear needs are created, good government demands coordination, not laissez faire. The delicate inter-dependence of environmental factors, and the consonant requirement for integrated policy, mean that the environmental cause suffers as much from the willingness of local authorities to indulge an expedient *ad hocism* as it does from piecemeal national policy-making. Assurance that funds are being used in a manner consistent with programmatic objectives does not mean federal controls. Rather the emphasis should be on initial review of an obligatory plan to be submitted by the recipient authority. With the assistance of the R & D teams, the connections necessary for coherent policy would be incorporated into the early design and serve as the guide for efficient implementation.

Ample opportunity would exist for local communities to determine the designs and special features of the format they prefer, e.g., the modalities of a metropolitan transportation network. There is no reason to assume need for a federally imposed orthodoxy on the forms and modes for implementing projects. The oversight function would have the dual purpose of encouraging efficient use of resources and their application as part of a congruent plan. Restrictions need not be imposed by Washington on the degree or type of citizen participation local authorities favor, and important substantive matters would remain for determination by the communities involved. Indeed, once significant resources are made available through well-financed federal programs, the occasion would present itself for communities to express their distinct personalities, differentiating themselves through design in a way that financially cramped local programs do not permit. With a positive community objective, participation might also take a more constructive form than the present factional warfare over the petty perquisites and emoluments provided by enfeebled municipal governments that now offers such a degrading spectacle of perverted participatory politics.

The principle we are affirming is a very simple one: public decision should be made at the level of authority appropriate for the problem. The loss of social amenity (and pollution as well) is an expression of the imbalance between expenditure for collective needs and expenditure for private consumption. Political decisions determine that balance, and it is the federal government that is the prime agent for making that cumulative decision by virtue of its powers of taxation and allocation. (It also is the central force in influencing the magnitude and direction of overall national development.) Logically, it follows that rectification of existing disproportions in: (a) the public vs. private allocations of national product and (b) between areas of public expenditure, should be initiated in Washington.

Self-evidently, this means centralization of decision. But that is a statement of institutional reality that prevails already and will not be changed by denying ourselves the public goods that only the federal government, as the executive manager of American society, can provide. What is regrettable is that the sense of national community and national political loyalties are not commensurate with either the configuration of public power or the scope of our collective need. It is a condition that is both cause and effect of our abdication of public responsibilities for provision of common goods. Hopefully, the environmental movements' holistic approach, and the obligation to act comprehensively that it imposes, will begin to regain a semblance of national community as we launch new public undertakings.

However real the virtues of participatory democracy, the structure of political life in an industrial nation of our size does not lend itself to the intimate town meeting of fellows. This holds for city and state government every bit as much as it does for the federal government (it is an absurd travesty of the communitarian idea to presume that Albany can somehow be an object of personal political passion and affection for a Long Island commuter in a manner that Washington cannot be). What we reasonably can accomplish is the formulation of issues and problems in ways appropriate to their encompassing nature, the focusing of public attention on the arena of national debate and choice where the locus of authority lies, and the cultivation of a political capability to participate in the multiple if not so intimate ways our system permits, within our local communities and the national context simultaneously.

13 Knowledge and Education

Change in our approach to the environment will require a shift in our values and ideas as much as it does renovation of our institutions. Those shifts would have to occur both in theoretical knowledge and popular belief. Public attitudes can be expected to shift gradually as part of an expedient response to new, observable circumstances. One major factor determining the scope and depth of the reappraisal will be the leadership exercised by public authorities in defining environmental issues, formulating programs of action, and taking the urgent initiatives that demand a redrawing of priorities and budgets. A requirement for imaginative leadership, in turn, is a new vision of the industrial system such as only structured theory can offer.

Galbraith's Remedy: The Educational-Scientific Estate

Our view of industrial society parallels that sketched in John Kenneth Galbraith's, *The New Industrial State.* The strength of Galbraith's analysis, and the essential correctness of his position, grow out of his perceptive insight into the mechanical workings of the industrial system. He effectively argues that the distinctive feature of the environmental defects of our society is their inadvertent occurrence. Their existence, and their relative neglect, are not for the most part the result of willful actions by individuals or institutions consciously prepared to accept them as the costs of their own gain. There is little malevolent about the situation. Rather, conditions express the cumulative outcome of actions taken by a myriad of individuals and groups doing what they are professionally trained, institutionally conditioned and organizationally directed to do.

In his study of the technostructure, Galbraith powerfully demonstrates how little comprehension of the whole of a corporation's operation there need be for it to achieve its institutional ends. The same principle we have applied to government agencies in our critical sketch of interest-based pluralist politics is valid in regard to the industrial system as a whole. Based on his assessment of the industrial system's mechanical quality that is rooted in the very nature of its implicit purpose and values, one might have expected him to accept fatalistically our inability to manage our collective enterprise with prudent restraint. Galbraith resists this logic, though. Instead, he elaborates a strategy whereby the system of interdependence can be mastered, and put in the service of humane

133

social management. The prime actors in this salvage operation are members of the "educational and scientific estate" who are deemed to have requisite awareness, skills, and strategic location in society to exert significant leverage on public policy.

To appreciate fully Galbraith's advocacy, we have to begin with his belief that political authority in the new industrial state is dispersed, fragmented, and characteristically managerial. Official officeholders are the managers of interest coalitions who maintain a balance in representative institutions that in turn permits the managers of the technostructure to pursue the essential tasks of production upon which the industrial system ultimately depends. These managerial-brokers of democratic politics are a logical outgrowth of the system. They fulfill organizational functions that are as much a part of the mechanism as are the more technical functions of the private sector. But they do not act on behalf of any self-conscious dominant group or class that is capable of concerting efforts to achieve selfish ends. The technostructure's leadership is qualitatively different from any elite that has preceded it, and, in fact, the term *elite* fails to get at its essential formlessness. Thus Galbraith argues: "The technostructure is . . . handicapped in its political activity by its collegial character. Political leadership, persuasion and action are activities of individuals; they are not readily undertaken by men who are accustomed to operating as a group."[1] Moreover, there is not one leadership group but a multitude of them—as numerous as the organizational empires in which they reside and over which they preside. Each acts to advance its special interests within the confines of its domain, whether it be a field of manufacturing and commerce, a sphere of scientific research, or a bureaucratic fief in government. Functionally, they all interlock; the power to direct them, however, is fragmented, narrow in its outlook, and itself of a managerial bent. Given this dispersion and lack of directive leadership, it would seem that political power in our pluralist industrial democracy is open to a self-willed group of powerseekers aware of the system's weaknesses and character. For the reasons Galbraith articulates, no such elite faction with a distinct political identity and purpose is likely to come out of the world of technostructures.

This latent accessibility to power, though, is a precondition for the success of Galbraith's strategy. There is room at the top, or to put it more accurately, there is opportunity to use the discretionary power which potentially exists at the top, and which in the style of managerial politics now lies unexploited. Why, though, its susceptibility to activists of the scientific and educational estates?

The essence of Galbraith's position is that the technostructure, and the political managers who synchronize the multiplicity of corporate techno-structures, are dependent on the expertise and technical skills of the educated elite. No modern system can exist without them. Dependence means access and possible influence. The decisive rule of the educational-scientific estate is explained by Galbraith this way:

As the Trade Unions retreat, more or less permanently, into the shadows, a rapidly growing body of educators and research scientists emerges. This group connects at the edges with civil servants, journalists, writers and artists outside. Most directly nurtured by the industrial system are the educators and scientists in the schools, colleges, universities and research institutions. They stand in relation to the industrial system much as did the banking and financial community to the earlier stages of industrial development.[2]

Demonstration of the scholar's newly acquired status is his much sought presence in all the councils of social management:

While the corporation president has become increasingly a traditional or ceremonial figure in his association with education, the modern scholar of science, mathematics, information systems or communications theory is ever more in demand to guide the mature corporation through its besetting problems of science, technology and computerization.[3]

Their presence is taken as evidence of genuine power that can be successfully nurtured and directed. Looking confidently and encouragingly at the rise of the scientific-educational estate, Galbraith optimistically suggests that:

The real power is with the men of knowledge who, given disciplined self-awareness and clear sense of purpose, could reduce managers—private and public alike—to a proper vassalage.[4]

Thus salvation lies hidden in the halls of ivy.

Galbraith's hopeful view of the scholar as political actor requires some interpretation as well as critical scrutiny. The readiness to accord academics this potent role rests on an inclination: (a) to assess highly their capacity for humanely inspired social innovation, and (b) to estimate just as highly their political acumen. The view of the educator as a combination Mandarin and social reformer seems to presume that today's academic embodies the whole panoply of extraordinary individual and professional traits that have been attributed to men of learning. He appears simultaneously as intellectual, expert, and philosopher.

By *intellectual,* we mean someone who by virtue of his intelligent, self-conscious approach to the personal and social circumstances of his existence has both unique understanding and perspective. The latter element is the crucial one. The great failing of the industrial-democratic system is the narrowness of its vision, the specialization of training, the compartmentalization of social roles and the partitioning of fields of knowledge. As Galbraith accurately describes it, our society is a congeries of mechanically linked organizational entities which act without explicit reference to the nature or direction of the whole. The intellectual's role, by definition, has the quality of distance and detachment. Supposedly, he objectively looks at the world around him, asks why it is as he sees it, and inquires as to how it works. He is therefore more likely to have an acute awareness of its premises, operative principles and purposes.

The second element of which Galbraith's composite man of learning seems to be fashioned is the *expert* on whose specialized skills the technostructure and the industrial system is dependent. It is he who creates the intellectual order of science, technology, economics, and management principles without which society cannot function. Thus his critical place in the equation of social forces. Now his expertise is his entry card into the councils of corporate and political power. Soon it can be the resource that is parleyed into political power. Ultimately it can be used by the scientific-educational estate to influence public policy knowingly as well as humanely.

Third, the academic is taken to be wise. There are in this image of the intellectual elements of the classic humanist, i.e., of the scholar whose thought embraces the range of human experience. In addition to knowing how the system works, he is the *philosopher* who can say how it should work. Or, more modestly, he recognizes what society, as constituted, is failing to do; can indicate the requirements for assuring its citizens the "good life;" and he thus can offer touchstones by reference to which we can hope to achieve a more exalted state. As philosopher, the academic is expected to distill from the cultural heritage and social ideals of our civilization (of which he is custodian) guideposts for designing that social order. Thus, as intellectual, the personified scientific-educational estate has self-knowledge; as expert he has practical skills and access to the throne; as philosopher, he has strength of truth and a vision of the future.

But what resemblance does this portrait bear to the reality of the educational-scientific estate? Galbraith neglects to address this question with his usual skeptical intelligence. For he seemingly attributes (by implication) these traits to men who in fact are far more limited in their capabilities and prosaic in their ambition. It is less than evident that the educational-scientific estate is in the collective possession of some philosophical vision of the good society or the requisite skill to promote it.

The most cursory familiarity with the academic world makes abundantly clear how little overlap there is between the technical expert and the humanist (as *intellectual* and as *philosopher*). Specialization is as much a part of the university as it is of the corporation. Academia, like the society which has powerfully influenced its present form and purposes, has seen the proliferation of specialists each with a remarkably competent mastery over his field of study. Their training is thorough but deep rather than broad. Their professional obligation is to domesticate a body of knowledge so as to make of it a useful tool. The intellectual order they create in man's understanding of his natural environment serves utilitarian purposes, at least as much as it advances knowledge for its own sake, and rarely represents wisdom acquired.

It is difficult to reject the oft-heard criticism of student rebels that our educational system at the highest level exists to provide the fund of scientists, engineers, technicians, and administrators on whom the industrial system does indeed depend. It is, indeed, engaged in the manufacture of an intellectual "technology." From one vantage point, the educational-scientific establishment can be studied as the agency through which the human skills requisite for the efficient functioning of that system are cultivated. This symbiosis is recognized in the scale of government support for research and training, especially in technical fields. It understandably has become an axiom of industrial life that effective utilization of these talents can only be achieved if educational *cum* research institutions are brought into close working harmony with government and industry.

Galbraith prefers to view "support for education" not just as reflecting "the needs of the industrial system, but also the increasing political power of the educational and scientific estate."[5] This is a highly questionable proposition. The sharp cutbacks in support for education in recent years, most keenly felt in nonspecialized fields, underscore just how pragmatic and calculating these programs have been. It is hardly a tribute to the political clout of the university that, when it finds itself on the brink of financial disaster, it proves unable to pry loose from the state the support needed to the continued development or even maintenance of its present activities. It is apparent who holds the whip hand.

Our criticism of Galbraith's strategy does not imply a blanket rejection of his advocacy of a more active role for academics in making public policy. Their expertise does give them access, if not always leverage. Some among them do have unique perspective on the weaknesses and liabilities of our industrial system. And it is not inconsequential or coincidental that the university is the great source of strength for the attack on environmental degradation. Galbraith himself is a symbol of this informed critical activism. It the scientific-educational estate shared his views it could, indeed, be a potent force. However, his is obviously an exception even among his fellow social scientists—as evidenced by the controversy his views arouse and the antagonism they often engender. It is insufficient to define the educational-scientific estate, as Galbraith occasionally seems to do, in terms of its members' rejection of consumerism and contempt for the systematic bamboozlement by the technostructure's all-pervasive public relations. These are ingredients of intellectual subcultures, homey and part of a cultivated alienation. They are not adequate bases for a dramatic political campaign.

The University

We have argued that the university, with ancillary research institutions, is itself a technostructure lacking in capacity for fundamental self-examination and missing a conscious sense of communal purpose and perspicacious leadership.

The university's main job is the transference of codified forms of practical knowledge. Humanism today most often takes the form of ritual obeisance to the liberal arts and the culture of antiquity. Classical humanities are a scholarly precinct for pundits, preserved as a curator protects under glass the fragile remains of ancient objects. They are not a vital force that informs more specialized learning. More contemporary humanities—including the social sciences in their less methodological aspects—exist in bits and pieces and nowhere are fashioned into an integrated body of study aiming at giving the student an intelligent overview of contemporary civilization.

The intellectual resources of our universities are abundant, but their potential for enlightened understanding is prevented from being realized by the comparmentalization of knowledge. The department's stranglehold on curriculum represents the scholarly galaxies that comprise our universe of knowledge. This partitioning precludes the acquisiton of that philosophic understanding, founded on an image of the whole of our collective enterprise, that conceivably might enable academic activists to concert their efforts to exert political power in the interest of a higher ideal than that pursued incrementally by the technostructure in conjunction with political management.

It the model scholar is the narrowly trained technical specialist, and the university lacks a common humanist philosophy, doubts also exist as to whether members of the scientific-educational estate enjoy that perspective and social distance by which we identified the intellectual. Both the comparmentalization of knowledge, and the emphasis on technical skills, suggests otherwise. As René Dubos has argued:

Advanced academic programs pay lip service to the need for knowledge in areas different from the field of specialization of the candidate. In most cases, however, this requirement is just a facade; the so-called doctorate in philosophy is now a misnomer, a certificate of expertise in a narrow specialty rather than a philosophical understanding or even awareness of the interrelationships among the various fields of knowledge.[6]

The scientist or engineer certainly is very much part of the industrial system. His skills are those most in demand by industry and government. They are routinely asked to advise, to consult, to direct; and they just as routinely respond positively. How could they do otherwise? Their competence demands demonstration, application, and outlet. Only the most theoretical of the specialists can derive professional satisfaction from the joy of their intellectual endeavor. In this respect they are as much part of the embracing industrial system as are the managers and technicians of the technostructure. The university engineer, computer expert, agronomist or aerospace physicist is an integral gear enmeshed in the productive machine. Were Galbraith to apply his corporate sociology to this presumably unique estate, he would see their systemically defined sense of purpose, the casual assumption of implicit goals and objectives, and the unquestioning acceptance of organizational forms characteristic of the technostructure.

The same can be said of many social scientists. Although their "enmeshment" is less overt, their skills of less certain practical utility, they too have become cogs in the machine. (To stretch an analogy, if members of the technostructure see in profits symbols of professional achievement as much as material gain, the specialist views his consultantships as evidence of his professional attainment). Moreover, the social scientist shares with his more "technical" colleagues the larger problem created by the cultural values that underpin modern industrialism; their instrumentalism, commitment to growth as an end in itself, formalistic rationality, and so forth. Where these norms are not left unspoken in the educational-scientific estate, they normally are articulated with almost clichéd simplicity. What the radical critique views as complicity with the establishment might more properly be interpreted as the logical expression of the social scientist's increasing specialization, his new-found proclivity for method (with its attendant scientific pretense), his reliance on government funds to support his scholarly enterprise, his intellectual desire to do "practical" studies, and his loss of that philosophical perspective that would give a humanistic orientation to his professional efforts. The joining of professional commitment to the broader stream of the industrial value system tends to deny even the social scientist that sense of distance that presumably is the intellectual's hallmark and his conjectured strength as potential political actor. The present structure of our educational establishment hardly offers evidence to support the belief that, as Galbraith says, the "needs of the industrial system are secondary to the cultivation of general understanding and perception."[7] The strain between the humanistic ideal and the compulsions of the technology-based society is routinely resolved at the expense of the former.[a]

More might have been expected from the university. After all, as an institution its calling is one of critical observation and the formulation of ideas with which to understand and to explain the phenomena of human experience. Ideally, it would use these talents to examine itself and to formulate a design for reform. That it has not done so, except in very rare instances, says something about the university's structural defects and infirmities of leadership. In a sense it is a perfection (or caricature, depending on your perspective) of a pluralist political system. It is characterized by a disassociation of powers, a plurality of

---

[a]The technological faith of an earlier day avoided the dilemma by defining industrial progress in humanist terms. As Erik Erickson has phrased it, the notion of "a future in a permanent state of planning" replaced much of the power of tradition.[8] The promise of indefinite progress in improving human welfare gave social meaning to the otherwise neutral industrial processes; the belief that you become what you do added a dimension of psychological realism. Today's more insistent humanism considers man, in his existential being, as the measure of things. Faith in progress as an abstract has been undermined by the attention to personal unfulfillment and physical degradation. Technology is less the opiate of the intellectual than the predicament of the intellectual. It is now the task of education to join the sociological ideal with the technological requirement (no longer accepted as an imperative) for a humanistic industrial society.

vetolike constituent groups, an unconscious and amorphous consensus on underlying values and purposes, a managerial style of leadership that is more prone to respond to, and seek to reconcile, claims made on it than to conceive ideas and to direct. It also reveals all the shortcomings of that kind of system. The university seems unable to anticipate crisis, to recognize challenges to its essential structure when they appear, to make up its collective mind through any process resembling systematic rationality, to exercise independent judgement as to how it should change when change and innovation are deemed desirable, or to concert its will to make these changes work. Typically, it acts according to the precepts of disjointed incrementalism. Disdaining conscious planning, its mode of action is reactive and excessively pragmatic. Seemingly confident of guidance exercised by an invisible hand, it assumes that the disparate elements of academic activity somehow produce a coherent educational whole. Constantly in motion its direction is uncertain; and if direction is at all discernible, it is almost assuredly coincidental. Under normal circumstances this might be a tolerable *modus operandi;* in the present unsettled and demanding situation it is more likely a guarantee of frenetic irresolution.

This type of disjointed incrementalism is of course not entirely accidental. It fits nicely the tenor and structure of the modern university. The university is diffuse, fragmented, and temperamentally unresponsive to central direction; as such it severely limits the administrator's capacity to plan or to set priorities. The specialization of training, the resistance of the departmental structure to encroachment or supersedence, the encrusted layers of privilege and prerogative; they are all well-known and often-documented obstacles to change. However deeply ingrained these characteristics are, though, they too often serve as easy excuses for inaction. They certainly should not preclude university authorities from doing the *intellectual* job of determining what it would like the liberal university to do and to become. Prior to active initiative, rejuvenation demands ideas and a necessary sense of urgency. Without intellectual imagination it is delusory to expect a redress of failings.

Educational Reform

Adaptation of university studies is crucial to any social change. Every educational system is a precision instrument for the propagation of social values. For generations it has inculcated the dominant values of our industrial (and liberal democratic) modern society: science, positivism, efficiency, organization, and growth. It, of course, has also imparted the special skills that move the system. The need how is for a broader vision. What we face is not a problem of insufficient knowledge, but an inadequate intellectual framework in which to place it and an imperfect philosophy of social need to guide the application of technique.

The critical requirement in the training of our multiplicity of specialized professionals is to inform their expertise with a sensitive awareness of the industrial setting in which they will live and work. To break the mechanical logic of the technostructure, the technician or manager should have an understanding of how he fits into the whole and of the nonorganizational consequences of what he does. It is possible to do so only if there exists some common humanitarian vision of technology's place in society and of the paradoxes of industrial progress.

Short of a drastic shift in values and outlook, there is basis for more practical reforms. Speaking of the sciences, René Dubos has observed, "The scientific establishment is shockingly irrational in the selection of its priorities and in the determination of the relative amount of support it gives to various fields."[9] There is undoubtedly a bias, in both research and training, in favor of those fields made attractive by high levels of federal support and popular prestige. Aerospace engineering is the outstanding example of where the availability of grant money, inspired by defense needs and grandiose national objectives, has produced growth all out of proportion to utility. And it has done so at the expense of those fields whose development would help to abate pressing problems, e.g., transportation engineering. For years, the academic world has allowed its professional education to be distorted by federal preferences; and it has by no means been an unwilling accomplice. To quote Dubos again, "University scientists themselves are much more susceptible to para-scientific influences than they are willing to admit."[10] The spectacle of highly trained engineers and scientists entering the ranks of the unemployed because of cutbacks in aerospace programs and a lack of funds for elaborate research. equipment, without the opportunity to redirect their skills into new fields defined by an amended standard of social utility (and in many instances unable to do so if the opportunities were there) is stark evidence of how derivative of the industrial system our professional education has been.

The initiative for reform could come from the university or the government; preferably the pace and pattern of innovation will be worked out jointly on the basis of a common understanding as to social needs and educational requirements. An accentuation of federal research funds in new areas like environmental engineering, acting in part through the NSF and its RANN program (Research Applied to National Needs), a conjectured "Environmental Technology Institute" (perhaps patterned after the model of the successful nuclear and space research facilities), or some other instrumentality linked to the EPA and CEQ, could have a major impact on research and curriculum.[11] In conjunction with government development laboratories, they would also promise productive and challenging professional outlets. (Furthermore, the logic of money and ambition would in this case be accentuated by strong currents of popular and student sentiment.)

In the domain of science, a similar approach is indicated. The government's role in accenting training and research is a given of the present situation. It remains to make explicit the criteria and definitions of need according to which these preferences are expressed. Although proper vigilance is always in order to assure that the governmental disposition to seek immediate answers to short-term policy problems does not distort basic science, it seems entirely proper for public authorities to make considered judgments as to the pool of scientific skills it believes (on the basis of informed judgements about the technical dimensions of social problems) that the nation will need in ten or fifteen years time and to frame the appropriate support programs. (Perhaps, at this state, calling for relative emphasis on biological, environmental, and medical sciences). Of course, delineating the purposes of science policy and making decisions about the direction, magnitude, and form of support, depend on prior reforms that enable government to inaugurate the sort of strategic planning it now neglects. Without reference to some well-defined standard of need, science policy will either (a) perpetuate existing patterns of education and research which provide so inadequately for certain kinds of skills; or (b) create a patchwork intellectual field reflecting random initiatives and expedient compromises.

What to do about liberal arts? The need, as we noted earlier, is for coherent programs of humanities and social sciences that strive to provide that understanding of, and thereby create perspective on, our historically unique industrial civilization. First, it is imperative that the monopoly of curriculum by discipline-bounded departments be qualified. No significant innovation is possible so long as every course must be a reflection of a discipline's special sense of professional training. Exclusive concern with the standards of one's own field and its criteria of achievement is hardly the ideal condition for imaginative creation of new programs of studies. (One is struck by how little variation in curriculum is to be found among the nation's several hundred institutions of higher education. It is a strictly nominal pluralism. From the top to the bottom of the ranks, the same course structure presents itself in dreary repetition, punctuated by rare originality.) The intellectual means are there. All the more pity that the potential for academic stimulation and enlightened understanding is so rarely realized.

Critical to the success of any reform are some fairly well-developed conceptions as to what the *substance* of general education should be. Piecemeal innovation makes no sense, and too often it gives the impression of substantial change when, in fact, a few eccentric whims have been indulged. A course here or a course there, expressing someone's passing interest, is not going to do much to give an arts degree direction and purpose. Despite the initiation of a spate of environmental programs in the last few years, they are for the most part only grafts onto the main body of learning and university organiztion whose ability to take a powerful hold is questionable. There is need for a concurrent pattern of courses intended to provide a comprehensive overview of our society.

Such a teaching program would include some hard economics, history, sociology and political science, as well as an infusion of layman's science and technology. The courses would be structured so that they build on each other and aim in their senior year at highlighting contemporary problems: environmental effects of uncontrolled economic expansion; alienation and anomie in modern society; centralization and community need; and so forth. At some point in the sequence it might be feasible to allow students to branch off and focus their interests. Empahsis, though, would be on continuity and integration so as to maximize its interdisciplinary effect and to avoid the program degenerating into a holding company for pet departmental schemes.

The training of environmental specialists in the social sciences (and the professional schools) would be a logical extension of both a purposeful liberal arts and a reorientation of technical education toward imparting the skills for human-use planning. Whatever the nominal major—economics, law, political science—the graduate would be attuned to public policy issues, aware of the dimensions of the problem, and would have a specialized competence in the technical aspects of his field as well. With this combination of skills he would be prepared to act effectively either as professional activist or as teacher. These trained people would perform for the environmental cause the same function as those education experts or social welfare experts do for their areas of activity.

Over time these educational innovations could be expected to produce significant results in shifting the emphases of the industrial system. One, it would make available competences and technologies that do not now exist. Two, it would create the capacity for informed political action that would depend on a sympathetic public and trained leadership rather than concerted "black-mail" by a clandestine scientific-educational estate. Third, and most vital, it would attenuate the impulsive logic of technological innovation and industrial growth. The characteristic feature, and ultimate danger of the industrial system as we find it today, is its seemingly blind, inexorable movement. With the educational reforms noted above rote behavior becomes that much more difficult. Once instilled with a certain knowledge of consequences, and hopefully some modicum of concern for repercussions, persons in various occupational roles will no longer act without at least some consideration of environmental consequences. With this modification of the definition of social need, and assimilation of a quotient of environmental awareness, the engineer, or manager, or legislator, will automatically take into account this element of collective interest and hopefully weight it appropriately. Regulations and coercive sanction probably will still be needed. We are speaking of an attenuation of outlook, not its total redesign. But casual disregard based on skewed perceptions will be broken and environmental factors would enter into individual and public decision-making *as a matter of course.* Inertia then would begin to work on the side of the "good guys."

14 Moral Dilemma and Personal Choice

For many people, particularly students, the environmental issue understood: (a) as pollution and (b) as loss of social amenity, unite with an even deeper estrangement from the dominant modes and institutions of our industrial civilization. The prevalence of this alienation introduces a special element of paradox into their approach to the environmental problem and into their attitude toward various efforts at reform. They do not cavil about the dimensions and saliency of environmental degradation as do some of their seniors who are hesitant and unprepared to call into queston what they have so long taken for granted. The paradox takes the form of a latent contradiction between their search for a gratifying personal existence and their concern for the collective condition of society. For there are private answers to the perceived randomness and oppressive quality of modern society that do not respond to communal needs. To drop out and to tune in to one's inner self implies insulation from what is going on anywhere else but in the immediate surroundings. It is a statement of fatalistic rejection, of denial, a shout, or a whisper, or "no" cast into the world. The person who seeks authentic meaning within himself as an alternative to what society fails to provide will not engage himself in the task of rectifying the conditions that are the source of his grievance. Participation itself becomes disturbing and corrupting with its taint of compromise of aesthetic standard and ethical principle.

The response one makes to the spiritually impoverishing climate of the industrial system is likely to reflect, if it does not wholly depend on, the way one interprets the problem. Are these conditions the inevitable, inexorable outcome of patterns of thought and action so deeply rooted in modern civilization that there is little expectation that they can be attenuated or redirected? Or are they more in the way of a coincidental convergence of circumstance that once adjusted can be managed in the interest of more humane ends and purposes? If the condition of things is viewed as immutable, there is no reason to commit oneself to public action. In that case, it is every man for himself and the cultivation of one's own soul becomes not a selfish or restrictive act but the only sensible course to take. If on the other hand we perceive the problems as tractable, the industrial system as malleable in some significant respects, then the strain toward engagement and commitment takes on force and logic. It is under those circumstances that the estranged individaul must measure his hope of achievement for the collectivity against his inclination to privatize. For then the hardest choice is posed. Whereas there is the longing for realizing

145

one's better, more genuine self in a society fashioned by principles other than numerical efficiency and formal order, the cost might be a dulling of sensibilities and the paling of vision which are the sources of creative striving.

This dilemma, admittedly somewhat esoteric, is nevertheless real, and occasionally acute. Earlier we defined the intellectual by his self-observant awareness of conditions around him. He perceives the danger to individual personality in the industrial system and has had the luxury of leisure in which to become sensitized to the nuanced disposition of his own being. To work for change, to hope against hope in modifying the technical impluses of the society, or to do one's own thing and to seek private answers to the quest for meaning and gratification? This is the reformist dilemma. So rich in irony and paradox, it permits no predictable response. The factors that will determine the ultimate decision are several: material considerations and the need to make a living not least among them. (In part, it will depend on how tolerant one is of imperfection. Does active commitment to remedy only the most pernicious effects of environmental degradation warrant acceptance of social obligation?) But what we are referring to is more than a vocational choice—the decision to drop out and join a commune or work out one's destiny in Middle America. Rather, it is a question of the whole orientation of mind and personality. Is public action to assure the simple physical survival requisites sufficiently compelling to overcome the reluctance to enmesh oneself in a debilitating industrial system?

To state it in very mundane terms, the reformer's paradox is how much of the tedium that must be endured in pursuing any professional activity is an individual prepared to put up with? The hours spent in the time-consuming, soul-killing banalities of conferences, committees, brief writing and report compiling are a painful cost for a hypersensitized potential privatizer. How many hours in a committee room are worth a municipal regulation, imperfect to boot, to control industrial effluent into the local river?[a]

They are not the questions to ask of the potential radical actor. His dilemma is of a different order. In the radical view, environmental damage and the abuses of technology are neither inevitable nor coincidental. Instead, they are attributed to the callous self-interestedness of those ruling groups who benefit from the industrial system's present structure. As we outlined in our discussion

---

[a]One answer to the reformist dilemma is that exemplified by the culturally schizoid professional, outstanding among whom are the "hippie computer programers" found in places like San Fransisco and Cambridge. These are people who have dropped out of society insofar as they do not hold to the conventional values and behavioral norms of the society. Their private lives are idiosyncratic in the extreme. Yet they perform as skilled professionals because it is intellectually challenging and a source of sustenance. Normally they are engaged in work that is emotionally neutral and has no immediate social referrant. The schizophrenia is thus rendered tolerable. The morality and psychological viability of cultivating private responses to a social problem while lending one's talents to the mechanical operation of that society is a fascinating question, beyond the scope of these comments, however. The professional engaged in environmental problems, though, is permitted no such divorce of work from his private life.

of radical doctrine, there are formidable hurdles of logic and evidence to be overcome before a resurrected neo-Marxism can provide persuasive explanation of industrial society's contemporary ills, much less formulate guidelines for its reconstruction. It nevertheless remains captivating for those with an acute sense of personal grievance and keen social conscience. First, it offers the comfort of an established position. Marxist terms, concepts, and symbolism dominate contemporary radicalism. Whether it is existential, Maoist, or whatever in orientation, it lives in a vivid world of Marxist imagery (thus the illogical attachment to an unconvincing and inappropriate class analysis). Neo-Marxist doctrine carries a tradition that imparts broader meaning to discrete bits of social criticism and implies direction for action that otherwise is prone to be random, if not aimless. Indeed, it reinforces a commitment to action itself, as opposed to introspective insularity, by implying a moral obligation to extend the struggle for equality and human dignity. The kind of anomic disaffection characteristic of the rebel in the contemporary setting constantly poses to strategies for sustained political movement the threat of estrangement from any organizational effort, revolutionary included. The Marxist link creates a modicum of responsibility, even where disciplined organization is lacking.

As always, Marxism also offers something approximating an embracing intellectual system. The incomprehensibility of the condition in which the alienated person finds himself, the difficulty in using conventional ideas to conceptualize the problem, are sources of that common feeling about the meaninglessness of things. For all its distortion, revolutionary doctrine pretends to explain the whole. And where it cannot, it substitutes the force of moral imperatives.

There is a two fold paradox for the radical individual inspired by a very personal dislike for the system that is more aesthetic-spiritual than based on issues of injustice. First, given the deeply felt need for community and belonging, the movement is liable to satisfy its members' psychological purposes by the very fact of its existence without achieving programmatic ends. The latter remain poorly defined and the strategies rudimentary. But the radical meaning is in being there, rapping, sharing the good vibes and acting communally. Practical accomplishment, therefore, is often demonstrably slight. Second, just as there is meaning in community apart from achievement, so there is individual meaning in action apart from direction. To throw oneself body and soul, literally and figuratevely, against the establishment is as tangible an expression of grievance as possible. It is existential politics with a vengeance. Whereas the hippie bores within himself to discover something authentic or genuine without which he feels the neurosis of total randomness, the radical by contrast seeks meaning through action. It is the movement that counts, not the accomplishment of a practical plan or the attainment of the desired state. As the French radical students asserted, ideas for building something new would come en route. For the existential movement, the action of negation was sufficient.

There is yet another paradox more abstract but more fundamental and common to all the estranged potential political actors. It is the paradox of will and consciousness. Faced with the kind of encompassing environmental malaise that is widely perceived, and viewing the systematic obstacles to substantial change as arduous, if not insurmountable, the alienated feels two strong, antithetical impulses. The one is to seek his own solution privately. He feels viscerally that the only thing ultimately that counts is inner contentment whether it be achieved through introspection or existential politics. It is what you are and not what you are doing that determines the quality of your relationship to people and yourself with nature. The other is the instinct of a social being to affect his communal existence. The response can be the existentially active one of striking out at the object of grievance. Or it can take the form of considered efforts at fashioning a more favorable social setting. The impulses toward some form of action are strong.

There is first what we might term the *intellectual imperative*. Knowledge implies that it be acted upon. Once one is consciously aware of the reasons for discomfort and pain, however imperfect the analysis, it is difficult to reject. Responsibility follows knowledge. One does not readily forget or lose awareness once acquired. Private answers, if they are to be successful, require not just isolation but loss of memory.

Second, there is the *communal injunction.* Man is a social animal who does not cut himself off from society easily. He has a yearning to share feelings, thoughts, and experience. For most it is not enough to share them with one other person, or with a self-enclosed group of fellow communicants. It is almost impossible to do so when that relationship exists primarily in contradistinction to the surrounding madness. A viable existence seemingly requires some reconciliation of one's private self with social realities. Under present circumstances it means a certain tolerance of imperfection in all things temporal. The closer that individual perfection is approached the strain placed on tolerance is greater. We might be reminded that "he who seeks the salvation of souls, his own as well as others, should not seek it along the avenue of politics."[1] But what he can seek, and what he tends to feel socially compelled to seek, are the common conditions of life that favor, or at least permit the quest for personal salvation. The "ethic of ultimate ends" and the "ethic of responsibility" are always in somewhat tenuous relationship to each other but neither can they be left divorced.

To expect that a modern industrial society will approximate the utopia of aesthetes is fantasy. Public action can only hope to secure relatively more agreeable surroundings. Anything else would assume changes of an order and a swiftness that are historically unprecedented. For what would be needed is not programmatic reform but a thorough transformation of consciousness.

An illuminating analogy might be drawn between the dilemma of the pacifist and that of the aesthetic-perfectionist. The pacifist holds to a position of principled opposition to kill. He himself will not murder his fellow man under any circumstances. His activism properly takes the from of proselytization for the cause of nonviolence. Yet he knows that he lives in a world where few now accept that proposition. Their morality is more proximate. If his intellect leads him to study the world of international politics he is aware that war is not a random phenomenon; nor do all men who are not pacifists routinely kill each other. There are some attitudes, some doctrines, and some policies that are less likely to lead to war than others. There is no logical or moral contradiction for a man of this nature and inclination (and understanding) to lend his support to the course of action that holds the least potential for initiating violence and the damage it inflicts even if it does not exclude violence. Even as he attests to his pacifism and argues in its name, he can state preferences for that which, given the undeniable imperfections of man and states, will reduce death and suffering. Moral neutralism under the circumstances is denial of ethical responsibility.

Similarly, one who believes in a life totally uncorrupted by dehumanizing procedures and expedient compromise can build his private life on that principle, proselytize in the name of those standards and social ideals, and yet act to further efforts to remove the most dangerous of environmental conditions. Even if those efforts are imperfect in conception and less than ideal in objective, even if society is unlikely ever to exhibit those human feelings of which he individually is aware, the communal injunction dictates his aiding the cause.

Appendixes

Appendix A: Reductionism and Proceduralism

There is a striking parallel between the dominant proceduralism of our public institutions and the reductionist methodology that characterizes the social sciences. Just as the political system is fragmented into semiautonomous bureaucratic fiefs so is the universe of knowledge partitioned among scholarly specializations. As a consequence, there is a strong tendency arbitrarily to carve political issues into analytical parts without later resort to constructive synthesis. These parts are structured by academic field or even more narrowly within the scholarly confines of a particular discipline. In political science, for example, the theoretical and professional pressures combine to divert attention from systemic properties and to focus it on selective facets of American political life: electoral choice, legislative behavior, the procedures of bargaining and coalition formation, and so forth. The conservative bias expressed in taking the parameters of present arrangements and practices as given is as pronounced in the academic writing as it is in practice. If our manner of conducting the public business is rife with unstated preference and bias, so do political studies accept them uncritically. The upshot in practice is gross systemic irrationalities; in political science, it is failure to point out and to illuminate those same conditions.

Similarly, the political system's reliance on correct, i.e., democratic and workable, procedure at the expense of substantive output is matched by the academic's inordinate concern with method. Emphasis on elaborate means as the basis for acquiring knowledge, rather than on the theoretical understanding of political phenomena, is a species of formalistic proceduralism in its own right. It expresses the faith that a mechanical formula can be found that will achieve a stipulated goal (in this case knowledge and understanding) without individual, conscious comprehension. If the industrial system is a network of interlocking institutions, acting according to the organizational inertia of the modern administrative body, so is the academic world based on the principle that loosely linked congeries of specialization, wherein each perfects its methodology (organizational structure and regulations) can satisfy our societal needs in the way of organized knowledge.

To note another parallel: the confidence in "procedural fixes" to deal with problems when defects in the output of the system become undeniable has its analogue in the compulsive search for new methodologies, but less often theories, when our dominant formulations prove unable to predict or to explain adequately. Thus the "methodological fix."

Appendix B: Cultural Norm and Standards of Progress

It is illuminating to consider what kinds of comparative figures (among national societies or states or municipalities) are the source of pride and anxiety. Gross National Product is the most obvious; indexes of steel production or some other essential industrial indicator, e.g., power output, rank high as collective status symbols. Advanced technology as represented by space or nuclear engineering is another common source of prideful symbols. The former express our economic strength and promise material rewards. The latter are seen as evidence of our intellectual prowess and engender confidence in our ability to provide for the common security as well.

International competition in this league of industrial growth is a pervasive topic in legislative debates; in the utterances of statesmen promising either to "catch up," "stay ahead," or just to "do better;" and in electoral campaigns; as well as in economic texts. Enjoying an enormous lead in the standings, the United States appears as the perennial champion who methodically goes on, adding $30 or $40 billion a year to its total. In the area of advanced technology, the United States is more susceptible to competition. Although present research capability and the regular provision of heavy financial backing give us an advantage, there is always a new sphere of discovery opening up which creates yet another arena in which threats can develop to our scientific and/or technological machismo.

Periodically, we are treated to cries of alarm that the nation is failing to maintain its lead in some prestigious field or other, with the implication that the "good society" is that which has the biggest and newest of whatever our fertile, and well-financed expert minds can concoct. A striking example of this line of reasoning was offered in the spring of 1970 by the National Science Board, composed of prominent figures in the natural sciences, which advises the National Science Foundation—the federal agency that is the financial rudder of our nation's scientific efforts.[1] Bemoaning the slowdown in support of research and development (in fact, only a slowdown in rate of increase), their report sketched in vivid colors our national plight. If present trends continue, was the foreboding prognostication, the United States will no longer boast the world's largest high-energy particle accelerator; some European countries might match our use of modern chemical research instrumentation; and even our lead in space might be lost. In anticipating this day of reckoning for United States science, and by implication for the national well-being, the board's august members simply took for granted that the health of science and national well-being were one and the same. Their tone suggested that the contention was not open to any refutation or qualification. They were operating on the conventional wisdom that there is a natural flow of beneficence from science through technology to the production of more and better goods.

155

In fact, historically, most technical advances have not depended on basic scientific research. Nor is our prosperity at the present necessarily a function of innovative research in those fields more prominently noted. There is real question as to how crucial to general levels of affluence esoteric areas of technology like electronics and aerospace engineering are. Of the research fields selected for special attention by the NSB, "solid-state science, atomic and molecular physics, and astronomy," none would appear to have a direct bearing on normal industrial activity. As for a 250 GEV accelerator and space exploration, their economic utility is remote at best. The former, even by the testimony of its advocates, is a indulgent piece of experimental equipment for theoretical physicists whose work is purely academic. The latter's costs are well established, and out of all proportion to the benefits in practical engineering spinoff. Both projects' primary economic function seems to be to consume huge quantities of national wealth that could better be devoted to other capital infrastructures; hospitals, mass transit, sewage systems, and so forth. Similarly, the funds urged for *pure research* in these nonfunctional, if intellectually gratifying fields, could be more fruitfully channeled into studying the chemistry, physics, biology, and engineering of pollution control and environmental management.

The episode of the National Science Board underscores our point about the distorted character of our society's dominant indicators of progress and well-being. At present, for those who determine the allocation of resources, they are economic growth and technical virtuosity. Others are conceivable, and rather more persuasive as standards for the good society; infant mortality, longevity, malnutrition, suicide, alcoholism, psychic disorder, to name a few. Each of these allows for some objective measure and minimizes the difficulties in assessing the aesthetics of "the quality of life." Of course, an indicator like longevity has its own ambiguities. It can be viewed in good part as a function of medical technology; and it is certainly possible for people to live long *miserable* lives. Suicide rates also are open to multiple interpretations and need to be placed in cultural context. Nonetheless, this straightforward set of indicators is almost assuredly a better measure of collective well-being and national good than the size of our largest nuclear accelerator or the number of automobiles per capita. That would seem to be a simple enough, commonsensical proposition. Yet where in our public life, in the press, in political debate, does one find these comparative statistics receiving a fraction of the attention, evoking any portion of the concern, elicited by the figures on GNP, growth rate, and rocket thrusts?

Within the last several years, the United States has dropped to fourteenth place among the nations of the world with regard to life expectancy, just below Greece and Bulgaria. We hold only a slightly higher rank in the standing of infant mortality. One could imagine the breast-beating and public soul-searching if we were to find ourselves at such a low position in the table of industrial productivity. Of course, matters would never be allowed to come to that pass.

So sensitive are we to those latter indicators that strenuous efforts to restore our place at the top of the heap would be launched immediately. As it is, social decline—in the instance of life expectancy itself on an absolute as well as on a comparative scale—of the former type is seemingly worthy only of academic study and statistical notation. No National Science Board, or its equivalent, has come forth with a forceful, publicized call to action. Our present National Science Board rarely even acknowledges the requirements for social research (while also downplaying the biological sciences). As constituted, and given its rigid conception of science, it hardly could be expected to be responsive to anything as "intangible" as longevity or the psychic health of the citizenry whose nation enjoys facilities to shoot atomic particles faster than anybody else can.

The bias is similar to one we have noted in other areas. Institutional mechanisms are so structured as to monitor certain kinds of events rather than others. The implicit determinants of consequence are the open-ended commitment to growth and technological virtuosity. Our conceptual technique more easily defines readily quantifiable, material factors than the intangibles, if not always unquantifiable condition of amenity and health. And some problems are simpler to solve than others. If the United States is falling behind in theoretical physics, then the solution is simple: use our resources and talents to build a larger, superior facility. But what is the ready answer to reduced longevity, to use the most basic of our social indicators? Improve health services? Yes, in part. That in itself requires a more difficult political strategy and entails more social strain than constructing a 250 GEV accelerator. Moreover, there are important environmental elements that impinge on health—e.g., psychological strain and social pressure resulting from our industrial life style—that are neither easily comprehended nor easily controlled. Imagine the challenge of estimating, assessing, and acting upon the social-psychological maladies created by the industrial system. At the moment, we do not have the knowledge or the conception of health required to act intelligently. Nor do we have the will. However, we do have some negative knowledge. Certain conditions are clearly deleterious and damaging to health: air and water pollution outstanding among them. We can go a long way to improve these conditions just by refraining from doing certain things. There our will could be meaningfully applied. Our political and economic structures, and the theories that propel them, are impediments to generating that will.

Appendix C: The Scientist

The paradoxes of the intellectual as potential actor are most evident among scientists. They are the personifications of the rational positivism that is modern society's intellectual trademark. Their methods, their achievement in advancing knowledge, the profound impact—for both good and evil—of their discoveries, and their consonant prestige in society, combine to give them a very special place in the industrial system. Their success is unique, as is public recognition of it.

It is not surprising, therefore, that scientists now should find themselves in a quandry as to the ultimate purposes and moral consequences of their work. Their dilemma is that of our whole civilization. At a time of growing pessimism, they are characteristically optimists. Steeped in a tradition that understands knowledge to be a good in itself, they find mounting fears that the acceleration of knowledge is taking man's fate out of his own hands and possibly leading us to dire ends. Accustomed to believe that progress is desirable by definition, they are now troubled by widespread doubts as to whether the gain is not outweighed by painful and potentially disastrous costs.[1]

The abuse of intellectual power and technological means is having its repercussions for science, as a profession, whereas the more appropriate culprit (if we were to think in terms of individual or collective guilt) is the technologist. But science and technology are so closely linked in the public mind, and in many scientific minds as well, that scientists tend to see in the attack on runaway technology an attack on the scientific enterprise itself. Science and restraint do not go well together. Talk of slowing down the production of knowledge, of directing research into more beneficial areas, combined with the retrenchment in the government science budget, have aroused a mild paranoia. Recent public manifestations of a general disenchantment touch a sensitive nerve among scientists whose own personal sense of meaning is closely tied to the dominant imagery of science serving human advancement in the vanguard of progress. Comments to the effect that "science gives man everything to live with but nothing to live for" strike to the quick of men whose lives are defined largely in professional terms.

In fact, there are some differences in philosophical outlook and vocational orientation between scientists and engineers or technologists. Science is the mastery of knowledge, technology is the mastery of mechanical devices. The later's work is more immediate to practical application, he is more engaged in technique, and less likely to see his labor in philosophical terms.[a] Many scientists

---

[a]We should also note significant differences in overall outlook on the world between physical scientists (and engineers) and biological sciences. The former share the modern vision of man as the master of nature and believe in his capacity to domesticate it for his own ends. The biologist is much more cautionary in his approach to nature. He is aware of

159

find it easy to cultivate a humanism, even if it is often a bland variety that exists cosily with their socially neutral scholarship. Today they feel an increasing estrangement from an increasingly critical public. The sensation mounts that scientists and nonscientists are no longer speaking the same language, that there is a breakdown in communication because their concepts and premises are not mutually comprehensible. Actually, there is probably less incomprehension than disagreement. Ever so gradually, the public's confidence in the common cultural values that the scientist exemplifies is being frittered away. Until very recently, most people understood their world in terms that were popular extensions of the same optimistic, positivist view that largely inspires science. It is the qualification of their universal public acceptance that disturbs many scientists. It leads some to activism in antiwar and ecological causes; among others it only engenders incomprehension.

Outstanding scientists are among the leading figures in the attack on the abuses of technology in defining the moral issues of nuclear weapons and in trumpeting the environmental cause. These men are carrying on the classic scientific tradition. For centuries the scientists' self-definition was a humanistic one. They saw their work as a labor of intellectual love whose practical applications were either nonexistent or of no regard. Technology in the eighteenth and nineteenth centuries, for the most part, developed independently of scientific discovery, and inventors were disdained intellectually and socially. Science was the elegant, cultured occupation of gentlemen. Their sense of status was not primarily dependent on utilitarian accomplishment. Indeed, they were often proprietary of the knowledge, integral as it was to their humanist self-image. Some residue of this attitude is found in their belief of a special responsibility for overseeing the public uses of their expertise. Nowadays it is

the fragile balance of nature, its sensitivity to ecological disequilibrium. His imagery is more organic than mechanical. The physicist tends to see the universe in terms of structured patterns whose components can be separated and reformed. Intellectual mastery is a likely prelude to manipulation. By contrast, the biologist's world is one of endlessly subtle interdependent functions, none of which can be affected without producing ramifying changes throughout. His watchwords are adjustment and accomodation: the danger is aberrant mutation. The physicist is prone to think in terms of control, the danger is imperfect fabrication. Man for the biologist lives in a finite world, part of a balanced natural system. The former accordingly sees a wider latitude for man's assertion on nature; nature is less vulnerable to imbalance. Although the physicist too knows the physical universe to be finite, it might be fair to say that he nevertheless sees near infinite possibilities for human endeavor. These differences manifest themselves on the environmental issue. The physicist is attracted by solutions that entail technical adjustment; he is chary of any limitations on technological development and controls on the uses of knowledge of any sort. The biologist is more likely to profess both individual and professional concern about ecological damage. (Biologists too are rationalists in method and study, but less positivist in regard to the active application of scientific knowledge to generate change. Here there is a certain strain between the structure and method of their research and the implication for human initiative that its subject-matter suggests. Thus their positivism is one with the growth and progress ethic of the culture. But they are intellectually better prepared to consider social ideas involving steady-state concepts).

also inspired by pride in their intellectual perspicacity. But science, like many another formerly elite vocation, has become institutionalized. With the rare exception of creative geniuses, scientific activity is routinized and professionalized. Humanism becomes a purely personal affair in proportion to this institutionalization, with its implications of specialization, organization, and occupational exclusiveness. Thus, apart from a unique competence in certain specialized areas of public concern, the scientist is professionally no better prepared to exercise tutelary guidance over, or to manage, the social effects of his research than any other expert.

Notes

Notes to Introduction

1. These philosophical and social paradoxes have been the subject of much contemporary thought, some of it illuminating. See especially Lewis Mumford, *The Transformation of Man* (New York: Collier, 1954), *The Pentagon of Power* (New York: Harcourt, Brace and Jovanovich, 1970), and *The City in History* (New York: Harcourt, Brace and Jovanovich, 1961); Jacques Ellul, *The Technological Order* (New York: Random House, 1959); René Dubos "Science and Man's Nature," *Daedalus,* Winter 1965; Kenneth Boulding "The Scientific Revelation," *Bulletin of the Atomic Scientists,* September 1970; and "The Dodo Didn't Make It: Survival and Betterment," *Bulletin of the Atomic Scientists,* May 1971; Lynn White, Jr. "The Historical Roots of Our Ecological Crisis," *Science* 155, March 10, 1969.

2. The initial effort to provide an overview of environmental effects was made in *Man's Impact on the Global Environment,* SCEP Report (Cambridge: MIT Press, 1970). More specific studies now have begun to appear in profusion. An excellent example, and one that carefully considers the imprecision in assessing environmental conditions, is *Air Quality Criteria and Guides for Urban Air Pollutants,* Report of a WHO Expert Committee (Geneva: World Health Organization Technical Report, Series No. 506. 1972).

3. The heraldic call to alarm about the population crisis is Paul R. Ehrlich's *The Population Bomb* (New York: Ballantine, 1968). The seriousness of population growth even in affluent Western societies is soberly outlined in *Population Growth and America's Future,* Commission on Population Growth and America's Future (Washington, D.C.: GPO, 1971).

4. Barry Commoner, *The Closing Circle* (New York: Knopf, 1971), ch. 8. See also his *Science and Society* (New York: Viking, 1968).
The classic statement of the conventional position linking population growth to environmental deterioration is Paul and Anne Ehrlich, *Population, Resources, and Environment* (New York: W.H. Freeman, 1970). See his exchange with Commoner in *Environment,* May 1972.

5. Dennis L. Meadows et al., *The Limits of Growth* (Cambridge, MIT Press, 1972). The problem was introduced in philosophical terms in the classic article of Kenneth Boulding, "The Economics of the Coming Spaceship Earth" in *Environmental Quality in a Growing Economy,* ed. Henry Jarrett (Baltimore: Johns Hopkins University Press, 1966). See also Hans H. Landsberg, Leonard L. Fischman, and Joseph L. Fisher, *Resources in America's Future-Patterns of Requirements and Availability: 1960-2000.* (Johns Hopkins for Resources for the Future, Ltd.) The Meadows conclusions have been criticized by the study at the University of Sussex excerpted in *Futures* (IPC: Science and Technology Press) February 1973.

163

Notes to Chapter 1
The Problem As System

1. Some of these issues were adumbrated by John Kenneth Galbraith in *The Affluent Society* (Boston: Houghton Mifflin, 1959).

2. For preliminary statements of this problem, see Donald N. Michael, *The Unprepared Society: Planning for a Precarious Future* (New York: Basic Books, 1968), and Lynton K. Caldwell *Environment: A Challenge to Modern Society* (New York: The Natural History Press, 1970).

3. John Kenneth Galbraith, *The New Industrial State* (Boston: Houghton Mifflin, 1967).

4. There are special features of American politics that exacerbate fragmentation and favor policy built around factional interest: the sharp separation of presidential and congressional authority, the decentralization of our parties, our liberal political traditions that emphasize procedure while downplaying doctrine, etc. They are all well known to students of American politics. Yet I believe our analysis is applicable, with only minor qualifications, to societies whose politics do not exhibit these distinctive American features, e.g., Great Britain, West Germany, France. The systemic properties common to all industrial democracies bulk larger in any analysis of environmental problems than do peculiarities of structure and political culture.

5. I discuss the element of economic corporatism in industrial, democratic politics in "Functional Representation and Interest Group Politics," *Comparative Politics,* October 1969.

6. The result is what Galbraith has aptly called "private affluence and public squalor," in *The Affluent Society.*

7. Quoted in *New York Times* editorial, March 9, 1972.

8. The shifting pattern of popular response to changing surroundings is considered in Hans Huth, *Nature and the American: Three Centuries of Changing Attitudes* (Berkeley: University of California Press, 1957). See also Roderick Nash, *Wilderness and the American Mind* (New Haven: Yale University Press, 1967).

Notes to Chapter 2
Pluralism and American Politics

1. The attitudes, concepts, and presuppositions we identify as pluralist are so pervasive in the writing of both scholars and nonacademic commentators that even a representative listing would be excessive. Seminal influences and characteristic works are: Robert Dahl, *A Preface to Democratic Theory* (Englewood Cliffs: Prentice Hall, 1965); *Modern Political Analysis* (Englewood

Cliffs: Prentice Hall, 1970); A. Kornhauser, *The Politics of Mass Society* (Glencoe: Free Press, 1959); David Truman *The Governmental Process* (New York: Knopf, 1951); Robert Lane, *Political Man* (New Haven: Yale University Press, 1962); Daniel Bell, "Notes on The Post-Industrial Society," in *The Public Interest* 1, no. 2, April 1967.

2. A sketch of the economic management of postindustrial society can be found in the comparative study of Andrew Schonfield, *Modern Capitalism* (New York: Oxford University Press, 1965). See also the critical essay of Robert Heilbroner, "What Is the Post-Industrial Society?" *Dissent,* Spring 1973.

3. See the considered analysis of Peter Bachrach, *The Theory of Democratic Elitism, A Critique* (Boston: Little, Brown, 1967). The more avowedly radical position is found in S.E. Gettleman and D. Mermelstein, eds. *The Great Society Reader: The Failure of American Liberalism* (New York: Praeger, 1962). Gettleman and Mermelstein have edited a companion volume *Economics: Mainstream Readings and Radical Critiques* (New York: Random House, 1970).

4. Sheldon, Wolin, *Politics and Vision* (New York: John Wylie, 1960).

5. Representative of this view is Aaron Wildavsky, "Aesthetic Power or the Triumph of the Sensitive Majority Over the Vulgar Mass" in *Daedalus,* Fall 1967 (which we discuss in detail in ch. 4).

Notes to Chapter 3
Incrementalism and the Distrust of Reasoned Policy-making

1. David Braybrooke and Charles Lindblom, *A Strategy of Decision* (Glencoe: Free Press, 1963); Lindblom, *The Intelligence of Democracy* (New York: Macmillan, 1965); Lindblom, *The Policy-Making Process* (Englewood Cliffs: Prentice Hall, 1968); Lindblom, "The Science of Muddling Through," *Public Administration Review,* 19, Spring 1959. See also the commentary of Yezehal Dror, "Muddling Through: Science or Inertia?" in *Public Administration Review* 26 September 1964.

2. Among the classic texts on organization theory are Peter M. Blau and W. Richard Scott, *Formal Organization* (San Francisco: Chandler Publishing Company, 1962) and Herbert Simon, *Models of Man.* The effort at updating and amending is both considered by, and reflected in, the work of Peter Drucker, *The Age of Discontinuity* (London: Heineman, 1969). The impression of theorists' preoccupation with the nuancing of models is reinforced by a perusal of journals in the field, e.g., *The Administrative Science Quarterly.* Michel Crozier's *The Bureaucratic Phenomenon* (Chicago University Press, 1967), an analysis of comparative bureaucratic styles is a notable exception. Aaron Wildavsky's *The Budgetary Process* (Boston: Little, Brown, 1964) stands out as a knowledgeable and finely attuned account of congressional decision-making. A

more sophisticated approach to policy-making, if still within the conventional frame, is Raymond A. Bauer and Kenneth S. Bergen, eds., *The Study of Policy Formation* (New York: Free Press, 1968).

3. Graham T. Allison *The Essence of Decision* (Boston: Little, Brown, 1971). In his impressive attempt to develop a typology of policy-making modes, Allison establishes the appropriateness of using variations of incremental analysis to study foreign policy decisions. However, he does not assess the desirability of present outcomes nor analyze the requirements for innovative policy.

4. Braybrooke and Lindblom, *Strategy of Decision,* p. 118, 81. Copyright © 1963 by the Free Press of Glencoe, a Division of Macmillan and Co., Inc. Reprinted with permission.

5. Ibid., p. 84.

6. Ibid., p. 88.

7. Ibid., p. 116.

8. Ibid., ch. 10.

9. Ibid., p. 134.

10. Ibid., p. 138.

11. Ibid., p. 126.

12. Ibid., p. 126.

13. Ibid., p. 129.

14. Charles L. Schultze, *The Politics and Economics of Public Spending,* (Washington, D.C.: Brookings Institution, 1970), p. 61. © 1970 by the Brookings Institution, Washington, D.C.

15. Aaron Wildavsky, "The Political Economy of Efficiency: Cost-Benefit Analysis, Systems Analysis, and Program Budgeting," in *Political Science and Public Policy,* ed. Austin Ranney (Chicago: Markham Publishing Co., 1968), p. 80.

16. Schultze, *Politics and Economics*, p. 62.

17. The problem of innovation is examined in a narrower organizational framework in Jerald Hage and Michael Aiken *Social Changes In Complex Organizations* (New York: Random House, 1970) and Victor A. Thompson, *Bureaucracy and Innovation* (University of Alabama Press, 1969).

Notes to Chapter 4
Economics and the Externality Problem

1. Charles Kindleberger, *Power and Money* (New York: Basic Books, 1970), p. 3.

2. For an attempt at extending the economic theory of choice, see Peter C. Fishburn, *Utility Theory For Decision-Making* (New York: Wiley, 1970).

3. Attributed in private conversation.

4. Nathaniel Wollman, "The New Economics of Resources," *Daedalus,* Fall 1967, p. 1100.

5. Ezra Mishan, *Technology and Growth: The Price We Pay* (New York: Praeger, 1969). See also the more favorable view of economic theory's capacity to handle externalities, R.V. Ayres and A.V. Kneese, "Production, Consumption and Externalities," *American Economic Review* 59, no. 3 (June 1969).

6. Ibid.

7. Richard Coffmann, "Economics, Ecology and Political Decisions," *Bulletin of the Atomic Scientists,* April 1971, p. 4.

8. Peter Self, *Administrative Theories and Practices* (London: George Allen and Unwin Ltd., 1972), p. 269. Some references on the problem of "welfare economics" and analogous efforts at employing cost-benefit analysis in an environmental context are: H.M. Bird, *The Economics of the Environment, A Survey* (London: Centre for Environmental Studies) Wns. 329, 330, 331, 332, and 333, August 1972; P. Bohm and A.V. Kneese, eds. *The Economics of Environment* (New York: St. Martin, 1972); D.W. Pearce, *Cost-Benefit Analysis* (London: Macmillan, 1971); A.R. Prest and R. Turvey "Cost-Benefit Analysis, A Survey," *Economic Journal* 75, no. 300, December 1965; J. Rothenberg, "The Economics of Congestion and Pollution: An Integrated View," *American Economic Review* 60, no. 2, May 1970; C. Tisdell "On the Theory of Externalities," *Economic Record* 46, no. 113, March 1970. For a critical review, see E.J. Mishan, *Cost-Benefit Analysis* (George Allen and Unwin Ltd., 1971); and "Pangloss on Pollution," *Swedish Journal of Economics* 73, no. 1, March 1971.

Some early attempts at applying economic theory to environmental problems are contained in: Harold Wolozin, ed. *The Economics of Air Pollution* (New York: W.W. Norton, 1964). More general discussion of the problem, most of it from a conventional theoretical perspective, is found in: Allen V. Kneese, "Background for Economic Analysis of Environmental Pollution," in *Swedish Journal of Economics,* March 1971; and *Problems of Environmental Economics* (Paris: OECD, 1972), especially the paper by Wilfred Beckerman. See also Beckerman's "Economists, Scientists, and Environmental Catastrophe," *Oxford Economic Papers,* November 1972, in which he soberly considers the need for adjustment of economic theory while simultaneously waxing optimistic about the laws of economics assuring avoidance of environmental catastrophe.

9. Coffman, *Economics,* p. 4.

10. This approach is presented, and the example noted, by John Maddox, *The Doomsday Syndrome* (London: Macmillan, 1972), pp. 147-49.

11. See Landsberg, Fischman, and Fischer, *Resources in America's Future Patterns;* R.U. Ayres and A.V. Kneese, "Pollution and Environmental Quality," in H.S. Perloff, ed., *The Quality of the Urban Environment* (Johns Hopkins Press for Resources for the Future).

12. Economic theory's enshrining of the market concept, and the assumption of an operative market even where one does not exist, is the critical theme of Joan Robinson, *Economic Heresies: Some Old-Fashioned Questions in Economic Theory* (New York: Basic Books, 1970). For a rare theoretical defense of the concept of public goods and attempt to integrate the group theory of political science with the economic concept of interest, see Mancur Olson, *The Logic of Collective Action* (Cambridge: Harvard Economic Series, 1965).

13. Wollman, "New Economics," p. 1110.

14. *Problems of Environmental Economics*, OECD.

15. Mishan, *Technology and Growth*, p. 52.

16. *New York Times*, February 12, 1972.

17. Wollman, "New Economics," p. 1111.

18. Again it is Kenneth Boulding who has pointed up the distortions and inadequacies of conventional theory: "Fun and Games with the Gross National Product—The Role of Misleading Indicators in Social Policy" in *The Environmental Crisis*, ed. Harold W. Helfrach, Jr. (New Haven: Yale University Press).

19. E. Boulding, *Economics As a Science* (New York: McGraw Hill, 1970).

20. Robert O. Overbury, "A Closed System Economy," *Nature*, April 27, 1973.

21. Aaron Wildavsky, "Aesthetic Power or the Triumph of the Sensitive Majority Over the Vulgar Mass," *Daedalus*, Fall 1967.

22. Ibid., p. 1115.

23. Ibid., p. 1121.

24. Ibid., p. 1122.

Notes to Chapter 5
The Environmental Protection Agency: An Attempt at Environmental Management

1. Message of the President, July 9, 1970.

2. *New York Times*, December 3, 1971.

3. *New York Times*, January 28, 1972.

4. *Washington Post*, October 16, 1971.

5. *Washington Post*, March 16, 1971.

6. Wildavsky, "Aesthetic Power," p. 1126.

7. *New York Times*, December 7, 1970.

8. *Second Annual Report*, p. 310.

9. Ibid., p. 327.

10. *New York Times*, May 4, 1971.

11. President Nixon's Energy Message to Congress April 19, 1973. A useful, independent analysis of electricity demand is "Electricity Demand Growth and the Energy Crisis," *Science* 17, November 1972.

12. Ibid., p. 8.

13. See the *New York Times,* June 4, 1973.

14. Nixon, Energy Message, p. 2.

15. See Alvin Weinberg, "Nuclear Hazards and Safety," *Bulletin of the Atomic Scientists,* December 1970. The debate over safety hazards continues, the question being liable to new data and interpretations.

16. See the excellent case study by Dorothy Nelkin, *The Cayuga Lake Nuclear Power Controversy* (Ithaca: Cornell University Press, 1971).

17. April 14, 1970.

18. See Stanford Research Institute, "Patterns of Energy Consumption in the U.S." (Office of Science and Technology, Washington, D.C., 1972); and Anthony Tucker "Fuel's Paradise?" *Guardian,* March 7, 1973.

Notes to Chapter 6
Transportation

1. A cautious discussion of some of these issues is contained in *OECD Fourth International Symposium on Theory and Practice in Transport Economics* (Paris: November 1972).

2. The strength of the highway lobby was exhibited in the fall of 1971 when Congress voted to transfer $350 million in alcohol tax revenues to the HTF as compensation for repeal of the excise tax on light trucks. (The action also punctured the defense often made for the HTF that its full coffers express economic transportation realities.) With entrenched power of this sort, there is little reason to look optimistically on more positive developments such as the recent Department of Transportation Report acknowledging the logic of emphasizing mass transit in future planning (*New York Times,* September 15, 1971).

3. See the comparative figures in the Brookings Institution's *Setting National Priorities: The 1973 Budget* (Washington: 1972).

4. Of the $900 million allocated for 1971, the administration chose to grant only $600; requests stood at $2.6 billion.

5. A sober review of revenue-sharing is Edward C. Banfield, "Revenue Sharing in Theory and Practice," *The Public Interest,* Spring 1971.

6. Theodore Lowi, *The End of Liberalism* (New York: W.W. Norton, 1969).

7. *New York Times,* March 18, 1971.

8. *New York Times,* June 15, 1971.

Notes to Chapter 7
Planning, PPBS, and Environmental Policy

1. Schultze, *Politics and Economics,* p. 7.

2. Ibid.

3. Ibid., p. 16.

4. See Arthur Maas, "Cost-Benefit Analysis, Its Relevance to Public Interest Decisions," *Quarterly Journal of Economics* 80 (May 1966).

5. These themes are treated to the context of regional planning in Harold Gillians, "The Fallacy of Single-Purpose Planning," *Daedalus,* Fall 1967.

6. Daniel Bell, ed., *Toward The Year 2000: Work in Progress,* (Boston: Houghton Mifflin, 1967). p. 5.

7. Raymond Aron, *Progress and Disillusion* (New York: Praeger, 1968), p. xi.

8. Galbraith, *New Industrial State,* p. 12.

Notes to Chapter 8
Legislative and Administrative Procedures: Costs

1. *New York Times,* editorial, November 14, 1970.

2. *New York Times,* July 19, 1971.

3. *Environmental Quality 1972,* pp. 278-79.

4. See the discussion of recent developments in *Environmental Quality, Second Annual Report,* ch. 5.

5. Grad makes the useful distinction between decentralization of authority to set standards and local enforcement powers in Frank P. Grad, et al, *Environmental Control: Priorities, Policies & the Law* (New York: Columbia University Press, 1971), p. 102. It is possible, and perhaps feasible, to combine a central determination of baselines and tolerances, as through the EPA, while allowing states and municipalities to devise the most effective means of enforcement locally. In practice, this is the present policy with regard to Clean Air Standards. Apart from the problem of oversight, it does have the liability of failing to assure active federal support for these ancillary programs essential to curb emissions.

6. *Environmental Quality 1971,* p. 138. See also the Brookings Institution, *Setting National Priorities: The 1973 Budget,* ch. 11.

7. *Second Annual Report,* p. 102.

8. Ibid., p. 89.

9. Ibid., p. 122.

10. *New York Times,* October 31, 1971.

11. See an incisive analysis of its limitations, "White House Presents Vapid Technology Plan," in *Science,* March 24, 1972. Various proposals have been made for endowing the EPA with its own research arm. The most persuasive is "A Program to Coordinate Environmental Research," by Bowers, Hohenberg, Likens, Lynn, Nelkin and Nelkin, in *American Scientist* 59, no. 2 (March-April, 1971).

12. The *Second Annual Report*'s extension discussion of "The Economy and the Environment," ch. 4, seems to assume that costs incurred by industry will be passed on to the consumer routinely, p. 126.

13. Robert Dahl, *After the Revolution* (New Haven: Yale University Press, 1971).

14. For a different view, see Rathjens in *Grad,* p. 34.

Notes to Chapter 9
Technology Assessment and Political Choice

1. *Technology: Processes of Assessment and Choice,* report of the National Academy of Sciences (Washington, D.C.: GPO, 1969).

2. Ibid., p. 3.

3. Ibid., p. 102.

4. *New York Times,* March 22, 1970.

5. *Technology: Processes,* pp. 80-81.

6. Ibid., p. 100.

7. Ibid., p. 48.

8. Ibid., p. 8.

9. Ibid., p. 15.

10. See Solly Zuckerman, "Science, Technology and Environmental Management," address to *International Institute for Environmental Affairs,* Stockholm, June 13, 1972.

11. *Technology: Processes,* p. 45.

12. Ibid., p. 48.

13. Ibid., p. 95.

14. *Science, Growth and Society: A New Perspective* (Paris: OECD, 1971).

15. Ibid., p. 15.

16. Ibid., p. 27.

17. Ibid., p. 39.

Notes to Chapter 10
Welfarists and Environmentalists: Another Liberal Dilemma

1. A rather considerable literature on environmental politics has appeared in the past few years. Rather little of it is analytically critical; its utility is either descriptive or an expression of a particular outlook. In the former category are: Davies, *The Politics of Pollution* (New York: Pegasus, 1971); Crenson, *The Un-Politics of Air Pollution* (Baltimore: Johns Hopkins, 1970); and Ridgeway, *The Politics of Ecology* (New York: Dutton, 1971). Readers in this category include: Roos *The Politics of Ecoside* (New York: Holt, Rinehart, 1970) and Foss, *Politics and Ecology* (Duxbury: Duxbury Press, 1972). A collection of largely radical, pro and antiecology, views is found in Jones, ed. *Finding Community* (Free Press, 1972), especially the articles by Nathan Hare and Barry Weisberg. A superior analytical assessment of the energy facet of the environmental problem is Gerald Garvey et al. *Energy, Ecology Economy: A Framework For Environmental Policy* (New York: Norton, 1972). Although not specifically related to the political and institutional requirements for effective environmental policy-making, Theodore Lowi's *The Politics of Disorder* (New York: Basic Books, 1971) notes how unrestrained interest competition distorts the political process.

2. Charles Reich, *The Greening of America* (New York: Random House, 1970).

3. A cogent statement of this divergence in outlook was recently made by Larry O'Brien, "The 'Ecology' of the Slums," *New York Times,* June 6, 1971. See also Jones, ed. *Finding Community.*

4. A striking example of this criticism from a more radical perspective is Richard Neuhaus *In Defense of People* (New York: Macmillan, 1971).

5. The recent Brookings Study, *Setting National Priorities, The 1973 Budget,* demonstrates the very considerable sums that would fill Treasury coffers were the most rudimentary tax reforms made. It points out that if 1959 tax rates prevailed (i.e., the late Eisenhower years, hardly a period of rampant socialism), annual receipts for 1972 would have been $23 billion greater.

6. See the story in the *New York Times,* May 25, 1971; estimates in the several tens of billions are also made in *Environmental Quality, Second Annual Report* of the Council on Environmental Quality, (Washington, D.C., GPO, 1971).

The split between welfarists and environmentalists has not gone unnoticed by those interests more directly threatened by pollution control measures. Witness the power companies' readiness to call upon the poor in defense of their uninhibited construction of polluting facilities. As an executive of the Nevada Power Company argued before the Senate Interior Committee investigating the unrestricted emissions of the huge plants recently built in the southwest, "although some people might be able to reduce their use of electricity marginally, there are a substantial number of disadvantaged Americans whose quality of life need desperately to be improved," (*New York Times,* May 25, 1971). One cannot help but wonder how much concern Nevada Power evinced about the social inequity represented by the dirth of refrigerators in homes of the underprivileged before coming under attack by the ecology forces.

7. The National Urban Coalition, *Counter Budget* (New York: Praeger, 1971).

8. Ibid., p. 160.

9. Ibid., p. 169.

10. Abundant evidence of the concentration of air pollution in the central city is provided by CEQ, *Second Annual Report,* pp. 191-96.

Notes to Chapter 11
Radical Doctrine and the Environment

1. A few characteristic works are: Robert Dahl, *A Preface to Democratic Theory* (Englewood Cliffs: Prentice Hall, 1965); Seymon Marlon Lipset, *Political Man* (New York: Doubleday, 1961); Clark Kerr, *Industrialism and Industrial Man* (New York: 1964); and Daniel Bell (ed.), *End of Ideology* (New York: Doubleday, 1962).

2. John Kenneth Galbraith, *The New Industrial State* (Boston: Houghton Mifflin, 1967); Lewis Mumford, *The Transformation of Man* (New York: Collier, 1964), *The Myth of the Machine* (New York: Harcourt, Brace and World, 1960); *The Pentagon of Power* (New York: Harcourt, Brace and World, 1970).

3. Daniel and G. Cohn-Bendit, *Obsolete Communism: The Left-Wing Alternative* (New York: McGraw-Hill, 1969), p. 6.

4. Norman Birnbaum, *The Crises of Industrial Society* (New York: Oxford University Press, 1969); Herbert Marcuse, especially *One-Dimensional Man* (Boston: Beacon, 1964); John McDermott, "Technology: The Opiate of the Intellectual," in *New York Review of Books,* July 31, 1969.

5. McDermott, Ibid.

6. Ibid.

7. Ibid.

8. Ibid.

9. Galbraith, *New Industrial State,* p. 62. Copyright © 1967, 1971 by John Kenneth Galbraith. Reprinted by permission of Houghton Mifflin Company. Also reprinted by permission of Andre Deutsch Ltd.

10. Ibid., p. 161.

11. Birnbaum, *Crises,* p. 2.

12. Raymond Aron, *Progress and Disillusion* (New York: Praeger, 1968), p. 128.

13. One of the few informed works on the subject is Ichak Adizes, *Industrial Democracy: Yugoslav Style* (New York: Free Press, 1971). See also Jaroslav Vanek *Participatory Economy: An Evolutionary Hypothesis* (Ithaca: Cornell University Press, 1971).

Notes to Chapter 12
Institutions and Public Policy

1. *Science, Growth and Society,* OECD.

2. Ibid.

Notes to Chapter 13
Knowledge and Education

1. Galbraith, *New Industrial State,* p. 302.

2. Ibid., p. 292.

3. Ibid., p. 291.

4. Ibid., p. 295.

5. Ibid., p. 345.

6. René Dubos, *Reason Awake* (New York: Columbia University Press, 1970), p. 37.

7. Galbraith, *New Industrial State,* p. 292.

8. Erik Erickson, "Memorandum on Youth," in *Toward the Year 2000, Daedalus,* Summer 1967, p. 864.

9. Dubos, *Reason Awake,* p. 235.

10. Ibid., p. 143.

11. An excellent assessment of RANN and related programs' potential is offered by Harvey Brooks, "Knowledge and Action: The Dilemma of Science Policy in the 1970's" in *Daedalus,* Spring 1973. See also the classic article of A.M. Weinberg, "Criteria for Scientific Choice," in E. Shils, ed., *Criteria for Scientific Development: Public Policy and National Goals* (Cambridge: MIT Press, 1968), and Jean-Jacques Salomon, "Science Policy and Its Myths: The Allocation of Resources," in *Public Policy* 20, no. 1, Winter 1972.

Notes to Chapter 14
Moral Dilemma and Personal Choice

1. Max Weber, "Politics As a Vocation," *Essays in Sociology* in *From Max Weber,* eds. Gerth and Mills (New York: Oxford University Press, 1958).

Notes to Appendix B
Cultural Norm and Standards of Progress

1. Report of the National Science Board, in *New York Times,* May 7, 1970.

Notes to Appendix C
The Scientist

1. The mixture of disquiet and faith that is so much the mood of the scientific community is poignantly stated in an article by Eugene Rabinovitch, "The Mounting Tide of Unreason," in *Bulletin of the Atomic Scientists,* May 1971.

Index

About the Author

Michael J. Brenner received the Ph.D. degree from the University of California (Berkeley) and has taught at the universities of Cornell, Stanford, California and Bristish Columbia. He was the recipient of Carnegie Endowment and NATO fellowships, and at present is a Fellow at the Center for International Affairs, Harvard University. His research interest is in the policy-making processes of industrial democracies and is the author of numerous articles in the field.